Richard Acklam   Araminta Crace

UPPER INTERMEDIATE

Lina Matiz.

Total English

Students' Book

PEARSON

Longman

Contents

UNIT	LESSON 1	LESSON 2
1 Connect page 5	**Grammar:** question tags **Can do:** check information	**Grammar:** *any/every/no/some* **Vocabulary:** making adjectives from nouns **Can do:** express agreement/disagreement
2 Work page 19	**Grammar:** futures overview **Vocabulary:** verb phrases about work **Can do:** talk about future plans and make predictions	**Grammar:** Future Perfect and Future Continuous **Vocabulary:** 'after work' activities **Can do:** do a survey and report the results
3 Old or new page 33	**Grammar:** narrative tenses **Vocabulary:** time expressions **Can do:** write a short story	**Grammar:** articles **Vocabulary:** materials **Can do:** talk about materials, possessions and inventions
4 Risk page 47	**Grammar:** *if* structures (1) **Can do:** write a diary entry	**Grammar:** expressing obligation **Vocabulary:** physical movements **Can do:** explain how to do something
5 The past page 61	**Grammar:** *used to/get used to/would* **Vocabulary:** appearance **Can do:** describe appearance	**Grammar:** expressing ability **Can do:** talk about memories
6 Explore page 75	**Grammar:** Present Perfect Simple and Continuous **Vocabulary:** adjectives with *-ed* and *-ing* endings **Can do:** write an informal email	**Grammar:** questions **Vocabulary:** weather **Can do:** ask and answer questions about unusual places
7 Excess page 89	**Grammar:** countable and uncountable nouns **Vocabulary:** food and cooking **Can do:** describe how to prepare and cook a dish	**Grammar:** passives **Vocabulary:** verb phrases about money **Can do:** write a formal letter of complaint
8 Success page 103	**Grammar:** *It's time/I'd rather/I'd better* **Vocabulary:** describing personality **Can do:** describe different types of people	**Grammar:** reported speech **Vocabulary:** adjectives and intensifiers **Can do:** report and describe what people say to you
9 Crime page 117	**Grammar:** sequencing devices. e.g. *After + -ing* **Vocabulary:** law and insurance **Can do:** tell a funny story	**Grammar:** past modals of deduction *must/might/can't have done* **Vocabulary:** compound adjectives **Can do:** speculate about past events
10 Mind page 131	**Grammar:** reflexive pronouns **Can do:** ask about and give your own beliefs and opinions	**Grammar:** gerunds and infinitives **Vocabulary:** advertising **Can do:** write the arguments for and against a point of view

Communication activities page 145   Film Bank page 152

LESSON 3	VOCABULARY	COMMUNICATION	FILM BANK
Grammar: present/future modals of possibility **Vocabulary:** noises **Can do:** make speculations	Phrasal verbs (relationships)	Your family history	Good relations
Grammar: *in case* **Can do:** write a formal letter of application	Collocations with prepositions	The best candidate	Dream career
Grammar: adjectives and adverbs **Vocabulary:** verb phrases with *take* **Can do:** give a presentation about a place	Making nouns	Lessons from history	Film heroes
Grammar: emphasis **Vocabulary:** phrasal verbs with *out* **Can do:** compare and contrast photographs	Distances and dimensions	Take a risk	Ellen MacArthur
Grammar: *although/but/however/nevertheless* **Vocabulary:** feelings **Can do:** talk about books	Idioms describing people	Time capsule	Home Road Movie
Grammar: making comparisons **Vocabulary:** verb phrases about moving/travelling **Can do:** make comparisons about places and people	Expressions with *go*	Travelling companions	Bhutan
Grammar: *have/get something done* **Vocabulary:** animal expressions **Can do:** talk about services	Prefixes	Can I help you?	Vikings
Grammar: *hard* and *hardly* **Can do:** write a report of survey findings	Phrasal verbs with three parts	Radio phone-in	Secrets of success
Grammar: relative clauses **Can do:** write an article	Newspaper headlines	Mind benders	Bullion Robbery
Grammar: *if* structures (2) **Vocabulary:** speaking **Can do:** talk about your regrets and resolutions	Commonly misspelt words	How does your mind work?	Yes Prime Minister

Writing Bank page 162   Tapescripts page 165

1 Read the text and match the parts of speech a–l below to each <u>underlined</u> word or phrase.

According to [1] the ancient Greek historian Herodotus, [2] in the 7th century BC the king of Egypt, Psamtik 1, decided to conduct a [3] scientific experiment. Using his absolute power over his subjects, [4] he took two newborn babies and handed them to a shepherd, with instructions that they were to be [5] brought up in total isolation. Most importantly, no-one was to speak in the babies' presence. Psamtik wanted to find out what language the children would speak if left to themselves. He thought that the language they produced would be the [6] oldest in the world - the original language of the human race. After two years, the shepherd heard the two children [7] repeatedly pronounce the word 'becos'. This was identified as meaning [8] 'bread' in the language of the Phrygians, a people then living in central Turkey. From this experiment, Psamtik deduced that the Phrygian language [9] must be the first ever spoken. Nobody now believes Psamtik's [10] conclusion – a few commentators suggest that the infants [11] were imitating the sound of the shepherd's sheep, but no-one since [12] has had any better success in discovering what man's very first spoken language was like.

a) Present Perfect	g) countable noun
b) Past Continuous	h) superlative
c) uncountable noun	i) adjective
d) phrasal verb	j) adverb
e) article	k) pronoun
f) preposition	l) modal verb

2 Find the grammar mistake in each sentence.

1 They've been to Brazil last year.

2 This cathedral built in 1590.

3 She's the person what told me I should study economics at university.

4 I was reading in my room when I was hearing a loud crash downstairs.

5 My grades this year are a lot worst than last year unfortunately.

6 You work for IBM, aren't you?

7 If I'll have time, I'll paint my bedroom this weekend.

8 Can I give you a small advice?

9 He's always wanted to be teacher.

3 **a** Complete the word maps with words/phrases from the box below.

do aerobics   souvenir   application form
sense of humour   take up a hobby
be promoted   go sightseeing   father-in-law

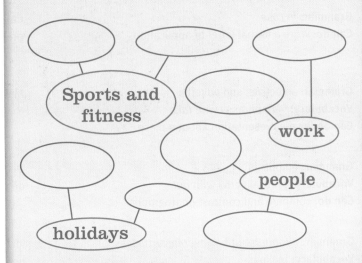

b Underline the main stress in each word/phrase.

c Add three more words to each word map.

4 **a** Look at the dictionary extract below from the Longman Active Study Dictionary. What does it tell you about each of the following: grammar, pronunciation and meaning?

sen·si·ble /ˈsensəbəl/ *adj* **1** showing good judgement: *a sensible decision* **2** suitable for a particular purpose, especially a practical one: *sensible clothes* – sensibly *adv*

b Complete the dictionary extracts below by writing a definition for each one.

1 re·tire /rɪˈtaɪə/ *v* [I] _____:
   I'd like to retire before I'm 60.

2 a·broad /əˈbrɔːd/ *adv* _____
   ___: Did you go abroad for your last holiday?

3 get on with sb *phr v* [T] _____:
   I get on well with both my sisters.

4 pitch /pɪtʃ/ *n* [C] _____:
   The players ran out onto the pitch.

c Now compare your definitions with the definitions in a dictionary.

d Add the words/phrases above to the word maps in Ex. 3a.

1 | Connect

Lead-in

1   Look at the photos. Who are the people? How do you think they are connected?

2   a   What is the difference in meaning between the words in each pair below? Use a dictionary if necessary.

1   step-sister/half-sister
2   colleague/acquaintance
3   soulmate/close friend
4   partner/wife

b   Read the sentences. What do the phrases in *italics* mean.

1   I don't think I *made a very good first impression* on your parents. They didn't seem very interested in me.

2   The first time we met, we *just clicked*. It was amazing. We started going out soon after.

3   We *have a lot in common*. Of course, we both work for the same company but we also like doing lots of the same kinds of things outside of work.

4   My sister and I don't really *see eye to eye* on much. We've always argued – even as children.

5   She thinks about things in the same way as me. I really *feel on the same wavelength* as her.

3   Discuss.

Who are the people you feel you have most in common with? Do you always feel on the same wavelength? Why/Why not?

Reading

1 **a** Discuss. What are three important characteristics of a 'good friend'?

b Read the text. Does it refer to any characteristics you thought of?

What makes a good friend?

On average each person makes an amazing 363 friends in their life – but only six of them will be true friends! We carried out a global survey to find out what makes a 'good friend'.

A friend should be there for you all the time, not just when they want to be. They will keep in touch even though you may be far apart. Some of my closest friends live abroad but it doesn't really make a lot of difference.
Maciek, 19, Poland

To me a good friend is someone who you have a lot in common with. You can share your beliefs and passions with them. I'm very lucky as I have three or four people like that but I'm still looking for my soulmate.
Haruki, 25, Japan

I think a good friend is somebody who you can trust and tell secrets to. They will never lie to you. If I ever found out that a friend of mine had lied to me, I know I couldn't be friends with them anymore.
Emily, 14, Britain

I think that a true friend is someone who you can feel completely comfortable with and you don't have to make yourself into someone you're not. They should accept you for who you are and not try to change you.
Mercedes, 31, Spain

I don't think you need to have known someone for ages for them to be a really good friend. But I do think that they should be there when you feel down or whenever you really need them.
Rachel, 15, New Zealand

A good friend is someone who listens to you but, at the same time, doesn't just agree with everything you say. They should definitely tell you if they think you're making a mistake although that can be hard.
Debbie, 23, South Africa

I think you know someone will be a really good friend as soon as you meet them. You just click straightaway. Then, the most important thing is trust. You have to know they will always look out for you and be totally loyal to you.
Stefano, 21, Italy

It's someone who is kind, has a good sense of humour, someone who forgives easily! Sometimes I'm not very nice to my best friend but she knows I don't mean it, so she doesn't mind really.
Lanza, 16, USA

For me to call someone a really good friend, we have to see eye to eye on most things. I don't need to have contact all the time but, when I do, I definitely want to feel we're on the same wavelength.
Mick, 36, Ireland

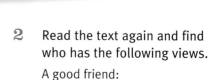

2 Read the text again and find who has the following views.

A good friend:

1 finds the same things funny that you do

2 is similar to you

3 doesn't want you to be different

4 doesn't always say that you are right

5 supports you when you feel miserable or upset

6 doesn't only support you when it's convenient for them

7 is always on your side

8 won't tell other people your secrets

3 Discuss.

1 Which views from the text do you have?

2 Do you think people look for different things in friends as they get older? If so, why and how?

3 Have you ever fallen out with a good friend? What happened?

Writing

4   Discuss. When do you write or get notes/ messages?

5   **a** Look at these notes and messages and decide which one is:

   1   making an apology
   2   enclosed with something else
   3   trying to rearrange an appointment
   4   reminding someone to do something
   5   passing on a message from somebody else

b Read them again and decide who might have written each one: a) wife, b) friend, c) flatmate, d) work colleague, e) brother.

A

Julie,
Sorry I didn't have time to talk about the sales figures earlier. I have to go to a meeting now.*Should be back by 1p.m.* Fancy lunch?

Alistair

B

Don't forget to pick up*jacket from*dry cleaner's. *See you at the restaurant*about 7p.m. xxx

C

This is the book I was telling you about. *Hope you like it. (Mum and Dad did!)
Vijay

D

Tony Robinson called about tennis.
*Ring him – ok?! (01279) 623 645

E

Hi! How r u? Cd u meet me b4 Sat.? Coffee Fri? Teri

c Which words have been left out in the notes/messages above? They are marked with*.

d Message E is a text message. What do the abbreviated words, e.g. 'r' mean?

6   **a** [1.1] Listen to three answerphone messages. What is the purpose of each one?

b Listen again and make notes of the important information. Then, write a brief message to each person using your notes.

7   Read the following statements and tell other students which ones you agree with and why.

  • It's important to hold on to your good friends.
  • Having one very close friend is the most important thing.
  • New friends will replace old friends.
  • Family are always more important than friends.

8   [1.2] Listen to Harry and Fiona talking about their ideas of friends and friendship. Which of the views from Ex. 7 does Harry have?

9   Listen again. Make notes about the people they talk about and how they are significant.

Angelina – Fiona's best friend at school

10 Discuss. Is your situation with your friends more like Harry's or Fiona's? In what ways?

Lifelong learning

Getting advice

Which of your friends or family speak English better than you do? What did they do to reach this level of English? Find out and see if any of their strategies might help you.

Grammar: | question tags

11 a Complete the examples in the Active grammar box with the missing auxiliary verb, e.g. *is*, *don't*, etc.

> ### Active grammar (1)
>
> 1 *You have a best friend, _____ you?*
> 2 *You had a best friend at school, _____ you?*
> 3 *That's just the way life is, _____ it?*
> 4 *You can't keep in touch with everybody, _____ you?*
>
> A We usually put negative question tags after affirmative sentences and affirmative tags after negative sentences.
> B If the main sentence has an auxiliary verb, e.g. *is, can*, etc., this is repeated in the question tag.
> C If the main sentence has no auxiliary, the question tag is a form of the verb *do*.

b Which examples does Rule B apply to and which examples does Rule C apply to?

see Reference page 17

12 a Read the interview below between Simon and his boss, Jo. Three of the question tags are incorrect. Find and correct them.

Jo: So, Simon, you've been with the company for nearly a year now, aren't you?

Simon: Yes, that's right.

Jo: You worked for Thomson International before then, didn't you?

Simon: Yes, for five years.

Jo: And you feel happy here now, don't you?

Simon: Absolutely, it's a great job and everyone's been really friendly.

Jo: Now, you're clear about your targets for this year, isn't you?

Simon: Yes, I think so. We have to increase last year's sales by 15%, don't we?

Jo: That's right. If that happens then everyone gets a 20% bonus which everyone will be very happy about, won't they?

Simon: Definitely.

Jo: Now, on the subject of your punctuality. That hasn't been particularly good, was it?

Simon: Ah yes, now I can explain that ...

b `1.3` Listen and check your answers.

13 a Complete the examples 1–6 in the Active grammar box.

> ### Active grammar (2)
>
> 1 *I'm too late, _____ I?*
> 2 *Help yourself to a coffee, _____ you?*
> 3 *Let's get a sandwich, _____ we?*
> 4 *You never go to the theatre, _____ you?*
> 5 *Nothing went wrong today, _____ it?*
> 6 *Nobody has complained, _____ they?*
>
> A The question tag for *I am* is _____ .
> B After imperatives we often use the question tag _____ to invite people to do things.
> C After *Let's* we use the question tag _____ .
> D After negative words like *never, no, hardly*, etc. we use a positive/negative question tag.
> E After *nothing* we use *it/they* in question tags.
> F After *nobody, somebody*, etc. we use *it/they* in question tags.

b Refer to the examples 1–6 and complete the rules A–F in the Active grammar box.

see Reference page 17

14 a Complete the sentences.

1 She's getting very tall, _____ ?
2 They don't seem to like their present, _____ ?
3 You haven't been waiting long, _____ ?
4 We can't leave the party early, _____ ?
5 Let's go and see a film, _____ ?
6 Do sit down, _____ ?
7 Nothing seems to be going right, _____ ?
8 I'm being a bit silly, _____ ?

b `1.4` Listen and check your answers.

c Decide whether each sentence is a) checking information, b) asking for agreement, c) asking someone to do something, d) making an offer or a suggestion.

Person to person

15 a Write one or two facts you think you know about three other students in your class.

b Check your facts by asking the person, using an appropriate question tag.

Listening

1 Discuss.

1 Do you know any large families?

2 What do you think are the good and bad things about being brought up as part of a large family?

3 How would you feel about working with a member of your family?

2 **1.5** Listen to this extract from a radio programme and answer the questions.

1 How big is this family now?

2 What is special about them?

3 What trip are they excited about?

3 Listen again and answer these questions.

1 Why did Larry Boehmer start juggling?

2 How did his children become interested in juggling?

3 When and where did the family first juggle for a public audience?

4 What does Larry believe about the skill of juggling?

4 **a** In pairs, look at the following phrases/expressions in the tapescript on page 165. Say what you think they might mean.

1 to juggle several tasks at once (l.2)

2 to get your hands on something (l.9)

3 to put your mind to something (l.21)

4 a big family man (l.24)

5 to be only too happy about something (l.25)

6 to go from strength to strength (l.28)

7 to pick up on something (l.35)

b Summarise the information in the radio programme. Use the phrases above.

Grammar: | any/every/no/some

5 **a** Decide if each example sentence in the Active grammar box is correct or not.

> ### Active grammar
>
> A *Anybody can learn to juggle.*
> B *Everybody can learn to juggle.*
>
> C *Do you want something to eat?*
> D *Do you want anything to eat?*
>
> E *I've looked anywhere for my keys.*
> F *I've looked everywhere but I can't find my keys.*
>
> G *She hasn't got anything to do.*
> H *She hasn't got nothing to do.*
>
> 1 *Any/Every* looks at things one at a time, separately.
>
> 2 *Any/Every* looks at all the things together.
>
> 3 We use *any/every* to mean it doesn't matter which, who, etc.
>
> 4 *Nothing/Something* means *not + anything.*
>
> 5 We use *any/some* in questions when we expect the answer 'Yes'.

b Choose the correct alternative for each of the rules 1–5.

see Reference page 17

6 Choose the best alternative.

1 I'm going to try and see my boyfriend *every/any* weekend.

2 *Everybody/Anybody* was thrilled to see Naomi.

3 Get me *every/any* soup you can find. It doesn't matter what kind.

4 I can't get rid of this cold. *Nothing/Anything* seems to help.

5 The market had flowers of *every/any* kind.

6 I'd like to go *everywhere/somewhere* hot for my holiday. I need the sun.

7 You can come *every/any* time after 5p.m. I'll be at home all evening.

8 I know you're very busy so I don't suppose you've got *some/any* time to help me tonight?

Reading

7 Discuss.

1 What are the advantages/ disadvantages of being born first, middle or last in a family?

2 Do you think it is good to be an only child? Why/Why not?

8 **a** Read the text. Which of the following does it do?

1 Say which type of child it is best to be (i.e. first born, middle born, last born, only child).

2 Give advice to parents about dealing with each type of child.

3 Describe the possible career consequences according to the position you are born in the family.

4 Advise children how to cope with their position in the family.

b Read the text again. Are these statements true (T) or false (F)?

1 Parents usually expect different things from their first and last children.

2 Only children and first-born children often follow similar types of career path.

3 The results of this research contradict existing research into the effects of birth order.

4 The researchers found first-born children easier to analyse than the other groups.

5 Younger children tend to take more risks as a result of their parents' attitude towards them.

6 Only children often prefer more physical occupations.

9 Discuss. Which of the points in the text are true for your family or other families you know?

WHO comes first?

A child's place in the family birth order may play a role in the type of occupations that will interest him or her as an adult, new research suggests. In two related studies, researchers found that only children – and to a certain extent first-born children – were more interested in intellectual, cognitive pursuits than were later-born children. In contrast, later-born children were more interested in both artistic and outdoor-related careers.

These results fit into theories that say our place in family birth order will influence our personality, said Frederick T.L. Leong, co-author of the study and professor of psychology at Ohio State University. 'Parents typically place different demands and have different expectations of children depending on their birth order,' Leong said.

'For example, parents may be extremely protective of only children and worry about their physical safety. That may be why only children are more likely to show interest in academic pursuits rather than physical or outdoor activities. Only children will tend to get more time and attention from their parents than children with siblings. This will often make them feel special but the downside is that they may suffer occasional pangs of jealousy and loneliness when friends discuss their brothers and sisters and family life.'

The first-born is an only child until the second child comes along – transforming them from being the centre of attention, to then sharing the care of parents. Parents will also expect them to be responsible and 'set an example'. The change from being the focus of a family may be quite a shock and so shape the first-born's subsequent outlook on life. Therefore first-borns may try to get back their parents' attention and approval by achieving success and recognition in their careers. It has been noted that first-borns are significantly more often found as world political leaders than any other birth order position.

'As they have more children, parents tend to become more open and relaxed and that may allow younger children to be more risk-taking,' Leong said. 'If the first-born or only child wants to be a poet, that may concern parents. But by the fourth child, parents may not mind as much.'

Being the youngest in the family can sometimes be a stifling and frustrating experience, especially if they're looking to be taken seriously and treated like an adult. The last-born is more likely than the other birth order positions to take up dangerous sports. This may be a sign of the last-born's rebellious streak – a result of being fed up with always being bossed about by everyone else in the family.

Middle children, however, have different issues. 'Middle child syndrome' can mean feeling sandwiched between two other 'more important' people – an older sibling who gets all the rights and is treated like an adult and a younger sibling who gets all the privileges and is treated like a spoilt child. Middle-borns have to learn to get on with older and younger children, and this may contribute to them becoming good negotiators – of all the birth order positions they are most skilful at dealing with authority figures and those holding inferior positions.

Leong said the biggest differences in the study were between only children and later-born children. 'First-born children are difficult to classify because they start out as only children but later give up that position. It may be that the length of time a first-born child is an only child makes a difference in his or her personality.' ■

Vocabulary | making adjectives from nouns

10 Complete the table.

NOUN	ADJECTIVE
intellect	
art	
	jealous
	lonely
responsibility	
	successful
importance	
skill	
frustration	

11 Complete the following sentences with the most appropriate word from the table.

1 Do you realise the _____ of these exams? They will decide which university you can go to.
2 My sister is very _____ . She can paint well and writes poetry.
3 It's so _____ trying to phone my bank. You have to wait for hours before a real person will answer the phone.
4 You shouldn't be _____ of Bob. He's not my type!
5 He's lived alone for ages but he says he never feels _____ .
6 There's a lot of _____ involved in juggling.
7 I wish someone would take _____ for the train crash.
8 His last film was an incredible _____ . Apparently, it won five Oscars.

Speaking

agree/disagree

Expressing agreement	*That's absolutely right.* *I completely agree with that.* *I couldn't agree more.* *That's probably true.* *I think there's some truth in that.*
Expressing disagreement	*I'm not sure if I agree with that.* *I don't think that's completely true.* *That's not true at all.* *I totally disagree.*
Reporting agreement/ disagreement	*We all felt pretty much the same about this question.* *There were a number of differences of opinion in the group.* *One or two people had quite strong views about this.*

12 a 🔊 1.6 Listen to the conversation. What are the two people talking about?

b Listen again. Which of the expressions from the How to box do you hear? Which word(s) is/are stressed?

13 a Discuss the following statements. Use expressions from the How to box as appropriate.

- Parents tend to be more strict with their first-born children.
- Middle children have the worst time.
- Youngest children are usually spoilt.
- Only children tend to be self-sufficient and not need many friends.
- We are attracted to people who are born in the same position within the family.
- Our position in the family affects the kind of career we choose.

b Report your group's discussion back to the rest of the class.

Speaking

1   Look at the photos. Describe what you can see in each one.

Mobile mad

2   Discuss.

1   Do you have a mobile phone? How much do you use it? What do you use it for?

2   Do you know anyone who doesn't have a mobile phone? Why don't they have one?

3   Do you think mobile phones are generally a good or a bad thing?

4   Where (if anywhere) are you not allowed to use mobile phones in your country (e.g. the cinema)? Do you think there should be other places where you can't use mobile phones?

5   What age do you think is appropriate for children to have a mobile phone? Why?

Reading

3   Read the text. Which of the following subjects does it refer to?

1   the number of young people who have a mobile phone

2   when the first mobile phone was invented

3   the reasons why young people want a mobile phone

4   how parents feel about their children having a mobile phone

5   mobile phones and noise pollution

6   the amount of contact teenagers feel they need with their friends

7   the effect of mobile phones on reading for pleasure

8   the future design of mobile phones

9   the health risks of mobile phones to children

10 some possible educational uses of mobile phones

4   Read the text again. Make brief notes about the subjects in Ex. 3 it refers to.

There are good reasons to be worried about children and mobile phones, reports Michael Fitzpatrick. Sociologists in Japan, where mobiles have been common among the young for some time and offer sophisticated services, see an alarming trend.

In Tokyo, for example, one-quarter of all four to fifteen-year-olds has a mobile phone. Well over half of Japan's high school students own one, many of them Internet enabled. Half the children polled recently said their lifestyle 'required' them to have a mobile phone, while 41.5 percent said their parents 'forced' them to have one.

An informal survey conducted on the Tokyo streets by *Japan Today* magazine, however, suggests that the nations' teens have other reasons for keeping hold of 'their best electric friend'. 'If I can't find my phone I feel really isolated from

5 Discuss.

1 Which two facts in the text did you find most interesting? Why?

2 How important do you think mobile phones are for young people in your country?

3 How do you think mobile phones will change over the next 5 years?

Vocabulary | noises

6 Tell other students. What noises do you typically hear every day? Which ones do you particularly like/dislike?

7 **a** **1.7** Listen and match the words in the box to the noises you hear.

> ring scream creak bang thud shout bark snore crash

b What typically makes each of these noises?

A: *Well, obviously, phones ring. Anything else?*

B: *And doorbells.*

8 **1.8** Some of the noises you heard make part of a story. Listen to these noises and with another student discuss how to link them to make a story. Use *may, might, could,* etc.

The crash might be the sound of someone breaking into the house through a window. Then the dog barks but maybe the burglar gives him some meat or something to keep him quiet. After that ...

my friends,' says 16-year-old Asuka Maezawa. Emi Inoue, seventeen, agrees, adding: 'It's great for talking to friends about gossip I don't want my parents to hear.' Another survey also revealed that about 22 percent said they talked at least ten times per day, while 45 percent said they used their mobile to send ten or more text messages each day.

Parents were also surveyed, with more than a third feeling their children spent too much time on the phone, while 23 percent said the mobile made it difficult for them to keep a check on who their children were communicating with. Tokyo parents may have good reason to be worried, since 26 percent of the children said they were regularly corresponding with people they had never met.

Such density of mobile ownership, especially among the young, has lead to a new type of neurosis, say sociologists. Japanese teens, in particular, have become fanatical about being 'always available'. 'Teenagers can be seen taking advantage of every spare minute to touch base with their friends. It is not the content of the communication but the act of staying in touch that matters. Indeed, many become extremely uneasy if unable to contact their peers countless times each day, fearing they are becoming socially isolated,' writes the sociologist Hisao Ishii, the author of *The Superficial Social Life of Japan's Mobile Phone Addicts.*

'If this trend continues,' he adds, 'two things are likely to happen. One is mobile phone addiction, where a person is incapable of forming and maintaining relationships without the help of mobiles. The second: Genuine conversation will be driven out by superficial communication, in which the act of contacting one another is all that matters, leading to a deterioration in the quality of relationships. Indeed, the very fabric of society may be threatened.'

The sociologist, Ms Maiko Seki, has also suggested that: 'Children read books less and less as they are too busy playing with their technological tools.' As well as this it may be that academic performance is being affected: 68 percent of children who responded to the DoCoMo survey and owned a mobile phone said they got poor grades at school.

In addition to this, a recent UK government report has highlighted the increased health risks to children under sixteen using mobile handsets and a circular sent to schools suggests that children below this age should be allowed to make calls only in emergencies.

On the other hand there are clear benefits for children, particularly if their connection is Internet enabled. One company has recently produced a revision/mock exam question service for delivery via SMS, and teachers are already using texting and mobile email to keep in touch with pupils.

Grammar | modals of possibility

9 **a** **1.9** Listen to the phone conversations and match them to the sentences A–E in the Active grammar box.

> ### Active grammar
>
> A *It **could** be someone talking to his boss.*
> B *He **might** need help finding his way.*
> C *The weather **can't** be very good.*
> D *He **must** be late.*
> E *They **may** go to the cinema later.*
>
> 1 It is possible
> 2 It is not possible
> 3 It is certain

b Match the sentences A–E in the Active grammar box with the meanings 1–3. Does each one refer to the present or the future?

c Make other sentences using *may/might/ could, must, can't* as appropriate. Refer to the tapescript on page 165 if necessary.

1 *He might be speaking to his girlfriend.*

see Reference page 17

10 Complete the second sentences so they have the same meaning as the first sentences. Use *may/might/could, must* or *can't.*

1 I'm sure that Terry is stuck in traffic. He's never normally late.

Terry _____ stuck in traffic. He's never normally late.

2 It's possible that we'll go and visit my brother in Manchester.

We _____ and visit my brother in Manchester.

3 It's not possible that Jane wants to go to Morocco this summer. She hates hot weather.

Jane _____ to go to Morocco this summer. She hates hot weather.

4 There's a chance that Susie will come to the party tonight.

Susie _____ to the party tonight.

5 I have no doubt that there are better ways of solving this problem.

There _____ better ways of solving this problem.

6 Perhaps Tarek will change his mind about lending you his car.

Tarek _____ his mind about lending you his car.

Person to person

11 **a** Choose eight of the following pieces of information and write them on a piece of paper.

- your father's first name
- the hour of the day you like best
- the name of a pet you have had or an animal you know
- the title of one of your favourite films
- the name of one of your favourite music bands
- a place you have never been to but would love to go to
- the first name of one of the people you admire most
- the place where you were born
- the language you most like the sound of
- the time you got up this morning
- the title of one of your favourite books
- the place where you spent your best holiday
- the foreign language you speak the best
- the first name of your best friend at school

b In pairs. Look at your partner's words and say what you think they mean. Use *might, must, can't* or *could.*

A: *Italian – This could be the language you most like the sound of.*

B: *Oh no, it isn't.*

A: *Oh. Well, it must be the language you speak the best, then.*

B: *Yes, that's right.*

1 Vocabulary

Phrasal verbs

1 **1.10** Read and listen to Tim's girlfriend (Mandy) and his sister (Gill) talking. Who are the people in the picture?

M: So.. do you think Tim **takes after** his dad?

G: Well, I suppose so, in some ways.

M: How?

G: Well, I mean, they're both very stubborn, aren't they!

M: That's for sure. It runs in the family.

G: But you know Tim really **looks up to** him. He always has, right from when we were kids and while we were **growing up**. I remember he used to always be **showing off** to him, trying to get his attention, one way or another.

M: And how about you?

G: Oh, I suppose I was always closer to my mum. She didn't have an easy time, **bringing us up**. Dad wasn't around much.

M: And how did you and Tim **get on**?

G: Oh really well … except when he'd put spiders in my bed!

M: … And how's life with you now?

G: Not bad. You know I'm **going out** with Kevin.

M: Oh yes? But, it's not so long since you **split up** with Max, is it?

G: Hey … it's nearly six months, and anyway, I've known Kevin for ages, it's just that it's never seemed to be the right time before.

M: And, how's Sally?

G: Oh … Sally. Well, we've kind of **fallen out**.

M: Really? Why? What happened?

G: Well, it's a long story but, in a nutshell, I told her something pretty sensitive about me and things going on at work.

M: Yes …?

G: And then I found out she'd talked about it to some other friends.

M: Oh no!

G: Yeah, I was really upset about it.

M: I can imagine. Do you think you'll be able to **make it up**?

G: I'm really not sure …

2 **a** Work in pairs. From the context, think about the meaning of each phrasal verb in **bold** and write a short definition.

take after – to look or behave like someone in your family

b Check your ideas in a dictionary.

3 Correct the mistake in each of the following sentences.

1 How long have you and your girlfriend been going out with?

2 You don't get on your boss very well, do you?

3 We made it out after we both agreed how silly we had been.

4 I think our parents did a great job of bringing up us with very little money.

5 David really looks up to. He thinks you're amazing.

6 Who do you take them after in your family, your mum or your dad?

7 I wish you would grown up and start behaving like an adult!

8 John's fallen out his brother again. I think his brother owes him some money.

9 Why did he tell us how much money he earns? I hate it when people show on like that.

10 Why did you and Lorraine split it up? I thought you were quite happy together.

4 Read the following statements. Which of them are true for you? Change the others so that they are also true for you.

- Of all the people in my family I probably get on best with my dad because we're so similar.

- I take after my grandmother in lots of ways. We both love travel and discovering new places.

- In my opinion, couples should go out for at least two years before they get married.

- If I have children in the future, I'll probably bring them up in much the same way that my parents brought me up.

- I really look up to my grandfather. He's incredibly kind and always ready to listen to you if you have a problem.

Your family history

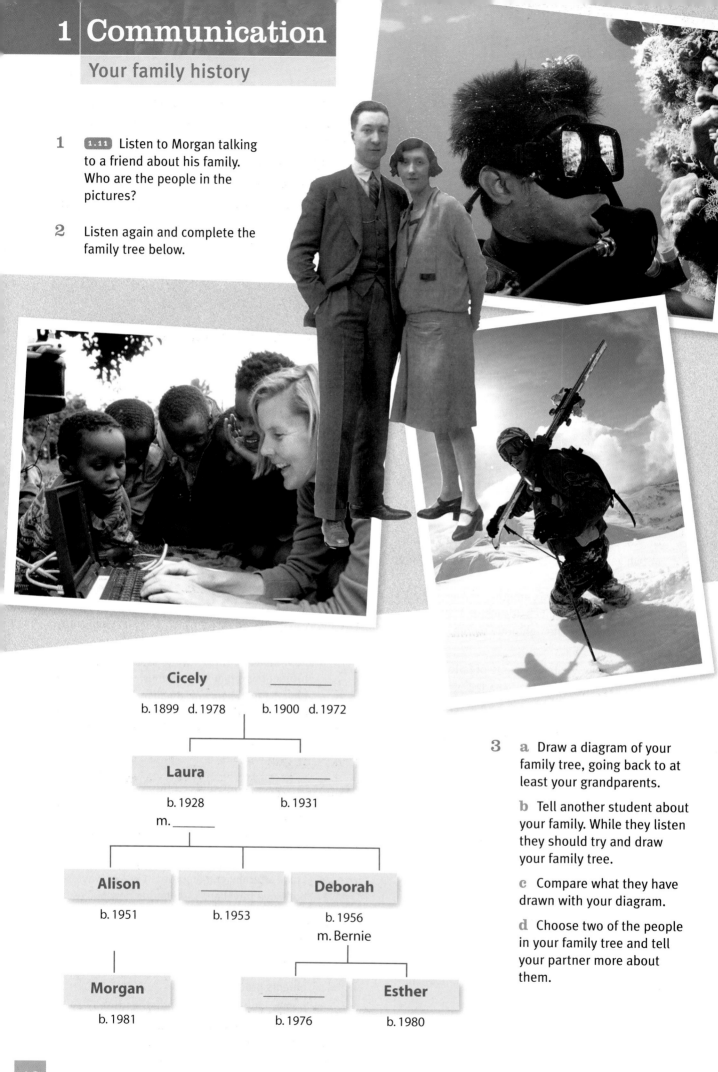

1   **1.11** Listen to Morgan talking to a friend about his family. Who are the people in the pictures?

2   Listen again and complete the family tree below.

Cicely
b. 1899   d. 1978

_____
b. 1900   d. 1972

Laura
b. 1928

_____
b. 1931

m. _____

Alison
b. 1951

_____
b. 1953

Deborah
b. 1956
m. Bernie

Morgan
b. 1981

_____
b. 1976

Esther
b. 1980

3   a Draw a diagram of your family tree, going back to at least your grandparents.

b Tell another student about your family. While they listen they should try and draw your family tree.

c Compare what they have drawn with your diagram.

d Choose two of the people in your family tree and tell your partner more about them.

1 Reference

Question tags

Use question tags in speech and informal writing to check information or ask for agreement.

We usually put negative question tags after affirmative sentences and affirmative tags after negative sentences.

It's warm today, isn't it?

He doesn't like me, does he?

If the main sentence has an auxiliary verb, e.g. *is*, *can*, etc. this is repeated in the question tag.

You can't play tennis this evening, can you?

If the main sentence has no auxiliary, the question tag is a form of the verb *do*.

They went to Australia last Christmas, didn't they?

In speech, use intonation to show the meaning of the question tag. If the tag is a real question (we want to know something and are not sure of the answer), use a rising intonation. If the tag is not a real question (we already think we know the answer), use a falling intonation.

The question tag for *I am* is *aren't I*.

I'm wrong, aren't I?

After imperatives we often use *won't you*? to invite people to do things.

Have a seat, won't you?

After *let's* use *shall we*?

Let's walk along the beach, shall we?

After negative words like *never*, *no*, *hardly*, etc. we use an affirmative question tag.

You never want to go out to clubs, do you?

After *nothing* we use *it* in question tags.

Nothing happened, did it?

After *nobody*, *somebody*, *everybody* we use *they* in question tags.

Nobody wants to go out tonight, do they?

Any/Every/No/Some

Any and *every* can both be used to talk in general about all the members of a group.

You can get an excellent meal in any/every restaurant in this street.

They are different in meaning, however. *Any* looks at things one at a time. It means *this or that or the other*. *Every* looks at things together. It means *all* or *this and that and the other*.

Haven't you anything to do?

There's enough food for everyone.

Any can also mean 'It doesn't matter which one'.

A: *Which bag shall I bring?* B: *I don't mind. Any of them are fine.*

Nothing means *not + anything*.

There's nothing we can do to change his mind.

Some is used in questions when we expect people to answer 'Yes'.

Would you like some more coffee?

Present/Future modals of possibility

Use *could, may* or *might* to talk about present or future possibility.

A: *Where's Jean?* B: *I'm not sure but she might be in the garden.*

A: *I think there will be an election before the end of the year.* B: *You could be right.*

Use *can* to talk about more general or theoretical possibility.

The sea can get rough here with almost no warning.

Use *must* to say that you believe something is certain.

You haven't had anything to eat all day. You must be starving.

Use *can't* to say that you believe something is not possible.

They can't know many people. They've only just moved here.

Key vocabulary

Family/Relationships

step-sister   half-sister   colleague   acquaintance   soulmate   close friend   partner   ex-wife
to make a good impression   to click (with someone)
to have a lot in common   to see eye to eye (with someone)   be on the same wavelength

Adjectives/Nouns

intellectual/intellect   artistic/art   jealous/jealousy   lonely/loneliness   responsible/responsibility   successful/success   important/importance   skilful/skill   frustrated/frustration

Noises

ring   scream   creak   bang   thud   shout   bark   snore   crash

Phrasal verbs (relationships)

to take after (someone)   to look up to (someone)   to grow up   to show off   to bring (someone) up   to get on (with someone)   to go out (with someone)   to split up (with someone)   to fall out (with someone)   to make (it) up (with someone)

1 Match the question tags a–h with the sentences 1–8.

1 Everything will be ok,
2 Have some more dessert,
3 I'm talking too much,
4 We don't have much time,
5 Somebody's moved the desk,
6 That's the law,
7 There's hardly any bread left,
8 Let's make a fire,

a) do we?
b) is there?
c) shall we?
d) haven't they?
e) isn't it?
f) won't it?
g) aren't I?
h) won't you?

2 Which of the following sentences are not correct? Correct the ones with mistakes.

1 Do you have every idea how I can get to Croydon by public transport?
2 Would you like something else to eat?
3 That dog will eat anything. It's amazing.
4 Every help you can give with the redecorating would be much appreciated.
5 FlyFast say that you can go anywhere in Europe with them for under £50!
6 Holiday companies go somewhere now so there are no undiscovered places left.
7 As regards the housework, John does the washing-up and I do everything else.
8 Every student needs to take the test before they can join a class.
9 Anyone said how much they enjoyed the party. It was a great success.
10 There isn't nothing else we can do today.

3 Choose the correct alternative.

1 Your dad *might/can* want some tea. Will you ask him?
2 You *must/can't* get the job. You're easily the most qualified person.
3 They *can't/could* win the next election. Nobody trusts them anymore.
4 This cat *may/can't* belong to the people at number 43. Why don't you go and find out?
5 You *must/could* be David. I've heard such a lot about you.
6 We *might/must* need some help at the weekend. Will you be free?
7 You realise he *could/can't* be lying. Are you sure he wants to borrow your car to visit his grandmother?
8 She *must/can't* be very ill if she didn't come to school today. She never misses school.

4 Complete the following sentences with one of the words from the Key vocabulary on page 17 in the correct form.

1 Mike and I stopped _____ out last June. It was about something I said about his sister. I apologised but he hasn't spoken to me since.
2 I get on very well with my _____ , Barbara, although we've been divorced for nearly seven years.
3 I have a lot more _____ in my new job than before. I manage twenty-five people and have a budget of nearly £1million.
4 I just bought my _____ a really nice engagement ring. It was incredibly expensive though.
5 I wonder why next door's dog keeps _____ . I don't think they look after him very well.
6 He really _____ after his dad you know. He's got an amazing sense of humour and he's terribly generous.
7 My dad _____ so loudly that it stops my mum sleeping at night.
8 Janine is just a work _____ of mine. We share an office.

5 Rewrite the sentences so that each one ends with a question tag.

I'd like you to go to the shops soon.

You will go to the shops soon, won't you?

1 I think her brother's name is Ivan.
2 I suggest we go for a swim this afternoon.
3 I'm pretty sure he never eats meat.
4 Please make yourself comfortable.
5 I don't think anybody told him we were having a party.
6 I think I'm in time for the start of the film.
7 I don't think anything was taken out of her bag.
8 I don't think she can sing very well.

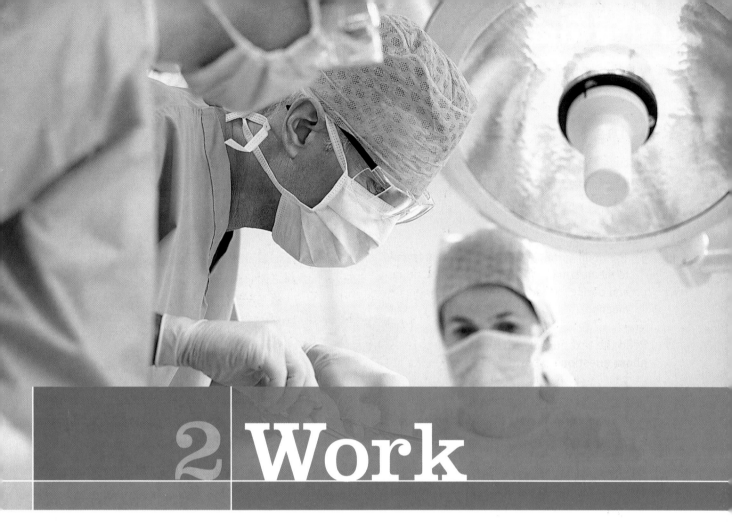

2 Work

Lead-in

1 Discuss.

1 Which of the following jobs can you NOT see in the photos: journalist, civil engineer, social worker, nursery nurse, surgeon

2 Briefly, what do you think each of the jobs involves?

3 Which of the jobs would you most/least like to do? Why/Why not?

2 a **2.1** Listen and match each person with the correct job.

b Listen again and explain the meaning of the phrases in the box.

> a change of career   a labour of love   a career path
> to take a year out   job satisfaction

3 In pairs, think of a job which fits each of the qualities in the box below.

> be good with figures   be a people person   be a good listener
> have a 'can do' attitude   work well in a team
> have an eye for detail   get the best out of other people
> be good at using your own initiative
> be able to meet tight deadlines   keep calm under pressure

4 Which of the phrases in Exs. 2b and 3 do you think apply to you? Give details.

Reading

1 Discuss.

  1 What can you see in the pictures?

  2 How do you think 'work' has changed over the last 1000 years? In what ways do you think it is the same?

  3 The noun 'grind' in the title of the text is used to mean 'something that is hard work, tiring and boring'. What do you think the whole title means?

2 Read the text quickly. What does it say about question 2 above?

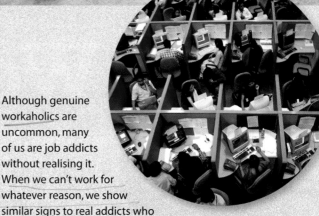

WORK

the daily grind we just can't do without

Work may sometimes seem like hell, but when we haven't got it, we miss it. We miss it, we want it and perhaps we even need it. Everyone wants to be valued and a salary is proof that we matter.

Not any job will do, however. Housework and voluntary work tend to be seen as non-jobs. In our work-centred culture, a 'proper job' means paid employment. Being paid for a job is better for our self-esteem. Of course, we would also prefer work to be useful and interesting, as well as paid. But you don't have to enjoy your job to get psychological benefits from it. According to some experts, achieving unenjoyable tasks during our work actually contributes to our sense of well-being.

The obligation to be in a particular place at a particular time, working as part of a team towards a common goal, gives us a sense of structure and purpose that we find difficult to impose on ourselves. For a lot of us, the workplace has also taken over from the community as the place of human contact. For most of us, work often functions as a social club, an information network, an informal dating agency and a marriage bureau.

Although genuine workaholics are uncommon, many of us are job addicts without realising it. When we can't work for whatever reason, we show similar signs to real addicts who are deprived of their 'fix' – we become irritable and lethargic. Among newly-retired men, death rates increase significantly in the first six months after leaving employment. For most of their lives, their personality, self-esteem and status have been defined by work; without it, they lose their appetite for life.

Life wasn't always so driven by employment, however. Work in the pre-industrial age was task-oriented not time-structured, focussing not on money but on tasks necessary for survival. Whole communities worked together so there was less division between work and 'free time'. The Industrial Revolution radically changed how people worked. Suddenly, work was no longer structured by seasons, but by the clock. Work was separated from the rest of life, and began to provide money rather than food and goods.

More recently, the revolution in Information Technology has again changed the nature of work and employment. The workplace itself may become redundant. Two million employees in the UK now work from home, keeping in touch via email and phone. Many employers say that working 'remotely' improves productivity, as workers are happier and waste less time commuting. There are downsides too, however, as workers lose touch with the workplace and people there.

We will undoubtedly have to accept that the nature of work has changed and will continue to do so. After all, we were conditioned into accepting the nine-to-five working day and there is no reason why we can't be conditioned into accepting something else. This article was written at home in the country during bursts of hard work interspersed with periods of inactivity. Perhaps that's the natural work-rhythm to which we will return?

sawing

3 **a** Read the text again and decide if these statements are true (T) or false (F).

1 Being paid to work makes many people feel better. T ✓

2 Non-paid work is just as good as paid work in terms of increasing self-esteem. F

3 Doing tasks you don't enjoy at work is always bad for your mental health. F

4 Most people find it difficult to find a purpose to the day without work. T

5 The social aspect of work is very important for the majority of people. T

6 People who work too much become irritable. T

7 When people retire, they sometimes feel less happy than when they worked. T

8 Two million workers in the UK work 'remotely'. T

9 One disadvantage of working from home is people feeling isolated. T

10 The writer is convinced that the work-rhythm of the future is a nine-to-five working day. F

b Summarise the main argument of the text by completing this sentence.

Although the nature of work has changed over the years, ... still Working is a important activity in people's life

4 Discuss.

1 Why do you think that being paid for a job often gives people greater self-esteem than doing voluntary work or looking after children at home? Do you think that this is always true?

2 In what ways (if any) does your job increase your self-esteem? What other things (apart from work) do you think are important for increasing people's self-esteem?

3 Is it common for people to work from home in your country? What do you think the advantages and disadvantages of working from home are? If you don't work from home, would you like to? Why/Why not?

Vocabulary | verb phrases about work

5 In pairs, find the difference between the verb phrases in *italics* in the sentence pairs. Use a dictionary if necessary.

1 **a** I *do voluntary work* in a charity shop once a week.

   b She *worked part-time* in a shop while she was studying for her degree.

2 **a** My uncle was very wealthy and *took early retirement* at the age of fifty-two.

   b 2000 workers *were made redundant* at the car factory last month.

3 **a** I like *working flexitime* because I can choose the hours to suit me.

   b She decided not to be a nurse because she didn't want to *do shift work*.

4 **a** Bus drivers *are on strike* until the unions can agree a new pay deal.

   b I'm afraid he will *be on sick leave* at least until the end of the month.

5 **a** He *was sacked* after he was caught stealing office equipment.

   b I'm going to *resign from my job* and go travelling for a year.

6 Complete the questions with the correct form of the phrases in Ex. 5. Use each phrase once.

1 Would you like to voluntary job, e.g. gardening for old people?

2 For what reasons do people sometimes choose to part-time instead of full-time?

3 Have you ever resign from a job to go and do something completely different?

4 How would you feel about shift, e.g. working nights and weekends? taking early retirement

5 Would you ever consider taking, e.g. at the age of forty-five or fifty?

6 For what kinds of reasons can people resign and have to leave their work? be sack

7 Which groups of workers (if any) in your country have be strike recently? What were they asking for?

8 Which do you think is the most common reason for being on sick in your country (backache, flu, etc.)?

9 Which do you think is more common in your country: working nine-to-five or flexi? part time flexi time

10 Are there any particular industries in your country in recent years which have declined and workers have been sacked?

7 Choose six of the questions in Ex. 6 to ask and answer with a partner.

Grammar | futures overview

8 **2.2** Listen to four conversations and answer these questions about a) Julia, b) Simon, c) Fran and d) Patrick.

1 Why does he/she want to change his/her work situation?

2 Has he/she got any definite plans? What are they?

9 **a** **2.3** Complete examples 1–6 in the Active grammar box from memory. Then listen and check your answers.

Active grammar

1 *That's a good idea! I think I* __'ll go__ *to the library now and do it there.*

2 *I've decided I* __'m not going to leave__ *work and go back to college.*

3 *I'm* __m meeting__ *them at 10 o' clock tomorrow morning.*

4 *I think they* __'ll give__ *Sally the job of departmental manager. She's really good and she's been there ages.*

5 *David* __is going to be__ *assistant manager. I heard him talking to James about it.*

6 *He* __is bound to__ *get the job. It's obvious. He's being fast-tracked for it.*

(3) A Use the Present Continuous to talk about a future arrangement (when details, e.g. about time and place have been decided).

(2) B Use *going to* to talk about a plan or intention (but no details have been decided).

(5) C Use *going to* to make predictions based on what you can see/hear now.

(4) D Use *will* to make predictions based on what you know/believe. We often use *think*, *hope*, *believe*, etc. with *will* in this case.

(1) E Use *will* to talk about a decision made at the time of speaking. We often use *I think* with *will* in this case.

(6) F Use *be bound to* to express certainty about the future. *bound is not use negative*

b Match the rules A–F with the correct examples 1–6.

see Reference page 31

10 Choose the correct alternative.

1 I've decided. I'm definitely not *bound/going to* apply for that job.

2 We*'ll meet/'re meeting* after work at the café on the corner.

3 She*'s getting/'s bound to get* the job. She's got the right experience.

4 I bought a newspaper this morning. *I'll look for/'m going to look for* a better-paid job.

5 Oh, there's the personnel officer. I *won't go/'m bound to go* then because I need to talk to her.

6 I*'ll play/'m playing* tennis with a colleague at 5p.m. this afternoon.

7 He's doing shift work at the moment so he *won't be/'s bound to be* tired tomorrow.

11 Complete the How to box with the words in the box below.

depends   idea   probably   sure   thinking

talk about future plans

HOW TO …		
Describe plans, intentions and arrangements		*I'd like to* have a complete break.
		I think I'll do some voluntary work.
		I've decided I'm going to leave work.
		I'm meeting them at 10.00 tomorrow morning.
		I'm planning to retrain.
Express some uncertainty about future plans	1	*I'm* __thinking__ *about* resigning.
	2	*I'm not* __sure__ *yet but* I think I'll leave soon.
	3	*One* __idea__ *is to do* some voluntary work.
	4	*It* __depends__ *on* being accepted on the course.
	5	*I'm* __probably__ *going to* start in September.

Person to person

12 **a** Tell your partner about your work/study/life plans for the future using the How to box above.

I'd like to train as an astronaut. When I've taken my exams I'll probably move to the city.

b Are any of your plans very different from your partner's plans?

Grammar	Future Perfect and Future Continuous
Can do	do a survey and report the results

Nek Chand

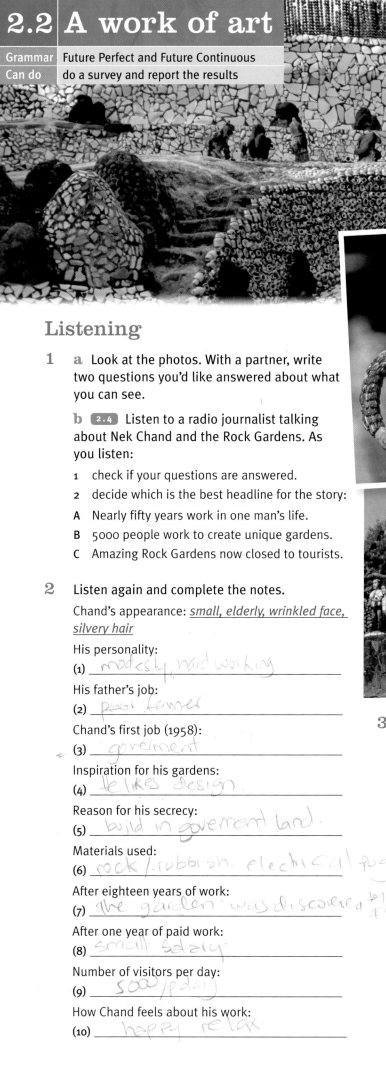

Rock Gardens of Chandigarh

Listening

1 **a** Look at the photos. With a partner, write two questions you'd like answered about what you can see.

b 2.4 Listen to a radio journalist talking about Nek Chand and the Rock Gardens. As you listen:

1 check if your questions are answered.

2 decide which is the best headline for the story:

A Nearly fifty years work in one man's life.

B 5000 people work to create unique gardens.

C Amazing Rock Gardens now closed to tourists.

2 Listen again and complete the notes.

Chand's appearance: *small, elderly, wrinkled face, silvery hair*

His personality:
(1) _modesty, hard working_

His father's job:
(2) _poor farmer_

Chand's first job (1958):
(3) _goverment_

Inspiration for his gardens:
(4) _He likes design_

Reason for his secrecy:
(5) _build in goverment land._

Materials used:
(6) _rock / rubbish. electrical plug_

After eighteen years of work:
(7) _the garden was discovered by a chan_

After one year of paid work:
(8) _small salary_

Number of visitors per day:
(9) _5000 / pday_

How Chand feels about his work:
(10) _happy relax_

3 Discuss.

1 **a** What do you think of Nek Chand?

b Would you like to visit the Rock Gardens of Chandigarh? Why/Why not?

c Do you know anyone with an unusual talent, hobby or job?

2 **a** What types of materials and things can be recycled? _Pastic, clothe,_

b What are the arguments for and against recycling?

c How much recycling of rubbish happens in your area? Do you think it's enough?

3 **a** Which environmental issues concern you most (e.g. recycling, pollution from cars, over-fishing, deforestation, etc.)?

b Would you consider your lifestyle to be 'environmentally-friendly'? Why/Why not? What could you change?

Grammar | Future Perfect and Continuous

4 **a** Match the examples 1–4 in the Active grammar box with the correct tense.

> ### Active grammar
>
> 1 *Tomorrow morning, he'll be doing the same as he's doing today.*
>
> 2 *Soon, Chand will have spent half a century working on this garden.*
>
> 3 *What will he be doing in five years' time?*
>
> 4 *He won't have finished the garden by the time he retires.*
>
> A Future Perfect – a description of something which will be completed before a definite time in the future
>
> ←————————————————
>   ————————x————————x————————
>   present   future
>
> B Future Continuous – a description of something in progress at a definite time in the future
>
>   ————————x————————x̃————————
>   present   future
>
> **Form**
> Future Perfect: *will/won't + have +* _____
> Future Continuous: *will/won't + be +* _____

b Complete the rules of form with the correct part of speech.

see Reference page 31

5 Complete the sentences with the Future Perfect or Continuous form of the verbs in brackets.

1 By this time next week, he ~~will have finished~~ _____ (finish) his Art project.

2 I'm sorry I can't come. I ~~will be playing~~ _____ (play) football tomorrow afternoon.

3 My boss won't be at work at 5.30p.m. She ~~will be going~~ _____ (go) home already.

4 Between 10.00 and 12.00 tomorrow I ~~will be having~~ _____ (have) a meeting so I'll phone you after that.

5 I hope you ~~will have finished~~ _____ (finish) making dinner by the time I get home.

6 I can't wait! This time next Friday, we ~~will be~~ _____ (lie) on a beach in Australia! *Lieing

7 This article says that when you're 50, you ~~will have spent~~ _____ (spend) a total of 16.7 years asleep.

8 Don't phone between 7.00 and 7.30 because I ~~will be having~~ _____ (have) my piano lesson.

Person to person

6 Ask and answer these questions with a partner.

1 What do you think you will be doing …
   a … at 2.00p.m. this Saturday?
   b … exactly one month from now?
   c … this time next year?
   d … when you're sixty-five?

2 What do you hope you will have done …
   a … by this time next week?
   b … by the end of this year?
   c … within the next five years?
   d … by the time you retire?

Vocabulary | 'after work' activities

7 **a** Match each verb in column A with the most appropriate words in column B to make ten verb phrases.

1 *do research on the Internet*

A	B
1 do	a) up to date with (your email, your diary, …)
2 visit (d)	b) the (bedroom, kitchen, …)
3 study (g)	c) an evening class
4 work (e)	d) chat rooms
5 spend (h)	e) late at the office
6 keep (a)	f) with friends
7 redecorate (b)	g) for a (law, business, …) qualification online
8 socialise (f)	h) quality time with (your children, family, …)

b Add three more 'after work' activities to the table above. Compare your ideas with a partner.

8 **a** Complete the sentences with the correct form of the most appropriate phrase from Ex. 7.

1 On a typical weekday evening I ___work___ – I've taken on a lot of extra responsibility and I often don't leave until after 9p.m.

2 I love ___visiting my friend___ in my free time. I've made loads of friends without having to even go out!

3 My evenings are very busy. On Mondays, I ___study___ in pottery, on Wednesdays, it's Spanish and on Thursdays, I do jazz dance.

4 I want to make the living room look nice and I can't afford to pay someone else to do it so at the moment I'm spending my weekends ___socialise___

5 I'm ___studying___ at the moment. I'm doing the next level in my accountancy training and it's a great course that I can do at home.

6 Whenever I'm not working I try to ___spend quality time___ with my children. They're growing up so fast.

7 I've been writing a diary since I was twelve. I try to ___keep up___ with it so I write a bit every day. ___socialise with friend___

8 ___is a big part of my life, either having dinner parties at home or going out.

b [2.5] Listen and check your answers.

9 Discuss.

1 Which of the sentences in Ex. 8 are most/least like you?

2 Do you think you spend your spare time wisely?

Listening and speaking

10 The questions below are from a 'work/life balance' survey. What do you think the results of the survey were?

1 *I think that less than half the group often works late at the office.*

2 *I think that hardly anyone has ever done any voluntary work.*

1 Do you ever work/study late either at the office/school or at home? *60% : 40%*

2 Have you ever done any voluntary work? *60%*

3 How many evening classes do you do? Which one(s)? *1/10%*

4 Do you usually switch on your computer in the evenings? *80%*

5 Do you find it easy to switch off after work/school? *Yes*

6 How good do you think your 'work/life balance' is? *30% : rest 70%: 8 hours*

11 **a** [2.6] Listen to the results and see if you were right.

b [2.7] Try to complete the sentences in the How to box from memory. Then listen and check your answers.

HOW TO …

report the results of a survey

Report exact results	nine (1) ___out___ of twenty people stay at work late at least three times a week.
	25% of the group had done some voluntary work.
	(2) ___Everyone___ said that a good way of relaxing was watching TV.
	Nobody liked doing this every evening.
Report approximate results	(3) ___nearly___ half the group regularly works late at the office.
	Hardly (4) ___any___ of them thought this was a bad thing.
	Many people are doing some kind of online course.
	Only a few people said they switched their computer on every evening.
	The (vast) (5) ___majority___ say they do at least one evening class.
	Only a (small) (6) ___minority___ would like to do more evening classes, however.

12 **a** Write some questions for a survey. First, underline the parts of the questions in Ex. 10 that you can use, e.g. *Do you ever...?*

b In pairs, choose which survey to do: the Internet in people's lives or the Arts in people's lives. Write six–eight questions for your survey.

c Ask your questions to as many students as you can and make a note of their answers.

13 **a** In pairs, collect the results of your survey and prepare to report them to the rest of the class. Use the How to box to help you.

b Report the results of your survey to the class.

c Were the results of any of the surveys surprising?

Grammar	*in case*
Can do	write a formal letter of application

Reading

1 a Look at the book cover and answer the questions.

   1 Where do you think the story is set?

   2 What do you think the main character does?

  b Read extract 1 and check your ideas.

1

Mma Ramotswe had thought that it would not be easy to open a detective agency. People always made the mistake of thinking that starting a business was simple and then found that there were all sorts of hidden problems and unforeseen demands. She had heard of people opening businesses that lasted four or five weeks before they ran out of money and stock, or both. It was always more difficult than you thought it would be.

She went to the lawyer in Pilane, who had arranged for her to get her father's money. He had organised the sale of the cattle, and had got a good price for them. 'I have got a lot of money for you,' he said. 'Your father's herd had grown and grown.' She took the cheque and the sheet of paper that he handed her. It was more than she had imagined possible. But here it was – all that money, made payable to Precious Ramotswe, on presentation to Barclays Bank of Botswana.

'You can buy a house with that,' said the lawyer. 'And a business.' 'I am going to buy both of those.' The lawyer looked interested. 'What sort of business? A store? I can give you advice, you know.' 'A detective agency.' The lawyer looked blank. 'There are none for sale. There are none of those.' Mma Ramotswe nodded. 'I know that. I am going to have to start from scratch.'

c Read extract 1 again and explain each of these lines in your own words.

  1 It was always more difficult than you thought it would be. (l.6)

  2 It was more than she had imagined possible. (l.9)

  3 I am going to have to start from scratch. (l.15)

2 a Before you read extract 2, discuss these questions.

  1 What kinds of things will she need to do to set up her business?

  2 What problems do you think she might have?

  b Read extract 2 and check your ideas.

2

There was a lot to do. A builder was called in to replace the damaged plaster and to repair the tin roof and, again with the offer of cash, this was accomplished within a week. Then Mma Ramotswe set to the task of painting, and she had soon completed the outside in ochre and the inside in white. She bought fresh yellow curtains for the windows and in an unusual moment of extravagance, splashed out on a brand new office set of two desks and two chairs. Her friend, Mr J.L.B. Matekoni, proprietor of Tlokweng Road Speedy Motors brought her an old typewriter which was surplus to his own requirements and which worked quite well, and with that the office was ready to open – once she had a secretary.

This was the easiest part of all. A telephone call to the Botswana College of Secretarial and Office Skills brought an immediate response. They had just the woman, they said. Mma Makutsi was the widow of a teacher and had just passed their general typing and secretarial examinations with an average grade of ninety–seven per cent; she would be ideal – they were certain of it. Mma Ramotswe liked her immediately. She was a thin woman with a rather long face and braided hair in which she had rubbed copious quantities of henna. She wore oval glasses with wide plastic frames, and she had a fixed, but apparently quite sincere smile.

They opened the office on a Monday. Mma Ramotswe sat at her desk and Mma Makutsi sat at hers, behind the typewriter. She looked at Mma Ramotswe and smiled even more broadly. 'I am ready for work,' she said. 'I am ready to start.' 'Mmm,' said Mma Ramotswe. 'It's early days yet. We've only just opened. We will have to wait for a client to come.'

3 Read extract 2 again and answer these questions.

  1 What equipment and furniture did she get for her office?

  2 Who did she employ and how?

  3 Were they busy when they first opened? Why do you think this is?

4 a Before you read extract 3, discuss these questions.

    1 Do you think Mma Ramotswe's business is likely to do well? Why/Why not?

    2 Do you think they get any clients on the first day of business? Why/Why not?

b Read extract 3 on page 145 and check your ideas.

c Read extract 3 again and write one sentence to summarise each of the following:

    1 Your impression of Mma Makutsi

    2 Mma Ramotswe's feelings about new business

    3 Mma Ramotswe's feelings about her employee

    4 Mma Makutsi's feelings as she 'hurtled through the door'

5 Discuss. Have you ever started/thought of starting your own business? Why/Why not?

Grammar | *in case*

6 Choose the correct alternatives for the rules 1–4 in the Active grammar box.

Active grammar

- *She stayed behind in the office in case the telephone rang.*
- *I phoned my boss again in case she hadn't got my message.*
- *I'll stay here in case any clients come in.* Precaution
- *I might leave early just in case there are problems on the trains.*
- *I always leave plenty of time to get to work just in case.*

1 a We can use *in case* to talk about past situations, to explain <u>why somebody did something</u>/<u>how things could have been different</u>.

  b When talking about the past, the verb that follows *in case* can be Past Simple or Past Perfect.

2 a We can also use *in case* to talk about future situations, to talk about <u>certainties</u> (*things that will definitely happen*)/<u>precautions</u> (*things we do in order to be ready for a possible future situation*).

  b When talking about the future, the verb that follows *in case* is normally in the present. We can use the <u>present</u>, future or a modal verb in the other clause.

3 We can use *just in case* to make *in case* a little more <u>emphatic</u>/<u>polite</u>.

4 We can use *just in case* <u>in the middle</u>/<u>at the end</u> of a sentence to talk about precautions in general (rather than specific situations).

---

see Reference page 31

7 Write sentences using the prompts and *in case*. You may need to change the verb tenses and to add words.

I want/prepare/well/interview/interviewer/ask me/difficult questions.

I want to prepare well for the interview in case the interviewer asks me difficult questions.

  1 I always write/'things to do' lists/forget/something important.

  2 I usually leave/more time than I need/get to work/the traffic/be bad.

  3 I always take/glass of water to bed/I/be thirsty/in the night.

  4 I usually take/first aid kit on holiday/just.

  5 I/give you/phone number/you/get lost.

  6 He took/umbrella/just/rain/on the way to the interview.

  7 I/buy/extra food/the children/be hungry/after the football match.

  8 You should write/address/your suitcase/it get lost.

  9 I/not go out/this evening/just/Daniela/phone.

  10 They wanted me/enter my email address twice/I make a mistake/the first time.

Person to person

8 a Look at sentences 1–4 in Ex. 7. Tell your partner if they are true for you.

b Write 4 more sentences about you using *(just) in case* about the past or the future. One sentence should be false.

I'm going to buy a newspaper as soon as I leave the class just in case they run out later.

c Guess which of your partner's sentences is false.

Writing

9 Read the job advert and the letter of application and answer these questions.

1 What relevant experience and qualities does Helena have?

2 What is her aim for the future?

3 Do you think it's a good letter of application? Why/ Why not?

Assistant Manager

required for new pizza restaurant

We're looking for an Assistant Manager to help run our new restaurant opening next month. The successful candidate will be enthusiastic, hard-working and sociable. Previous management experience would be helpful, and although experience of working in restaurants/cafés is desirable, it is not essential.

Write to:

Mario Ruggiero, 22 Wood Lane, London, N6 2RR by 13th January.

Please enclose your CV.

Mario Ruggiero
22 Wood Lane
London, N6 2RR

Letter for Aplication.

10 Hatton Close
London, N2 2NX

Tel: 07745 346229

9th January 2006

Dear Mr Ruggiero,

A I am writing to apply for the job of Assistant Manager of your new pizza restaurant you advertised in this week's *Highgate Times*.

B As you can see from my enclosed CV, I have worked as a waitress in a pizza and pasta restaurant for the last nine months, and my previous jobs include working as a waitress in a small French café/patisserie and a busy lunchtime sandwich bar in the city centre. I believe that I have gained valuable experience in the restaurant business and now feel it is time to move into the management side of things. I feel that I would be suitable for the job as I am very keen and hard-working. I am sociable and easy to get on with, as well as passionate about working in the catering industry.

C I am particularly interested in this job because I'd like to be involved with the setting up of a new business. Ultimately I would like to set up my own restaurant business but I obviously need to get more experience first.

D I can be contacted on the phone number above. I look forward to hearing from you.

Yours sincerely, → *you know the name of the person*

Helena Taylor

Helena Taylor

yours faithfully → you don't know the person

10 a Read the letter again. Which paragraph:

1 says how you can be contacted

2 describes your experience and why you would be suitable for the job

3 includes any extra information you think is important

4 says which job you are applying for and where and when you saw it advertised

b Complete the box below with the expressions from the letter.

INFORMAL	FORMAL
Dear Mario,	1 Dear Mr Ruggiero,
Just a quick note because I'd like the job.	2 *I'm writing to apply*
I reckon I've got a lot of good experience.	3 *I believe that I have gained...*
I think I'd be good at the job.	4 *I am suitable*
I really want this job.	5
Phone me on 07745 346229.	6 *I can be contact*
Hope to hear from you soon.	7 *look forward*
Best wishes,	8

11 Look at the job adverts on page 151. Decide which job to apply for. Then write a formal letter of application.

Lifelong learning

English for work and study

1 In what ways might you need to use English for work or studying?

• to socialise with clients

• to understand textbooks written in English

• ...

2 In what specific ways could you improve your English for work or studying?

• go to a website which can help you with language you might need in a work situation, e.g. www.longman.com/business

• find out where you could do an EAP (English for academic purposes) course

• ...

2 Vocabulary

Collocations with prepositions

1 Complete the sentences using the correct preposition which collocates with the adjectives in **bold**.

1 I'm **interested** _____ (of/ in/about) training to be an architect.

2 Nek Chand is very **modest** _____ (of/for/about) his achievement.

3 A lot of people are **afraid** _____ (of/at/for) losing their jobs.

4 I'm really **worried** _____ (about/from/on) my interview tomorrow.

5 I'm **keen** _____ (about/on/ in) doing some voluntary work in a prison if possible.

6 This job is very **similar** ___ (of/for/to) my last one.

7 You look **different** _____ (to/from/of) your sister, don't you?

8 Marc is really **good** _____ (about/in/at) tennis. He always beats me.

9 I'm **proud** _____ (of/about/ for) passing all my exams this year.

10 My uncle has been **passionate** _____ (about/ of/for) jazz all his life.

2 Complete the sentences with the correct preposition from the box which collocates with the verbs in **bold**.

> about   of   for (x3)   from   in (x2)   on (x2)

1 Are you going to **apply** _____ that job at the local café?

2 He **resigned** _____ his job last month to travel round the world.

3 My colleague **insisted** _____ paying for the whole meal.

4 You must make sure you **prepare** _____ your interview properly.

5 Do you **believe** _____ things like astrology and horoscopes?

6 Would you **complain** _____ slow service in a restaurant?

7 I usually **pay** _____ things by credit card.

8 I'm not sure what we'll do tomorrow. It **depends** _____ the weather.

9 Have you **succeeded** _____ finding a job yet?

10 The interview procedure **consisted** _____ a series of group tasks.

3 **a** Match the sentence halves 1–10 with a–j.

A	B
1 I'm afraid	a) at drawing.
2 She believes	b) for the party.
3 The audience consisted	c) from her job after only two months.
4 I've prepared everything	d) of a lot of noisy children.
5 It looks different	e) in ghosts.
6 My brother's very good	f) about Spanish dancing.
7 I always insist	g) on getting a receipt.
8 Your shoes are similar	h) to mine.
9 She resigned	i) from last time I was here.
10 Ana is passionate	j) of flying.

b **2.8** Listen and check your answers.

4 Complete the questions with the correct prepositions.

1 What kind of job would you like to apply _____ ?

2 What music are you most keen _____ ?

3 Do you feel passionate _____ anything?

4 In your family, who are you similar _____ and who are you different _____ ?

5 What sports are you good _____ ?

6 Did your parents insist _____ a particular bedtime when you were young?

7 When you decide where to go on holiday, what does it depend _____ ?

8 How do you usually pay _____ things in shops?

9 Are you the kind of person who is often worried _____ things?

10 What are you most proud _____ in your life?

5 Choose five of the questions in Ex. 4 to ask your partner.

2 Communication

The best candidate

1 Discuss. How do you feel about interviews? Do you get nervous? Why/Why not?

2 **a** Look at the list below of things that can happen at job/university interviews. Which of them do you think are positive?

1 I was slightly late for the interview
2 I wore fairly casual clothes
3 I panicked and couldn't think clearly
4 I showed them that I was enjoying talking about myself
5 I wasn't very well prepared for the interviewer's questions
6 I maintained eye contact with the interviewer
7 I talked quite negatively about my previous experience
8 I didn't have any questions to ask the interviewer
9 I let myself visibly relax
10 I remembered to switch off my mobile phone
11 I didn't find out exactly what the job/course involved
12 I couldn't remember everything I wrote on my application

b Have you experienced any of the situations above?

3 **a** **2.9** Listen to parts of interviews with four different candidates (Karen, Jenny, Liz and Linda) and answer these questions.

1 Is each interview for a job or for a place on a university course?
2 Which of the things in Ex. 1 apply to each candidate. (There may be more than one for each.)

b **2.10** Complete the interviewer's sentences. Then listen and check your answers.

1 Thank you for _____ for the job and coming to the interview today.
2 I'd like to ask you _____ your experience.
3 You say you've worked in an _____ before. Tell me about that.
4 I'm Peter Manning and I'll be _____ you today.
5 Can I start by asking you about your _____ for applying for the course?
6 What are your _____ for the future?

4 Choose one of the adverts on page 146 and prepare to roleplay an interview with a partner. Follow the instructions below.

Interviewees should prepare for the interview by making notes about:
- any relevant experience and qualifications you've got
- qualities that make you a suitable person for the course/job
- your plans for the future
- any further questions you'd like to ask

Interviewers should prepare for the interview by making notes about:
- how to start the interview
- questions to ask about relevant experience and qualifications
- questions to ask about personal qualities that make the candidate a suitable person for the course/job
- questions to ask about plans for the future
- how to finish the interview

5 **a** In pairs, roleplay the interview.

b Change roles. Prepare and then roleplay another interview.

c Discuss. Would you give your interviewee the job/place on the course? Why/Why not?

Futures overview

For plans and intentions:

Use *will* to talk about a decision made at the time of speaking (including offers and promises).

I think I'll go shopping after lunch.

I don't think I'll have anything to eat.

Use *going to* to talk about a plan or intention (but no details have been decided).

I'm going to study law, but I'm not sure where yet.

Use the Present Continuous to talk about a future arrangement (when details, e.g. about time and place have been decided).

I'm meeting Sonia after my interview in the café.

For predictions:

Use *will* to make predictions based on what you know/believe. We often use *think, hope, believe,* etc. with *will* in this case.

I think Ben will be the new School President.

Use *going to* to make predictions based on what you can see/hear now.

Be careful! You're going to fall off that chair if you lean back like that!

Future Continuous and Future Perfect

Use the Future Continuous to talk about something in progress at a definite time in the future.

Form *will + be +* present participle

Don't phone me tonight. I'll be watching the football.

We can use the Future Continuous to ask about someone's plans, especially if you want something or you want them to do something.

Will you be using the car on Saturday?

Use the Future Perfect to talk about something which will be completed before a definite time in the future.

Form *will + have +* past participle

She won't have finished her essay by Friday.

We often use the Future Perfect with time phrases with *by*, e.g. *by that time, by this time next week, by tomorrow, by then, by the end of the trip,* etc.

In case

We can use *in case* to talk about past situations, to explain why somebody did something. When talking about the past, the verb that follows *in case* can be Past Simple or Past Perfect.

We took our swimsuits in case there was a pool.

I phoned her again in case she hadn't heard the phone the first time.

We can also use *in case* to talk about future situations or to talk about precautions. When talking about the future, the verb that follows *in case* is normally in the present. We can use the present, future or a modal verb in the other clause.

You should insure your bicycle in case someone steals it.

We can use *just in case* to make *in case* a little more emphatic.

I'm going to apologise again just in case she's still angry with me.

We can use *just in case* at the end of a sentence to talk about precautions in general (rather than specific situations).

I'll take some extra money with me just in case.

Key vocabulary

Jobs/Phrases about jobs

journalist   civil engineer   social worker
nursery nurse   surgeon
a change of career   a labour of love   a career path
to take a year out   job satisfaction

Personality traits for jobs

be good with figures   be a people person
be a good listener   have a 'can do' attitude
work well in a team   have an eye for detail
get the best out of other people
be good at using your own initiative
be able to meet tight deadlines
keep calm under pressure

Verb phrases about work

to do voluntary work   to work part-time
to take early retirement   to be made redundant
to be sacked   to resign from your job
to be on strike   to be on sick leave
to work flexitime   to do shift work

'After work' activities

do an evening class   visit chat rooms
study for a (law, business, …) qualification online
work late at the office
spend quality time with (your children, family, …),
keep up to date with (your email, your diary, …),
redecorate the (bedroom, kitchen, …)
socialise with friends

Collocations with prepositions

interested in   modest about   keen on   passionate about   good at   proud of   afraid of   worried about   similar to   different from   apply for   resign from   insist on   prepare for   believe in   complain about   pay for   depend on   succeed in   consist of

1 Choose the correct alternative.

Why have you got your towel?

I'll wash/m going to wash my hair.

1 A Why are you turning on the TV?

   B I'*ll watch/m going to watch* the football.

2 A What would you like to eat?

   B I think I'*ll have/m having* a cheese sandwich.

3 A Wow! Look at those black clouds!

   B Yes, I think it'*ll rain/s going to rain*.

4 A Did you get the bread?

   B Oh no! Sorry, I forgot. I'*ll go and get/m going to get* it now.

5 A Have you seen John recently?

   B No, but I'*ll meet/m meeting* him at 7p.m.

6 A Where is Eva?

   B Oh, she'*ll be/s being* late ... she always is!

7 A Where are you going on holiday this year?

   B We've decided we'*ll have/re going to have* a skiing holiday but I'm not sure exactly where.

8 A Can you come on Thursday evening?

   B No, sorry. I'*ll play/m playing* volleyball.

2 Insert the verb phrases in the box in the correct places in the email.

> 'll be waiting   won't be going   'll be revising
> 'll have left   'll have been   ~~'ll have finished~~

Sat. 23rd

Hi Antonio,

I can hardly believe it - but by next Friday afternoon, *I'll have finished* all my exams! Until then, I'm completely up to my eyes in revision. I for my exams the whole of this weekend and then every spare minute I get next week. I really can't wait to get them all out of the way.

I'm really excited though, because I've booked a holiday for immediately after. In fact, this time next week, I for my flight to Crete. I'm going with Daniel - we've both been there before and loved it. After this holiday, we there four times! Anyway, that's why I'm writing really. I just wanted to know if you your job by then. If you have, why don't you come with us? I know it's short notice, but it would be great if you could come.

Let me know as soon as you can. Either email me or phone anytime. I to bed early tonight because I've got so much to do. Really hope you can come.

Gianni

3 Complete the sentences using the words in the box. Three of the words cannot be used.

> retirement deadlines surgeon career
> figures voluntary ~~resign~~ redundant
> pressure quality detail initiative

He found his job very stressful and decided to resign from it last month.

1 I don't think I'd be a good architect because you need an eye for _____ .

2 I'd love to be able to take early _____ and spend my time painting.

3 To be a successful vet, you have to be good at using your own _____ .

4 My father regrets not spending more _____ time with my sister and me when we were young.

5 My cousin Isabella is the best heart _____ at that hospital.

6 In my spare time I do a lot of _____ work with deaf people.

7 Thirty people were made _____ in our office last week because there isn't enough work for them now.

8 As a journalist, I'm always having to meet very tight _____ .

4 Complete the sentences with one word from box A and one word from box B. You will sometimes need to change the form of the verb.

> A prepare depend succeed complain
>   ~~consist~~ worried modest

> B about (x3) for on (x2) in ~~of~~

The flat *consists of* a kitchen, a large living room and three bedrooms.

1 My flatmate always _____ the noise when I'm listening to music.

2 Why are you so _____ her? She'll phone if there's a problem.

3 I'm so pleased that I _____ passing my driving test first time!

4 I'm not sure if I can come tonight. It _____ what time I finish work.

5 I haven't _____ my test tomorrow. I'm sure I'm going to fail.

6 She's so _____ her exam results. She never tells people how well she's done.

3 Old or new

Lead-in

handwritten: ↳the Parthenon

1 Discuss.

handwritten: A.D (anno Domini) despues de cristo.

1 What do you know about the places in the photos? What are they called? Have you visited any of them? If so, what were they like?

2 When do you think they were built?

- about 2000 AD
- about 1960 AD
- about 440 BC
- about 3000 BC

handwritten: conventional ↳ casual.

2 a Three of the <u>underlined</u> adjectives in the questions below are wrong. Correct them using the table and a dictionary.

handwritten: the Pyramids

PLACES	BUILDINGS	THINGS	PEOPLE	CLOTHES
ancient	old/new	old/new	old/young	old-fashioned
modern	modern	traditional	elderly	trendy
		second-hand	traditional (values)	fashionable
		modern		second-hand
		antique		traditional

handwritten: trendy → popular

1 Do you prefer <u>ancient</u> or modern furniture? Why? *handwritten: conventional casual.*
2 Are you interested in wearing <u>fashionable</u> clothes? Why/Why not?
3 Does your country have <u>traditional</u> dress? If so, what is it?
4 Do you live in an <u>elderly</u> building?
5 What do you think about using <u>second-hand</u> things?
6 Are there any interesting <u>antique</u> places near where you live?
7 Are there any <u>elderly</u> people in your family? Who are they?

b Ask and answer the questions with a partner.

Reading

1 Discuss.

1 Do you have a favourite hero or heroine from a story or film? What makes him/her heroic in your opinion?

2 Do you know who the heroes are in the ancient Greek story of Troy (made into a film in 2004)?

2 a Look at the pictures and read the text about the story of the Trojan War. Then answer these questions.

1 Which characters are mentioned in the story? What are the relationships between them?

2 Who is/are described as the hero(es) in the story?

b Read the text again and decide if these statements are true (T) or false (F).

1 Homer's story is mostly about war. T

2 The purpose of the party was for King Menelaus to declare victory over King Priam. F

3 Paris and Helen left the party without telling anyone. T

4 One reason why Agamemnon went to war was to win the city of Troy. T

5 Achilles wanted to help Agamemnon to become as powerful as possible. F

3 Now read the film review on page 146 quickly and answer the questions.

THE TROJAN WAR

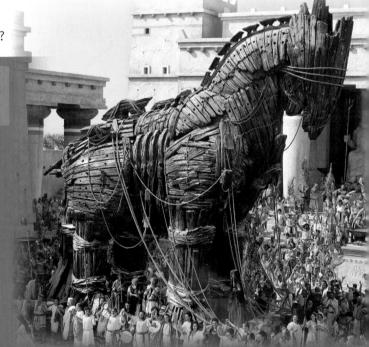

In the 8th century BC, the Greek poet Homer wrote about the Trojan War in his classic book, *The Iliad*. This epic story is full of love and passion, as well as the triumphs and tragedies of the war. King Menelaus of Sparta decided to have a party to make peace with King Priam of Troy and his eldest son Prince Hector. For the previous few centuries, the two kings had been fighting, trade had been declining and many cities had fallen into ruins. Now, the two kings were looking forward to a better future.

At the party, however, Hector's brother Paris fell in love with Menelaus's beautiful wife, Helen. Secretly, while the guests were enjoying the feast, Paris and Helen left the party together. From that point on, war between these two nations was inevitable. King Agamemnon of Greece (Menelaus's brother) ordered his warriors to fight for the honour of his brother and for the chance to become even more powerful by taking the city of Troy, which, up until that point, no army had been able to enter.

Agamemnon knew that the key to his success was the legendary Greek warrior, Achilles. At that time, all enemies feared Achilles who was known as the greatest warrior alive – a hugely skilled and heroic soldier. Although Achilles was willing to fight for Agamemnon, his motivation was not Agamemnon's victory since he despised the king's desire for power. For Achilles, the only reward he was interested in was the promise of eternal fame.

4 Read the text on page 146 again and complete these notes.

1 Main focus of the book *The Iliad*: _____
2 Main focus of the film *Troy*: _____
3 Two main characters in the film: _____
4 Number of extras: 2 000
5 Film reviewer's favourite character: Hector
6 Reviewer's favourite moment in the film: _____
7 Main criticism of the film: story is not the same
8 Reviewer's overall opinion: _____

5 Discuss.

1 If you've seen the film, do you agree with the reviewer's opinions? Why/Why not? If you haven't seen it, does the review make you want to see it? Why/Why not?
2 Do you think it matters if a film is not exactly the same as the book? Why/Why not?

Grammar | narrative tenses

6 **a** Match the <u>underlined</u> verbs in the Active grammar box to the list of narrative tenses A–D.

> ### Active grammar
>
> *Trade <u>had been declining</u> and many cities <u>had fallen</u> into ruins.*
>
> *Secretly, while the guests <u>were enjoying</u> the feast, Paris and Helen <u>left</u> the party together.*
>
> A Past Simple
> B Past Continuous
> C Past Perfect Simple
> D Past Perfect Continuous
>
> 1 Use _____ to talk about completed actions in the past.
> 2 Use _____ to talk about completed actions that happened before another action in the past.
> 3 Use _____ to talk about actions in progress at a particular time in the past.
> 4 Use _____ to talk about actions or situations which continued up to the past moment we are talking about.

b Complete each explanation 1–4 by writing the name of the correct narrative tense A–D.

c Look at paragraphs 1 and 2 of the text in Ex. 2. Find more examples of narrative tenses.

see Reference page 45

7 **a** Read the story of Hannibal and choose the correct alternative.

Until the 3rd century BC, Carthage (1) *was being/had been* a powerful city which controlled most of the Mediterranean Sea. For the previous few hundred years, the Carthaginians (2) *had been trading/traded* with people in India and the Mediterranean area. There (3) *had been/were* many battles between the Romans and the Carthaginians to try to control the area. Although Carthage (4) *had been taking/had taken* control of many important places, they (5) *weren't managing/hadn't managed* to take Sicily, the island on their doorstep. So, when the Romans won total control of Sicily, Carthage (6) *decided/was deciding* to attack Rome.

The leader of the attack (7) *was/had <u>been</u>* a brilliant young general called Hannibal. He had forty war elephants, trained to charge at the enemy. As Hannibal's army (8) *was marching/had been marching* northwards towards the Alps, soldiers from Spain and other areas (9) *joined/had joined* them. The icy mountains were difficult to cross, however, and by the time they (10) *reached/were reaching* Italy in 218 BC, many of his soldiers and elephants (11) *had died/had been dying*. They famously (12) *won/were winning* three battles but in the end the Romans were stronger and they took the city of Carthage.

b 3.1 Listen and check your answers.

Person to person

8 **a** Work in groups. Student As look at page 147 and student Bs look at page 148. Use the notes to practise telling your part of the story.

b Now work in pairs (one A and one B) and take turns to tell the story of Romeo and Juliet together.

Vocabulary | time expressions

9 **a** Look at the underlined expressions in the box. Do they talk about a) a time before, b) a time after, c) a specific time or d) actions at the same time?

> At that time   From that point on   Since then
> In 218 BC   Up until that point   Eric Bana is
> brilliant throughout the film.   During the war,
> trade declined.   Until the 3rd century BC
> For the previous few centuries.   After that
> In the 8th century BC   While the guests were
> enjoying themselves, Paris and Helen left the
> party.

b Add other appropriate expressions you know to the box above.

10 Choose the correct alternative.

1 *While/During* the summer we travelled around seven European countries.

2 I changed schools when I was twelve. *From that point on/Throughout*, I loved school.

3 I moved house last week. *For/While* the previous few months, I'd been living with my parents.

4 The Great Fire of London happened *at/in* 1666.

5 She was chatting *throughout/since then* the whole maths lesson.

6 A cinema opened in my town last year. *Up until that point/At that time*, the nearest one had been 40 km away.

7 I met James last year. *After that/Since then* we've been seeing each other a lot.

8 China was ruled by Emperors *until/while* the beginning of the 20th century.

9 I had a great time when I was at university. *At that time/Throughout*, I was sharing a flat with four friends.

10 *While/During* I was waiting for you, I finished my book.

11 **a** Complete the sentences about you.

1 Throughout most of last year I _____ .
  Previously, I _____ .

2 The best year of my whole childhood was _____ . At that time, I _____ .

3 I couldn't believe it when _____ . From that point on, I _____ .

4 One of the most important things to happen to me was _____ . After that, I _____ .

b Compare your sentences in pairs. Give more details about one or two of your sentences.

Writing

12 Discuss.

1 Do you think any groups of people who do particular jobs are modern-day heroes, e.g. firefighters, aid workers, nurses, etc.? Why?

2 Can you think of any other famous people or particular jobs that you think are heroic? Give reasons.

13 **a** You are going to write a short story about a hero or heroine. Choose one from this list:

a a famous modern-day hero/heroine, e.g. Princess Diana, Gandhi, Tiger Woods.

b a hero/heroine from a story or film

c Achilles, Hector, Hannibal, Romeo or Juliet

b Write brief notes about the events and the characters in the story.

c Divide your notes into three paragraphs:

1 What happens at the beginning of the story and events leading up to that time

2 The main events of the story

3 What happens near or at the end of the story

14 **a** Write your story using your notes. Don't write the name of the hero; just write *he/she* (or appropriate nouns). Use narrative tenses and time expressions.

b Read another student's story. Do you know the hero or heroine in his/her story?

Grammar	articles
Can do	talk about materials, possessions and inventions

Materials → uncountable   thing - countable

Vocabulary | materials

1   a   Describe the items in the photos using the words in the box.

> leather   porcelain   denim   bronze   silk   *iron*   Lycra   wool
> gold   rubber   cotton   silver   *fur*
>
> *cashmere / Glass / plastic / ink*

b   **3.2**   How do you pronounce the words? Listen and check.

c   Add four more materials to the box above.

A iron →   A Glass.

2   Think of five things you own. Describe the materials used in each one using words from Ex. 1.   *→ It's made of*

It looks like a   It similar to... (up) of

3   a   Match the adjectives 1–8 with the definitions a–h.

Adjectives	Describing something that:
1 soft *(e)*	a) has an even surface
2 stretchy *(f)*	b) has an uneven surface
3 shiny *(g)*	c) feels/looks like fur
4 smooth *(a)*	d) feels uncomfortable to wear because it irritates your skin
5 rough *(b)*	e) isn't hard or firm, but is easy to press
6 furry *(c)*	f) is slightly elastic
7 slippery *(h)*	g) has a bright surface
8 itchy *(d)*	h) is wet or difficult to hold/walk on

b   Complete the sentences with the most appropriate adjective.

1   Be careful on the icy path. It's very _slippery_.

2   I really like silk because it feels so _smooth_ on your skin.

3   I've got some new winter boots with _furry_ insides.

4   I can't wear wool because it's too _itchy_ for my skin.

5   For the interview I wore a suit and my new _shiny_ leather shoes.

6   Wear something _stretchy_ for the gym class so you can move easily.

7   It was a very uncomfortable journey because the road was so _rough_ *bumpy*

8   This bed is too _soft_ for me. I need a mattress that supports my back more.

4   Think of an object you have used today. In pairs, try to guess each other's object by asking Yes/No questions. Ask questions which contain the materials or adjectives in Exs. 1 and 3.

some parts are (adjective

Listening and speaking

5   a   **3.3**   Listen to five mini-dialogues and write down which objects and materials are mentioned in each one.

b   Listen again and answer these questions for each dialogue.

1   What is the woman's problem?

2   What does the woman like about her jeans?

3   What is the woman's problem?

4   What kind of toys does the woman like?

5   What does the woman say about her friend?

6   Discuss.

1   Have you got a favourite item of clothing? Why do you like it?

2   What do you think about wearing fur?

3   Do you have any allergies?

Listening

7 **a** Discuss. What things do you associate with
a) modern-day China and
b) ancient China?

b ▶ 3.4 Listen to the radio programme. Do the speakers mention any of the things you talked about?

8 Listen again. Decide if these statements are true (T), false (F) or we don't know (DK).

1 China has over 3000 years of history. *T*

2 China has been a major world economic power for centuries. *DK* *F*

3 Paper was made in China in around 1005 AD. *F* *Printing*

4 The first paper was made of silk waste products. *T*

5 The wheelbarrow was invented by one person. *Don't*

6 Guns were developed by the Chinese in around the 10th century. *F* *Firework*

7 The invention of cast iron had a huge impact on people's lives. *T*

8 Agriculture accounts for about 50% of China's economy. *F*

9 Rice, tea, cotton and fish are the major agricultural exports. *Don K*

10 Iron production in China is a rapidly expanding business. *T*

11 The population of Shanghai is growing by 22% a year. *DK*

12 Production of goods like toys, clothes and cars account for more than 50% of China's economy. *T*

9 Discuss.

1 Has any of the information in the programme made you change your ideas about modern-day or ancient China?

2 Would you like to visit China? Why/Why not?

Grammar | articles

Sky scrapers
manufacturing

10 Complete the Active grammar box with the underlined examples in the tapescript on page 168.

– fake products

Active grammar

The definite article *the* is used:

With inventions and species of animal	(1) *the gun*, *the tiger*
With national groups (when described as one whole nation)	(2) *The German*
When there is only one of something	*the Moon*
With rivers, oceans, seas	*the Pacific Ocean*
With superlatives	(3) *The most*
With particular nouns when it is clear what we are referring to	(4) _____
With previously mentioned nouns	*I've got a red umbrella and a black one. I prefer the red one.*

Brist

The indefinite article *a/an* is used:

With jobs	*a scientist*
With singular countable nouns (mentioned for the first time or when it doesn't matter which one)	(5) _____

No article (the zero article) is used:

With most streets, villages, towns, cities, countries, lakes, mountains	*Oxford Street, Beijing,* (6) _____ , *Mount Everest.* For countries and groups of islands in the plural we use '*the*' – *the United States, the Himalayas*
With uncountable, plural and abstract nouns used in their general sense	(7) _____ , *umbrellas*

Generally 'the' noun # of) noun

see Reference page 45

- Agriculture   - ming
- simple life   -
- Dynasty

Person to person

12 a Prepare to talk about one of these topics.

    1 a country or city you like

    2 a football club you support

    3 a species of animal you're interested in

    4 a make of car you like

    5 a job you'd like

    6 the most exciting thing you've ever done

b In pairs, take turns to talk about your topic.

Speaking

13 a **3.5** Listen to two people talking and answer these questions.

    1 What are they trying to decide?

    2 What do they agree on?

b Listen again and complete the questions in the How to box.

11 Complete these sentences using *the*, *a/an* or the zero article (–).

    1 _____ giant panda mostly lives in _____ bamboo forests high in the mountains.

    2 _____ Yangtze River is 6380 kilometres long. It is the third longest river in _____ world.

    3 _____ China covers _____ area of almost six million square kilometres and is _____ most populous country on Earth, having more than one billion people.

    4 _____ Chinese mainly speak Mandarin but there are over 150 other languages and dialects spoken throughout _____ country.

    5 I've got three Chinese silk dresses: ___ red one and two black ones. I think I'll wear ___ red one for my party.

    6 Amy Tan is _____ famous Chinese–American novelist. In 1989 she wrote _____ book called *The Joy Luck Club*. _____ book has now become a best-seller.

    7 _____ umbrella was invented around 450 AD to protect _____ people from sun and rain.

    8 'Zong Zi' is ___ dish made of ___ rice and bamboo leaves and is traditionally eaten during the Dragon festival.

HOW TO …

communicate interactively

Asking for someone's general opinion	1 *What do you _____ ?*
	2 *What _____ you?*
	3 *What _____ do you think is important?*
Asking for someone's specific opinion	4 *Do you _____ that …?*
	5 *How do you _____ about …?*
	6 *Isn't it _____ that …?*

14 a Look at the inventions in the box and decide which three you think are the most important. Write brief notes about your reasons.

> the television   the wheel   the telephone   the light bulb
> paper   the car   the Internet   gunpowder   the computer

b With other students, try to agree on the three most important inventions. Use the language in the How to box to help you.

Lifelong learning

Using technology

How much do you use technology to help with your learning?

1 Do you do these things: often, sometimes or never? Why?

2 Which ones would you like to do more?

- do exercises on CD-Rom
- watch English-speaking films or TV programmes
- listen to songs in English
- email people in English
- access English websites or take part in online chat in English
- listen to English radio

HIGH ST. LEIGHTON BUZZA...

Reading

1 Discuss. In what ways do you think things nowadays are the same as or different from twenty years ago? Think about food, clothes, music, etc.

2 Read the extract from a newspaper article below. Does the writer mention anything you talked about?

The Good Old Days

Is the uniformity of globalisation here to stay? Is every high street in the world doomed to be the same? Is the English language killing other languages and taking over the world? Oliver Hughes reports on what he found in Europe and laments the passing of the good old days.

Recently, I took a trip around Europe with my family and was truly saddened by what I found. It seems that gone are the days when travelling meant finding new and different places. Everywhere I went, I found the same things.

I found towns with the same shops along their high streets. I found people wearing the same clothes, eating the same types of food and listening to the same types of music. When I tried out my language skills in shops and asked for something in French or Spanish or whatever, they generally answered me in English. In one or two of the places, I had to think hard to try and remember which country I was in.

3 Divide into groups.

Students A: read the text on page 147 and choose the best summary sentence below (A, B or C).

Students B: read the text on page 148 and choose the best summary sentence below (A, B or C).

A One major advantage of globalisation is the melting pot of cultures and the creation of new things.

B The most damaging aspect of globalisation is that people lose their sense of national identity.

C The incredible choice we have nowadays is much preferable to the limited availability of the old days.

4 Students A: Read your text again and answer the questions below.

1 Does the writer mostly agree or disagree with Oliver Hughes?

2 What does he mean by 'the tyranny of geography'?

3 What is the main point he makes about his own high street?

4 Why does he mention brands like Zara and Muji?

5 What does he mean by 'we increasingly define ourselves'?

Students B: Read your text again and answer the questions below.

1 Does the writer mostly agree or disagree with Oliver Hughes?

2 What is the main point he makes about food?

3 Does he agree with Oliver Hughes about music?

4 What does he mean by 'a new type of English has been created'?

5 What is the distinction he makes between a 'single' language and a 'common' language?

5 Work in pairs with one student A and one student B.

1 Tell your partner about your text using your answers from Ex. 4.

The writer of the letter I read disagrees strongly with Oliver Hughes. The writer says that the diversity and choice in the modern world is …

2 In what ways are the opinions in the two letters a) the same and b) different? Which of the two letters is closest to your point of view?

6 Discuss. Do you think the old days really were 'the good old days'?

Grammar | adjectives and adverbs

7 **a** Choose the correct alternatives for rules 1 and 2 in the Active grammar box. Find examples of adjectives in the texts on pages 147 and 148 to help you if necessary.

Active grammar *write 1 sentence for each category.*

Adjectives

1 Adjectives are used to modify (*nouns*)/ *verbs*

2 Position of adjectives: usually directly (*before*)/ *after* the noun

Adverbs

3 Adverbs (and adverbial phrases) are used to modify verbs, adjectives and other adverbs

4 Position of adverbs:

At beginning of a sentence

A Connecting adverbs (which join a clause to what came before), e.g. *Nevertheless, Then,* Besides. However

B Time adverbs (if the adverb is not the main focus of the message), e.g. *Tomorrow, Last year,* In the morning

In the middle of a sentence (before the main verb)

C Adverbs of certainty and completeness, e.g. *probably, nearly,* truly , almost .

D Adverbs of indefinite frequency, e.g. *often, sometimes,* generally

E Adverbs of comment, e.g. *stupidly, ignorantly,* _____ → opinion about someone did

F Some adverbs of manner (if the adverb is not the main focus of the message), e.g. *quickly, rudely,* widly

At the end of a sentence

G Adverbs of manner (also see F above), e.g. *slowly,* strongly

H Adverbs of place, e.g. *upstairs, in the corner,* throughout the world

I Adverbs of time (also see B above), e.g. *this morning, a while ago,* all the time

---

b Look at the underlined adverbs and adverbial phrases in the texts on pages 147 and 148. Write them in the correct place in the Active grammar box A–I.

see Reference page 45

8 For each sentence, decide if the underlined words are adjectives or adverbs.

1 She lives in a lovely village but it's quite a *adj* lonely place. *adj.*

2 He's a lively child but can be a bit silly *adj* sometimes.

3 A: How are you? B: I'm fine, thanks. *adj/adv*

4 Don't eat those mushrooms. They're deadly. *adj.*

5 He can jump really high. I'm sure he'll do well *adv* in the competition. *adv* *adv*

6 I got up very early and caught the early train. *adj* *adv*

7 He's a really friendly dog but quite ugly! *adj* *adj*

9 Write the missing adverb or adverbial phrase in **bold** in the correct place in the sentences. Two different positions may be possible.

1 I want to try the local food when I'm in Thailand. **definitely** (C) rule

2 I spilt my coffee all over my new jacket. (F) **accidentally**

3 I work in a really modern building. on the 19th (H) **floor**

4 I went on a tour of six capital cities in Europe. **last month** (B) or (I)

5 My grandmother has been on an aeroplane in her whole life. **never** (D) rule.

6 The new building is designed to be both (E) attractive and practical. **expertly**

Person to person

10 **a** Choose the correct alternatives for each pair of sentences. *adj* *adv*

complete/completely completely.

1 a Do you usually _____ finish a book before starting a new one?

   b How do you feel about working when your desk is a _____ mess? complete

definite/definitely adv

2 a Is there anything you _____ want to do this weekend? definitely

   b Have you got any _____ plans for your next holiday? definite

late/lately

3 a Are you the kind of person who is often _____ for things? late

   b Have you bought any new CDs _____? lately

b Ask and answer the questions with a partner.

adv → change mean of verbs

[handwritten notes at top: fuss → a lot of unnecessary fuss / worried / excited about something]

Vocabulary | verb phrases with *take*

11 Match the <u>underlined</u> verb phrases with the definitions a–h.

1 We <u>take it for granted</u> that we have huge choice nowadays. *(f)* *[handwritten: → abuse doing something 'cause we have but another nd. → no te wal a costumbre]*

2 Is English <u>taking over</u> the world? *[handwritten circle]*

3 Thailand's unspoilt beauty <u>took my breath away</u>. *(h)*

4 Thousands of people <u>took part in</u> a demonstration to save the old town hall. *(e)*

5 Tourism in my city began to <u>take off</u> about 10 years ago. *(a)*

6 I found it hard to <u>take in</u> what the tourist guide was saying. *(c)*

7 He's always very calm and <u>takes</u> everything <u>in his stride</u>. *(g)*

8 The Italian people I met were really friendly. I <u>took to</u> them immediately. *(b)*

a) to start to increase/improve
b) to start to like someone or something
c) to understand what you see, read or hear
d) to take control of or take responsibility for something
e) to do something together with other people
f) to believe that something is true without making sure
g) to cope calmly with things without making a fuss
h) to be very surprised because something is very beautiful or exciting

12 Complete the sentences with the correct form of the phrases in Ex. 11.

1 I didn't *take to* the piano at first, but now I love it.

2 Don't *take it for granted* that I'll cook for you. You should check.

3 I decided not to _____ the race because I hurt my ankle. *[handwritten: take part in]*

4 He's quite old now so his son is going to *take over* the business.

5 The view of the mountains will _____. It's absolutely amazing. *[handwritten: take your breath away]*

6 She hadn't done very well before but her career *took off* when she joined this company.

7 There will be a lot of changes in the department. We need someone who will _____ and not need too much support. *[handwritten: take in / their stride]*

8 It was hard to *take in* everything that was happening in the film because it was a very complicated story.

13 Discuss.

1 When was the last time you took part in a race or a competition?

2 Are you the type of person who usually takes things in your stride?

3 Is there anyone that you sometimes take for granted? *[handwritten: you expect someone do something for you]*

4 Was there a point when you felt your English really started to take off? If so, when and why?

5 Can you think of something that has taken your breath away recently?

Speaking

14 a Give a short presentation about a city you know. First, make notes about the following.

• main events in its history
• any recent changes
• main positive features of the place
• any difficulties or problems the place has
• main tourist attractions
• likely future situation/changes/problems

b Practise giving your presentation to your partner. When you listen to your partner's presentation, can you give any advice to improve it? Look at these questions to help you give advice.

1 Was the information organised clearly?
2 Did he/she speak slowly, loudly, clearly enough?

15 Give your presentation to the class. Which of the places you heard about would you most like to visit?

3 Vocabulary

Making nouns

1 **a** Read the rules about making nouns.

  b Look at the examples and write some more examples of your own.

RULES	EXAMPLES
-er/-or is used to make nouns from verbs (often for a person who does an activity or for a thing which does a particular job)	*write → writer* *invent → inventor* *open → bottle-opener*
-ist is often used to make nouns from nouns (often for jobs, for people who play musical instruments and for holders of particular beliefs)	*journal → journalist* *piano → pianist* *social → socialist*
-(t)ion/-sion is one way of making nouns from verbs	*invent → invention* *pollute → pollution*
-ness is one way of making nouns from adjectives	*happy → happiness* *weak → weakness*
other common endings for nouns are: *-ment, -ity, -hood, -ship*	*excite → excitement* *product → productivity* *mother → motherhood* *friend → friendship*

2 Complete the sentences with the correct noun form using the word in **bold**.

Paper is one of the most important <u>inventions</u> ever. **invent**

  1 My boss really is the best _____ I've ever had. **employ**
  2 She spent most of her _____ in Scotland. **child**
  3 Lots of money doesn't always lead to _____ . **happy**
  4 Wait until the _____ arrives. She'll know what to do. **supervise**
  5 The job offers a lot of _____ in terms of working hours. **flexible**
  6 We need to improve _____ between departments. **communicate**
  7 My cousin is a very talented _____ . **violin**
  8 There has been a _____ in the number of trains in service. **reduce**
  9 Fresh vegetables are important for a child's growth and _____ . **develop**
  10 There has been a big increase in the _____ of the golf club. **member**

3 **a** One noun in each group is wrong. Find the incorrect word and correct it.

  1 involvement, arrangement, producement, replacement
  2 friendship, partnership, membership, enjoyship
  3 brotherhood, employhood, manhood, neighbourhood
  4 typewritist, pianist, physicist, scientist
  5 forgetfulness, readiness, forgiveness, modernness
  6 alteration, donation, develoption, admission

  b **3.6** Listen to all the correct nouns in the groups above and <u>underline</u> the main stress in each word.

in<u>vol</u>vement

4 **a** In pairs, decide which words you think have the main stress in each of these sentences.

  1 Career development is very important to me.
  2 My longest and most important friendship started in my childhood.
  3 There is a lot of pollution in my neighbourhood.
  4 One of my biggest weaknesses is forgetfulness.
  5 I think scientists should be paid more than musicians.
  6 Good communication is essential in a successful relationship.

  b **3.7** Listen and check your ideas.

  c Think about how far each of the statements above is true for you.

  d Compare your reactions to the statements with another student.

3 | Communication

Lessons from history

3 Read the six quotes about history below and match two of them to each of these explanations.

   A Learning history is a waste of time

   B Learning about the past is important for the future

   C It is difficult but essential to learn from history

1 Discuss.

   1 What was your most/least favourite subject at school? Why?

   2 Which do you think are the three most important subjects to study at school? Why?

   3 Are there any subjects you had to give up before you wanted to? Why?

   4 Are there any subjects you wish you'd studied harder in? Why?

   5 Do you think it's important to do vocational subjects at school, e.g. mechanics, metalwork, cookery? Why/Why not?

   6 Do you think it's important for students to do sport, music and drama at school? Why/Why not?

'History teaches everything including the future.' Lamartine

'History is a useless heap of facts.' Lord Chesterfield

'To be ignorant of the past is to remain a child.' Cicero

'History is more or less bunk. It's tradition. We don't want tradition.' Henry Ford

2 **a** **3.8** Listen to two friends, Martin and Debbie, and answer these questions.

   1 How did Martin feel about maths when he was at school?

   2 What is he studying now? Why?

   3 What is 'one of the biggest lessons' that Martin has learned?

'Whoever wishes to foresee the future must consult the past.' Machiavelli

b Think about your school days and complete one of the sentences below to make it true for you.

   1 Looking back, I wish I'd ...

   2 Now I'm older and wiser, I realise ...

   3 It's only with the benefit of hindsight that I've realised ...

   4 One of the biggest lessons I've learned in life is ...

'Learning history is easy; learning its lessons seems almost impossibly difficult.' Nicholas Bentley

c Compare and discuss the sentence you completed with another student.

4 Choose one of the quotes in Ex. 3. Discuss the quote with other students. Do you have the same opinions?

Narrative tenses

Use the Past Simple to talk about completed actions in the past.

We got up early and caught the 11 o' clock train.

Use the Past Continuous to talk about actions in progress at a particular time in the past.

Form *was/were* + present participle

I was walking to work when I tripped and fell.

Use the Past Perfect Simple to talk about completed actions that happened before another action in the past.

Form *had* + past participle

I'd just finished my lunch when the doorbell rang.

Use the Past Perfect Continuous to talk about actions or situations which continued up to the past moment we are talking about.

Form *had* + *been* + present participle

Before they moved to this country, they had been living in Australia.

Articles

Use the definite article *the*:

With inventions and species of animal: *The giant panda is an endangered species.*

With national groups: *the British, the Ancient Greeks*

When there is only one of something: *the sun*

With rivers, oceans, seas: *the Mediterranean Sea*

With superlatives: *China is the most interesting place I've been.*

With particular nouns when it is clear what we are referring to: *Can you turn off the light, please?*

With previously mentioned nouns: *Would you like an apple or a banana? The banana is very ripe.*

Specifying which one we mean: *What did you do with the book I lent you?*

Use the indefinite article *a/an*:

With jobs: *a teacher, an engineer*

With singular countable nouns (mentioned for the first time or when it doesn't matter which one): *I'd like an apple.*

Use no article (the zero article):

With most streets, villages, towns, cities, countries, lakes, mountains: *Italy, Mount Fuji*

(For countries and groups of islands/mountains in the plural we use 'the': *the Netherlands*.)

With uncountable, plural and abstract nouns used in their general sense: *Accommodation is difficult to find.*

Adjectives and adverbs

Adjectives are used to describe nouns. They usually come directly before the noun.

I live in a really beautiful city.

Adverbs (and adverbial phrases) are used to modify verbs, adjectives and other adverbs. The position of adverbs in a sentence can vary, depending on the main focus of the message.

Position of adverbs:

At the beginning of a sentence

Connecting adverbs and Time adverbs (if the adverb is not the main focus of the message)

In the middle of a sentence (before the main verb)

Adverbs of certainty and completeness, Adverbs of indefinite frequency, Adverbs of comment, some Adverbs of manner (if the adverb is not the main focus of the message)

At the end of a sentence

Adverbs of manner (see above), Adverbs of place, **Time** Adverbs (see above)

Many adverbs end in *-y*, but some words ending in *-y* are adjectives not adverbs. e.g. *friendly, lively, lonely, silly*

There are also many adverbs which do not end in *-y*. e.g. *late, fast, fine, hard, high, well*

Sometimes the adjective and adverb have the same form: *fast, hard, fine, early, daily*

He worked really hard.   This chair is too hard.

Key vocabulary

Age

modern   ancient   antique   traditional   second-hand   elderly   old-fashioned   trendy   fashionable

Time expressions

while   during   throughout   at that time
in (218 BC)   in the (8th century BC)
from that point on   since then   after that
up until that point   until the (3rd century BC)
for the previous (few centuries)

Materials

leather   porcelain   denim   bronze   silk   iron   lycra   wool   gold   rubber   cotton   silver

Describing objects

soft   stretchy   shiny   smooth   rough   furry   slippery   itchy

Verb phrases with *take*

take off   take to   take in   take part in   take over   take my breath away   take it for granted   take it in one's stride

1 Five of the sentences have a missing word. Find the sentences and write the word in the correct place.

1 We had walking for twenty minutes when it started to rain.

2 You remember to bring that book yesterday?

3 When I got to the party, Jack already gone home.

4 I went back to my hometown after fifteen years and found that it had changed a lot.

5 While Cristina sitting on the bus, someone stole her wallet.

6 The doorbell rang and I hadn't even got dressed!

7 Someone finally answered the phone after I'd waiting for ten minutes.

2 Complete the sentences by writing the correct form of the verbs in brackets.

When you rang, I <u>was getting</u> (get) ready to go out.

1 I _____ (work) on the report for five days when she told me it _____ (not/be) necessary.

2 What _____ (you/do) when I phoned? It _____ (be) very noisy.

3 It wasn't until I _____ (get) home that I realised my wallet _____ (steal).

4 I can remember exactly what I _____ (do) at midnight last New Year.

5 I was embarrassed because she _____ (arrive) before I _____ (wrap up) her birthday present.

6 _____ (you/learn) the guitar for a long time before you gave up?

3 Put *a/an* or *the* in these sentences if necessary.

1 She lives in Alexandra Road. It's not far from post office.

2 People say that British are reserved.

3 I'm not sure but I think I'd like to be architect when I grow up.

4 Don't forget your suncream. Sun is very strong today.

5 Leisure time is increasing for most people in Europe.

6 We stayed at very nice hotel in Barcelona.

7 That was one of best books I've read for ages.

8 Shall we sit in garden for a while?

4 Complete the pairs of sentences with the correct adjective and adverb.

quiet/quietly

Could everyone be <u>quiet</u> during the exam?

You're speaking too <u>quietly</u>. I can't hear you.

1 **bad/badly**

a I fell and hurt myself quite _____ .

b The pollution is very _____ in this part of town.

2 **careful/carefully**

a Don't worry. He's a very _____ driver.

b You really need to do your homework more _____ .

3 **perfect/perfectly**

a Your pronunciation is absolutely _____ .

b Petra speaks English almost _____ now.

5 Choose the correct alternatives.

I was only slightly (late)/lately for the class.

1 The new shopping centre is *enormous/ enormously*.

2 I couldn't believe it. The exam was *incredible/ incredibly* easy.

3 He drove frighteningly *quick/quickly* along the motorway.

4 I can't go out until I've *complete/completely* finished my homework.

5 I thought the meal would be cheap but it was *surprising/surprisingly* expensive.

6 I'm absolutely *certain/certainly* that you got the answer right.

6 One word is wrong in each sentence. Find and correct it.

My grandfather lives in a home for ancient people. elderly

1 I don't usually wear wool because I find it too stretchy.

2 When I first visited Rome, it took my head away.

3 She's got all the most fashion clothes.

4 I've decided to take part of a writing competition.

5 I've been working in a café while the summer.

6 I like going to second time shops and buying old clothes.

7 There's too much information to take on at once.

8 I broke my leg last year. Since that, I haven't played football.

4 Risk

Lead-in

1 Discuss. In what ways do you think the people in the photos might be 'taking a risk'?

2 Which alternative in each of the sentences below is not possible?

1 Moving abroad without a job can be a bit of a *risk/gamble/hazard*.
2 You'll never get another *luck/opportunity/chance* like this to travel.
3 We need this contract. There are a lot of jobs at *stake/risk/gamble*.
4 My one real *ambition/dream/belief* is to go to the North Pole.
5 If we don't go back now there's quite a *big/substantial/vast* risk that we'll get caught in a storm.
6 For some people doing something that no one else has ever done can become an *obsession/infatuation/all-consuming passion*.
7 I think they're *hardly/amazingly/incredibly* brave to walk across that tightrope without a safety net. What if they lost concentration for a second?

3 **4.1** Listen to this young woman talking about her attitude to risk and answer the questions.

1 What amazing thing did her brother once do?
2 What adventure is she considering?

4 Discuss.

a When did you (or someone you know) last take a big risk?
b What did it involve doing?
c How did you (or he/she) feel before/during/afterwards?
d Would you (or he/she) do something like that again?

Reading

1 Discuss.

1 Do you like to spend a lot of time on your own? Why/Why not?

2 Do you prefer working in a group or on your own? Why?

3 Do you prefer team or solo sports?

2 Read the text and tick (✓) the topics mentioned.

1 Ellen's achievement ✓

2 Her attitude to her boat ☐

3 Her love life ☐

4 Her boat's facilities ✓

5 The qualities a solo sailor needs ✓

6 The costs of the voyage ☐

7 The differences between sailing in 1969 and today ✓

Ellen MacArthur

has been welcomed home by huge crowds after sailing solo around the world in record time. (A) _____ . 28-year-old MacArthur battled storms and high winds for much of the 44,000-kilometre journey. She finally completed her voyage in 71 days 14 hours 18 minutes and 33 seconds, beating the existing record by 33 hours.

I met up with her the day after her return and we went to see her boat. 'She talks,' says Ellen with complete sincerity. 'She talks to me.'

This is why she risked her life and sanity to become the fastest person ever to sail alone around the world: not fame or money or even winning, important though that is to her. (B) _____ .

Her boat, named *B&Q* after her sponsors, is 23m long and 15m wide, the cabin is no more than 2.5m by 1.5m. It contains a bunk, a chart table, twin computer screens and navigational equipment, a single gas burner and a sink the size of a large bowl. That's it. No toilet (just a bucket), no shower, no comforts except a cuddly toy or two. (C) _____ .

Did you ever get lonely, I ask. 'No,' she says without hesitation. She is also dismissive of fear. 'Often you don't know what's going to happen when there's a big storm coming so, when you're actually in it, it's better. Then you can get on and do what you have to do.'

Apart from breaking the time set by Francis Joyon last year, MacArthur is only the second person ever to sail solo non-stop around the world on a multi-hull boat. Six times more people than that have stood on the Moon. More than 1800 have climbed Everest. And four men, all great sailors, have already tried and failed to match the feat of Joyon. (D) _____ .

'That's the common misconception, that it's all down to size and muscle,' says Sir Robin Knox-Johnston, the first person to sail solo non-stop around the world. 'Single-handed sailing is really all about the mind.'

Knox-Johnston, 65, sailed into the record books in 1969 when he became the first person to sail non-stop around the world alone in his 10m wooden yacht, Suhaili. (E) _____ . 'You need to be able to focus, deal with things alone and have incredible levels of self-discipline. If you don't have an extreme mental toughness, you probably won't survive,' he adds.

The technology has changed greatly since Knox-Johnston's day. Now you can watch what happens on board via cameras, listen to audio links and communicate by email. (F) _____ . He used an old-fashioned sextant to work out his position and made crude weather predictions with a barometer taken from a local pub.

Today, sailors use GPS positioning for accurate plotting of their exact location and get highly accurate weather forecasts from their team onshore. However, as the veteran yachtsman says: 'If we'd had all the modern equipment, it would have saved us time but rescue is still not guaranteed and the hazards remain the same. I don't think the challenge is any less, it's just different. The course is the same.'

3 Each of the following sentences comes from the text. Read it again and decide where each one should go.

1 Ellen, standing at just 1.6m tall, is the first to succeed.
2 He finished in 312 days.
3 She tells me she washed twice on the trip, once in a rainstorm and once using some of her fresh drinking water.
4 This is very different to the early days of single-handed sailing when Sir Robin Knox-Johnston lost the use of his radio and therefore all contact with the outside world.
5 What matters is living as one with her boat and the sea.
6 This achievement establishes her as possibly the greatest sailor Britain has ever produced.

4 Discuss.

1 From the article what is your impression of Ellen MacArthur? In what ways do you think you are like her?
2 How would you feel about being alone on a boat like Ellen's for 71 days? What would you miss the most?
3 Do you agree with Sir Robin Knox-Johnston when he compares his voyage in 1969 and Ellen's and says: 'I don't think the challenge is any less, it's just different. The course is the same.'

Grammar | *if* structures (1)

5 **a** Look at the structures A–C in the Active grammar box and complete examples 1–3 with *don't, won't, would, have* or *had*.

Active grammar

1 _____ you be interested in sailing round the world, if you _____ the chance?
2 If we _____ had all the modern equipment, it would _____ saved us time.
3 If you _____ have an extreme mental toughness, you probably _____ survive.

A Use *If* + present tense, + *will* to talk about future possibility. (Often called the First Conditional).
B Use *If* + past tense, + *would* to talk about present or future unreal or imagined situations. (Often called the Second Conditional.)
C Use *If* + Past Perfect, + *would have* to talk about unreal or imagined situations in the past. (Often called the Third Conditional.)

b Now match the rules A–C in the Active grammar box to each of the examples 1–3.

see Reference page 59

6 Correct the mistake in each of the following sentences.

1 Do you phone me if anything goes wrong?
2 What you have done if a nearby boat hadn't picked up your distress call?
3 You had feel a lot better about things if you took a risk and left your job.
4 What you like to do if you had some free time and money?
5 If I didn't take a year off to cycle across Africa, I wouldn't have met my husband.
6 If you'll see John, can you ask him if he's going to come parachuting with us at the weekend?
7 I wouldn't suggest you come if I'd known you were afraid of heights.

Person to person

7 **a** Think of three different people you might see or talk to today. Imagine what you might say to them. Tell another student.

If I see Matt, I'll ask him if he wants to come to my party at the weekend.

b Imagine you had more time each week to do the things you enjoy. Tell another student how you would spend that time.

If I had more time, first of all I think I would have some piano lessons because ...

c Think about major decisions you have made in the past. Imagine if you had made a different choice. Explain to another student what you think you might have done.

If I hadn't had children in my 20s, I would have travelled more. I've always wanted to go to Brazil and ...

Writing

8 Read these extracts from Ellen's diary. What is the main thing she writes about on Day 1, Day 3 and Day 4?

Day 1
It was pretty amazing for me – the emotion of leaving the dock and seeing all the people wave me off down the Channel. It finally hit me during the night as I was working on the computer: This is it – I'm doing the [1] Vendée Globe. It hadn't really sunk in until then. So I'd better get on with it ...

Day 3
Approaching Spanish coast. Spoke to my uncle (a doctor) today, to ask him if I should stick a burning hot wire through my fingernail to release a bit of pressure as it was black after I trapped it while trying to open a valve last night. The answer was yes. The blood spurted out, leaving a still sore but less painfully throbbing finger.
I'm not totally happy with the boat speed. I guess this is partly due to the extra weight of what I'm carrying for the next three months.

Day 4
Steep, savage seas, with forty-five-knot blasts right on the Cape of NW Spain. Last night was the toughest I've spent on board. The wind went from fifteen to forty-five knots in thirty seconds. The seas were just horrific. I couldn't stop her leaping over each wave and crashing down on to the next. At one point, the carbon shelving on which the stores are stacked collapsed. Very tired.

> **Glossary**
> [1] *Vendée Globe* = a round-the-world yacht race

9 Discuss in pairs.

1 Which of the following do you think are the most typical reasons for keeping a diary?
- as a personal record of experiences
- as a way of practising your English
- as a way of thinking things through
- as a way of communicating with someone else
- as a way of helping you when you are studying
- as an emotional outlet
- as a place to put special private thoughts
- as a place to put ideas in case you want to write a novel

2 Have you ever kept a diary? If so, when and for how long? How often did you write in it? What did you write about? Did you mind if other people saw it or was it private? Which of the reasons in question 1 above applied to you?
If you haven't ever kept a diary, is it something you would consider doing? Why/Why not?

3 There are many different ways of keeping a diary. What do you notice about the 'style' of Ellen's diary? What do you notice about the grammar of the first and last sentences in her Day 4 entry?

10 a Read the definition below. Have you have ever read or written a 'blog'?
A blog (or weblog) is a diary/journal that is available on the web. The activity of updating a blog is 'blogging', someone who keeps a blog is a 'blogger'.

b Read the 'blog' on page 150 and answer these questions.

1 What reasons are given to explain why some people write 'blogs'?

2 Why do you think that people write 'blogs'?

11 a Prepare to write a diary entry or 'blog'. First decide what you would like to write about, e.g.
- what you did last night/last weekend
- how you are feeling
- something important that has happened recently
- what you think about 'blogging'
- something else

b Write your diary entry or 'blog'. (Write at least 100 words).

Lifelong learning

Keeping a diary

Keeping a diary can be a very good way to practise your writing in English. Buy a special book to write in and try and write something in your diary every day (even if it is only a few words).

Vocabulary | physical movements

1 Match the drawings to the verbs in the box.

> leap swing land bend balance
> stretch flip tuck roll lean

a) *stretch*

f) *leap / jump*

b) *bend*

g) *tuck*

c) *roll*

h) *balance*

d) *swing*

i)

e) *Lean*

j) *Flip*

2 **a** Look at the drawings on page 150 and read the description of three moves involved in free running. Complete each one with verbs from Ex. 1.

Standing/Basic jump: Bend the knees and (1) _____ the arms. Throw the whole body forwards and bring the knees up. (2) _____ with bent knees and roll.

The Parkour Roll: (3) _____ the knees and put your hands on the floor. (4) _____ across one shoulder, (5) _____ the body and roll diagonally. Stand up and continue running.

Wall flip: Run and put your foot as high as possible up the wall. Next, (6) _____ back and bring the free leg through. Finally, (7) _____ and land. (Hopefully!)

b How would you feel about trying any of these moves?

Listening and speaking

3 **4.2** Listen and follow these instructions to do a relaxation exercise.

4 **a** Work in pairs. Student A look at the pictures and read the instructions on page 148. Student B look at the pictures and read the instructions on page 149.

b When you understand the move, tell your partner what to do. Check that they do it correctly.

Reading

5 Read the article quickly and answer this question. What does it say you need to do to be able to do 'free running' successfully?

- training
- feel confidence

Running Free

1 'Parkour' – or free running – is the fast-growing extreme sport that turns everyday urban landscapes into obstacle courses. Caroline Williams meets the man who started it all.

2 Loosely translated, 'le parkour' means 'using every object in your path as an obstacle'. It began in 1987 in the Paris suburbs, where bored teenagers Sebastien Foucan and David Belle decided to make life more interesting. 'Interesting' involved climbing up buildings, swinging around lamp posts and vaulting anything that stayed still for long enough. 'We were just kids who started playing a game, and we've never really stopped,' says Foucan.

3 With six friends, they set up 'Yamakasi' – a group which later split when five of them opted to take work as theatre acrobats, but not before it had led to a 2001 film of the same name. Yet, despite all the splits and personal differences, what they refer to as 'the discipline' lives on.

4 Fifteen years later, it's a global phenomenon. The UK-based parkour website gets 10,000 visitors a day. Foucan is surprised to say the least. 'For me, it's amazing but it's my goal to meet people from all over the world and to spread the philosophy,' he says. This philosophy is all about challenging and improving yourself, while maintaining a zen-like calm. That's why there are no competitions in parkour, and definitely no world records. When asked what is the highest he has ever jumped, Foucan replies: 'I have no idea.'

5 There have been serious setbacks. One person died after trying some of the moves in the Yamakasi film. And since the rise of parkour's popularity amongst the general public there have been more than a few broken bones. 'The key thing,' says Ez (pronounced 'ee-zee'), a founder member of the movement, 'is that you must learn how to roll. It's very important because if you're moving forwards with a lot of momentum and you don't roll, your legs take the shock. If you can roll – across your shoulder, never on your spine – it transfers the energy so you don't get hurt. You land, you roll, you stand up and you keep running.'

6 And if you are going to leap from a tall building, or even just off the back of your sofa, you should know how to land properly. 'You might think you just bend your knees, but actually you have to land on the ball of your foot, bend your knees in a certain way and slap the floor with your hand. It takes the shock out of landing entirely.' It looks painful but he insists it doesn't hurt nearly as much as when he landed flat on his heels one time and couldn't walk for nine weeks.

7 Once you've mastered these moves, you can create as many jumps and death-defying handstands off the edges of buildings as you like. But, as the cliché goes, it's practice that makes perfect. And you have to be able to suppress any last-minute doubts or fears. 'When you get scared, you become more rigid in your movements, your muscles become tense and you're more likely to lose co-ordination,' says Professor Stuart Biddle, a sports psychologist. 'The mind plays a massive part,' agrees Ez. 'When you're standing at the edge of one building leaning to do a spot jump, you fall until the very last second and then jump. It's scary because you can see exactly how far up you are – it might be eighteen or twenty metres. If the fear gets to you, it's all over, so you really have to have confidence in your training.'

> **'We were just kids who started playing a game, and we've never really stopped'**

6 Read the article again and decide if the following statements are true (T) or false (F).

1 'Free running' was invented in France. T

2 It was originally a way of fighting boredom.

3 A group of friends created 'Yamakasi' and it still exists. F

4 Foucan knew it would become this popular. F

5 People who do free running aren't competitive. F

6 Ez says one of the most important things is to be fit. F

7 He has never hurt himself while free running. F

8 Fear has a bad effect on your co-ordination. T

9 Ez never feels any fear. F

7 Find words in the text which mean:

1 to jump over something in one move (para. 2)
2 to choose one thing over another (para. 3)
3 a problem that happens that stops you from making progress (para. 5)
4 the force or energy that makes a moving object continue to move (para. 5)
5 an expression that is used too often and no longer has any real meaning (para. 7)
6 stiff and not moving or bending (para. 7)

8 Discuss.

1 Is 'free running' a good thing for young people to be involved in? Why/Why not?
2 Who do you think might be opposed to 'free running'? Why might that be?

Grammar | expressing obligation

9 a Match each example 1–5 in the Active grammar box with one of the meanings A–E.

Active grammar

Present

1 You <u>should</u> know how to land properly. *D*
2 You <u>must</u> learn how to roll. *C*
3 You <u>have to</u> get permission to run across certain buildings. *E*
4 You <u>don't have to</u> wear special clothes. *A*
5 You<u>'re supposed to</u> do it in groups. *B* (expect)

A It's not necessary for you to do it.
B It is expected.
C The obligation comes from inside, e.g. how the speaker feels.
D It's a good idea to do it.
E The obligation comes from outside, e.g. a law.

Past

6 We should *have known* how to land properly.
7 We *had to* learn how to roll.
8 We *had* to get permission to run across certain buildings.
9 We *didn't have* to wear special clothes.
10 We *were supposed* to do it in groups.

b Complete the examples 6–10 to put the sentences in the past.

c Decide if there are any differences between each pair of sentences. Explain what they are.

1 a I must stop smoking. → obligation
  b I have to stop smoking. → no necessary
2 a You don't have to wear a tie. → it's a advice
  b You shouldn't wear a tie.
3 a You should tell her how you feel. → the same
  b You ought to tell her how you feel.
4 a You didn't have to wait for me. → the same
  b You didn't need to wait for me.
5 a We didn't need to run for the train.
  b We needn't have run for the train.

see Reference page 59

10 a The words in the box are missing from the text below. Note where each one should go.

> should to had (x2) supposed didn't

'One of the best things we did on holiday was to go whitewater rafting. However, I was a bit nervous at first when they told us we to sign something which basically said we wouldn't hold the company responsible if we got injured or died! Anyway, the guy in charge of our boat gave us some instruction before we started off. We to wear lifejackets of course but I was quite surprised that we have to wear any kind of crash helmet. We were also to wear trainers but I'd forgotten mine so I had wear my sandals. Finally, we got going and the whole thing was fantastic. There were eight of us in a boat and there really was a lot of 'white water'. It was a bit like being on a rollercoaster and I nearly fell in at one point. The one thing I'm sorry about is that I didn't get any photos. I have taken my camera but I was afraid I would drop it in the water.'

b 4.3 Now listen and check your answers.

Person to person

11 Tell another student one thing:

- you should do today
- you should have done by now
- you must do this week
- you have to do every day
- you had to do as a child
- you didn't have to do as a child
- you were supposed to do recently (but didn't)

Million Dollar Baby

Every Which Way But Loose

Dirty Harry

Listening

1 **a** What is the connection between the film stills above? Do you know any of the films?

b [4.4] Listen to this conversation. Which of the films are they talking about?

c Listen again and answer the questions.

1 Did both people like the film?
2 What is one important theme of the film?
3 In what way does the Clint Eastwood character <u>not</u> take a risk in the film?
4 In the beginning why does the Clint Eastwood character not want to train the young woman boxer?
5 Do we discover why Clint Eastwood doesn't have contact with his daughter?
6 What connection is suggested between the young woman boxer and Clint Eastwood's daughter?

2 Work in groups.

1 If you know the story of *Million Dollar Baby*, tell the other students in your group (who haven't seen it) what happens in the rest of the film.
2 If none of you have seen it, say what shocking thing might have happened that is referred to in the conversation above. Then check your ideas by reading the synopsis of the film on page 146.

Grammar | emphasis

3 Match the examples 1–4 in the Active grammar box with the ways of emphasising A–D below.

Active grammar

1 *I do like Clint Eastwood.* D
2 *It was much, much better than that.* A
3 *There are so many different themes running through the film.* B
4 *It's the film which I've enjoyed most this year.* C

A Use repetition.
B Add an emphasising word, e.g. *so*, *such*, *really*, *just*, etc.
C Use the structure: *It is/was ... which/that ...*
D Add an appropriate form of *do*.

see Reference page 59

4 **a** Match the sentence halves 1–7 with a–g. Add *do*, *does* or *did* for emphasis. Change the form of the verbs where necessary.

She does know the film starts at 7.30p.m.

1 She knows   a) for being so late.
2 I sent   b) some help with her homework.
3 They like   c) the film starts at 7.30p.m.
4 He apologised   d) you a message this morning.
5 You realised   e) oysters.
6 She needs   f) how you are feeling.
7 I understand   g) they were married, didn't you?

A Fistful of Dollars

Bridges of Madison County

5 **a** [4·5] Listen to the sentences below. Underline the words/phrases which you hear emphasised.

1 She had always wanted this job.

2 I went and saw my doctor yesterday.

3 I decided to ask if I could borrow his new Mercedes.

4 She really doesn't like the words to their new song.

5 He wants to study sociology or psychology at university.

6 He broke the kitchen window while he was playing with a ball.

b Now, give special emphasis to the parts of the sentences you have underlined by beginning each one with *It*.

It was this job that she had always wanted.

c [4·6] Now listen and check your answers.

Person to person

6 **a** Talk about one of the following:

1 a risk you have taken

2 an actor you really like

3 a place you love

4 a person who is very important to you

Make a few notes about what you want to say about it/them. Decide what points you particularly want to emphasise.

b Tell another student about it/them.

Vocabulary | phrasal verbs with *out*

7 Match the phrasal verbs in *italics* in these sentences to the meanings a–h.

1 Something has happened which we never really *find out* about.

2 She *turns out* to be a very good boxer.

3 I just couldn't *work out* why his daughter never replied to his letters.

4 We've *run out* of milk. Will you go next door and ask Tilda for some?

5 I've *fallen out* with my best friend. She won't speak to me at the moment.

6 Could you *give out* one of these papers to each student, please?

7 It took them several hours to *put out* the fire at the hotel.

8 There's been a mistake with the bill but they've said they'll *sort it out* as soon as possible.

a) give to each person

b) stop being friends

c) become, happen in a particular way

d) extinguish, stop a fire or cigarette from burning

e) discover, get information about something or someone

f) put something in order, correct a mistake

g) use all of something so there is none left

h) calculate, find a solution to a problem

8 **a** Complete the sentences with one of the verbs from Ex. 7 in the correct form.

1 Have you ever had to _____ out a fire? What happened?

2 When you want to _____ out about a piece of information (e.g. where you can go bungee-jumping), what do you normally do?

3 Have you ever been in a car which has _____ out of petrol? What happened?

4 Have any friends of yours ever done anything strange and you couldn't _____ out why they had done it?

5 Have you ever met someone who _____ out to be very different to what you imagined they were like at first? In what way were they different?

6 Have you ever _____ out with a good friend? If so, why? What happened?

b In pairs, ask and answer the questions.

Speaking

9 **4·7** Listen to someone comparing and contrasting the two photos. How would she feel about being in each situation?

10 **a** Look at these incomplete sentences from the tapescript in Ex. 9. Say what words/phrases you think complete each sentence.

1 They're _____ ironing.
2 In the first picture, I _____ _____ a young man ironing some _____ of brown t-shirt ...
3 But the ironing board is _____ fixed between the sides of a ravine ...
4 I can't _____ _____ he got there.
5 The second picture is of a _____ more ordinary situation.
6 His wife _____ be out at work.
7 He is also _____ _____ his children.
8 The guy in the first picture _____ more relaxed than the man in the second picture, _____ though it must be very dangerous.
9 I am _____ scared of heights ...
10 I wouldn't like to be in _____ situation!

b Listen again and check your ideas.

HOW TO ...

compare and contrast photos

Use comparing words/phrases	*also, as well as, both*
Use contrasting words/phrases	*on the other hand, but, however, whereas, while* *Mind you ...*
Speculate about the situation	*His wife might/may/could/must be at work.* *He doesn't seem/appear to be enjoying himself much.*
Give your own reaction	*I wouldn't like to be in either situation!* *You wouldn't get me up there in a million years!* *It puts me off having kids!* *It makes me want to give up my job and go travelling.*

11 **a** Work in pairs. Student As look at the two photos on page 149. Student Bs look at the photos on page 145. Prepare to talk about them to your partner.

b Show your partner your two photos and compare and contrast them using the suggestions in the How to box above.

4 Vocabulary

Distances and dimensions

homework ~100 hundred words. pop into words. — make a deep impact on me.—

1 **a** Check you know the words in the table below. Then, complete it with the missing parts of speech. Use a dictionary if necessary.

ADJECTIVE	NOUN	VERB
long	length *longitud largo.*	lengthen *alagar*
(1) *short*	xxx *shortness*	shorten *acortar*
wide */waid/ ancho*	width */wid/*	(2) *widen*
broad *amplitud*	breadth *amplid*	(3) *broaden* *expandir*
(4) *heigh*	height *altura*	heighten
deep *profundo*	(5) *depth*	deepen
low *bajo*	xxx *low*	(6) *lower*

b [4.8] Listen and check your answers.

2 Complete the following sentences with the correct form of one of the words from the table. *llano*

1 I know the length of this rug but I don't know the *width*.
2 The pool is quite shallow at this end but do you know the *height* at the other end?
3 They intend to *broaden / widen* this road and make it four lanes instead of three.
4 This skirt's too short. It needs *to lengthening* a bit.
5 If I go by car to work instead of by train, it *shortens* my journey by about fifteen minutes which is great.
6 This bed is very *low*. It's almost like sleeping on the floor!
7 He has very *broad* shoulders and is quite muscular.

3 **a** Work with another student and discuss the difference between:

1 a low-risk strategy/a high-risk strategy
2 a long-term plan/a short-term plan
3 a local phone call/a long-distance phone call *(take)*
4 a short cut to somewhere/a long way round
5 a broad-minded person/a narrow-minded person
6 saying a person is skinny/saying a person is slim
7 saying a person is shallow/saying a person is deep

b Describe a situation or a person. Can your partner decide which word or phrase above you are illustrating? *silly. superficial*

A: *I have a friend who has a very fixed view of the world. He thinks just like his parents and isn't prepared to see other people's viewpoints. He won't try different foods or go out to new places. He's really ... ?*

B: *Narrow-minded!*

this job makes a deep impression on me

4 Discuss. What do you think the following expressions mean?

1 to make a deep impression on someone *— something*
2 to be thrown in at the deep end *→ you are in a dificult situation*
3 to be deep in thought
4 to go off at the deep end *→ make angry → for not good reason. upset*
5 still waters run deep
person who is quiet is intelligent. calculated person

5 Choose the correct alternatives. Use a dictionary if necessary.

1 We'd like to *expand/heighten* our business and start producing different kinds of kitchen equipment.
2 We have *grown/extended* the house at the back and now we have a much bigger kitchen.
3 It's a wonderful beach. It *stretches/expands* for miles.
4 It's quite a *distance/length* to the next petrol station.
5 If the city keeps *stretching/spreading*, our local forest will disappear.
6 They had a *broad/lengthy* conversation about the problems in the company.
7 You know that metal *contracts/shortens* when it becomes cooler, don't you?
8 This jumper seems to have *shrunk/reduced* in the wash!

6 **a** Work with another student. Prepare to tell a story to other students. The story must involve someone taking a risk of some kind and include at least five of the words/phrases from Exs. 1, 3, 4 and 5.

b Tell your story and then listen to other stories. Which story involved the biggest risk?

1   Read the rules on page 151 and then play the game.

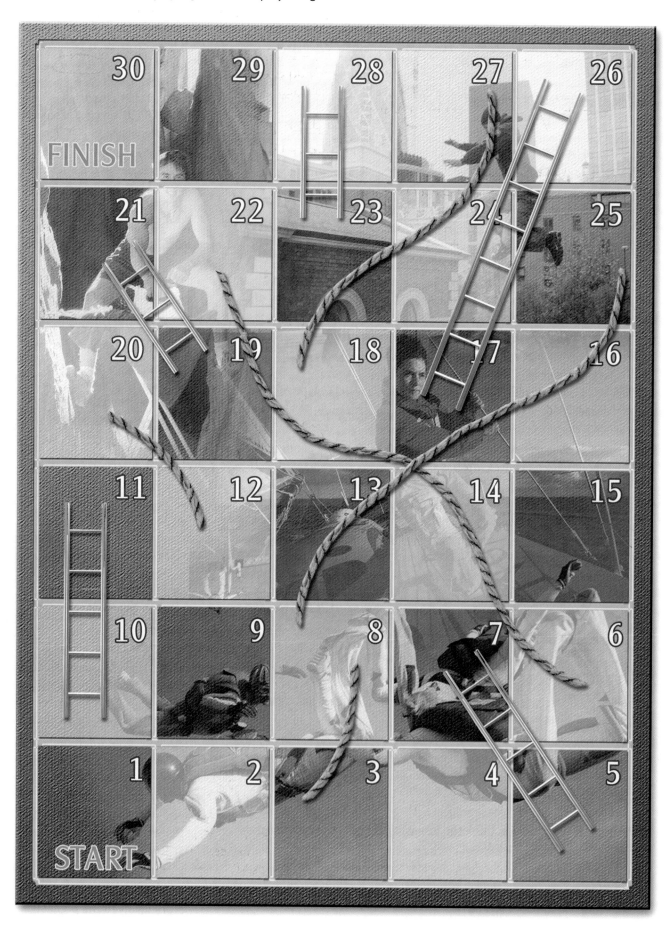

If structures (1)

Use the First Conditional to talk about a possible situation in the future.

If + Present Simple/Present Continuous/Present Perfect, Future/Present Continuous/Imperative + verb

The '*if* clause' can come first or second. When the '*if* clause' is first, we need a comma at the end of the clause.

If you need help, ask me.

We're going to get very wet if it rains.

Use the Second Conditional to talk about unlikely or imagined situations in the present/future.

If + Past Simple/Past Continuous, *would* (or *'d*) + infinitive

If I lived in the country, I'd do a lot more walking.

When we are less certain, we can use *might* instead of *would*.

If someone gave me a lot of money, I might take a year off work.

Also, use the Second Conditional to give advice.

I'd buy a good English–English dictionary if I were you.

Use the Third Conditional to talk about past situations that did not happen.

If + Past Perfect, *would have* + past participle

If she had answered all the questions, she would have passed the exam.

Expressing obligation

Use *must/mustn't* to talk about present and future strong obligations that come from the speaker.

I must go to bed early tonight.

Use *have to/have got to* to talk about present and future strong obligations that often come from outside the speaker.

We have to wear uniforms at our school.

You've got to show your ID before they will let you in this club.

Use *don't have to*, *don't need to* or *needn't* to talk about a lack of obligation in the present or future.

You don't have to come shopping with me if you don't want to.

We don't need to check in until an hour before the plane leaves.

Use *should* (or *ought to*) to talk about obligations and duties in the future, present or past, and to give advice.

I really should go and visit my cousins in Wales.

Use *should + have +* past participle to criticise your own or other people's behaviour in the past.

I shouldn't have spoken to Brian like that.

She should have asked me before borrowing my car.

Use *supposed to* to talk about what people have to do according to rules or about what is expected to happen.

You're supposed to wear a tie at work.

They weren't supposed to arrive until after 8p.m.

Use *had to* to talk about past and reported obligations.

When I was at school we all had to stand up when the teacher came in.

Emphasis

Use repetition.

She's a very, very nice person.

Add an emphasising word, e.g. *so, such, really, just,* etc.

I was so pleased to meet your sister.

They are such a nice couple.

The concert was just fantastic. You must go.

Use the structure: *It is/was ... which/that ...*

It's the kitchen that I particularly like about that house.

Add an appropriate form of *do*.

I do wish you could stay a bit longer.

They did enjoy themselves very much.

Key vocabulary

Risk/Achievement
risk gamble opportunity chance stake
ambition dream big substantial

Physical movements
leap swing land bend balance stretch flip
tuck roll lean

Parts of the body
elbows chest shoulders shoulder blades chin
forearm hands thumbs index finger
little finger palms finger tips

Phrasal verbs with *out*
find out run out (of) turn out work out fall out
give out put out sort out

Distances and dimensions
long/length/lengthen short/shorten
wide/width/widen broad/breadth/broaden
high/height/heighten deep/depth/deepen
low/lower

1 Match the sentence halves 1–8 with a–h.

1 If the cheque arrives today,
2 If I had more time,
3 If I had heard the weather forecast,
4 If I did more exercise,
5 If anyone spoke to me like that,
6 If I hadn't fallen in the race,
7 If I come to the party,
8 If I get my bonus at Christmas,

a) I would be extremely angry.
b) I wouldn't have gone walking in the mountains.
c) I'll buy a new car.
d) I would like to do a pottery class.
e) I would probably start losing weight.
f) I'm sure I would have won it.
g) I'll put it straight in the bank.
h) will you get them a present from both of us?

2 Complete the sentences with the appropriate form of the verbs.

1 What will we do if/taxi/not come/time?
2 If I/been born/year earlier,/ I done/military service.
3 What would you do if/you/ offer/better job?
4 If I/not home/11p.m./my dad/be/really angry.
5 I/not/hired/a car/if I/ known/expensive/it/going to be.
6 If she/work/hard/between now/the exams,/she/ probably pass.
7 We/gone/the cinema/if we/able/find/babysitter.
8 If I/you,/I/go/long holiday.

3 Rewrite the first sentence using the words in bold so that the meaning stays the same.

1 There was no need for you to wait for me.
   have
   You ...
2 The rules say I have to take some ID.
   supposed
   I ...
3 It wasn't necessary for me to get up early this morning.
   need
   I ...
4 It's necessary for us to be in our seats at the theatre by 7.30p.m.
   got
   We ...
5 It wasn't a good idea to forget Janine's birthday.
   should
   You ...
6 Were you obliged to do military service when you were 18?
   have
   Did ...

4 Find the extra and unnecessary word in six of the lines below.

1 My friend Jane it is probably one of the people I admire the most.
2 She's a journalist and travels all over the world, often to so incredibly dangerous
3 places. Her job is just very important to her. It's probably the thing which
4 drives her the most in life. She thinks it's vital vital that people know what's going
5 on in the world. As well as being very passionate about her job she's a wonderful
6 friend. She's so thoughtful and such a caring person that everyone who meets
7 her does loves her. She's married with two children. Her husband, Tony, is
8 such incredibly supportive but he does miss her sometimes, I know. He's very,
9 very good with the children and looks after them when Jane is away for work.

5 Unjumble each of the words in *italics* below.

1 I can't *kwro* out why Tim left so suddenly. It's very strange.
2 I banged my *bwelo* on the car door this morning. It really hurts.
3 Most children have a *aremd* of what they would like to do when they grow up.
4 It's very important to *tthcesr* properly before you play football.
5 Bob is a very *stnneei* young man. He shouldn't take life quite so seriously.
6 This film has *deeehhgitn* public awareness of the problem of poverty in our big cities.
7 Don't sit with your *rssduohle* back like that. It's not good for you.
8 Winning two gold medals at the Olympics is a marvellous *teeemvhcnai*.

5 The past

Lead-in "introduction"

1 **a** When do you think each photo was taken: 1940s/1950s/1960s/1980s? What details make you think this?

    b Match the sentences to the photos.

1 I get quite **nostalgic** when I see some of the old TV ads that I used to watch as a child.

2 Do you **remember** our holidays at the seaside? You always used to bring back a souvenir.

3 So, **remind** me, which company did you work for back then?

4 I've got such a terrible **memory**. When did we go to that music festival? It must have been in the 1970s sometime, I think.

5 What made it so **memorable** was the little song.

6 My mother is getting quite **forgetful** these days but she likes to **reminisce** about the family holidays we had when we were children.

2 **a** In pairs, decide if the words in **bold** above are verbs, adjectives or nouns. Can you explain their meanings?

    b Say how you think each of the words is pronounced. Where is the main stress in each word?

    c **5.1** Listen and check your ideas.

    d Write sentences that are true for you using the words in **bold** from Ex. 1b above.

3 Discuss. What is the most memorable evening or day you have had in the last year? What made it special?

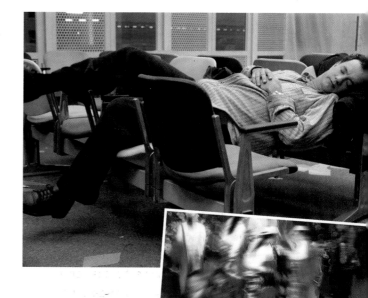

Reading

1 Discuss. What is happening in the pictures? What do you think *The Terminal* is about?

2 Read the article and answer these questions.
1 Who is Alfred?
2 What do we learn about Alfred's daily routine?
3 What does Alfred hope about his future?
4 What is the journalist's attitude towards Alfred?

The man who lost his past

I first saw him, many years ago now, staring out with an intense gaze from the pages of a newspaper. Seated alone on a bench, he had a slight, balding appearance, with amazing dark eyebrows and a small, neat moustache. Strangely noble, he seemed immune to the endless motion of the airport around him.

His name was Merhan Karimi Nasseri though he called himself 'Sir Alfred' and he was lost in a bureaucratic nightmare. That is to say he lived on a bench in Terminal One of Charles de Gaulle International Airport. He had been there since 1988. For a series of insanely complicated reasons, the Iranian-born refugee was now a man without a country. Alfred couldn't leave France because he did not have papers; he couldn't enter France because he did not have papers. (1) ___d___ Which he has done – for the last sixteen years. Recently, he was catapulted into stardom as the result of Steven Spielberg's film *The Terminal* which tells a heavily adapted version of his story. But what is the reality of his daily life?

He actually lives in the basement shopping mall of Terminal One. Alfred's red bench is the only anchor in his life. (2) ___C___ It is just about wide enough to sleep on if he keeps his hands tucked under the pillow but he never sleeps during the day.

Stacked around the back of the bench are boxes, suitcases and plastic bags containing everything Alfred owns in the world. This includes: an extensive collection of newspaper and magazine reports about himself; his drycleaning; a large collection of McDonald's straws and a diary which records in extraordinary detail every day of his strange existence since he first appeared at Terminal One. From the moment I sat down next to him I felt the force of his dignity. Alfred seemed totally content within himself. (3) ___G___ Everything in Alfred's life was conducted on his own terms. In some sense he was a freer man than most. *clean yourself*

Despite outward appearances, Alfred lives a life of total self-sufficiency and order. He keeps himself meticulously clean and groomed, using a nearby airport bathroom. (4) ___F___ He always eats a McDonald's egg and bacon croissant for breakfast and a McDonald's fish sandwich for dinner. He always leaves a tip.

Alfred had four brothers and two sisters, all of them middle-class people who lived in Tehran, except for one sister who was a dentist in Luxembourg. The relative he was closest to was his brother, Cyrus, who was two years older. 'We used to be very close and we usually had the same friends. We had a good life. I liked swimming and Merhan used to play table tennis. He was very good at it.' Alfred had lived with Cyrus and Mina for a time in London in the 1970s. (5) ___6___ 'He was an intellectual. He spent all his time studying and reading books and listening to the radio. He talked all the time about politics. It was very important to him.'

Last week I flew to meet Alfred, three years since I last saw him. He seemed quite content. (6) ___B___ That was the only thing that mattered to him any more. Not his family or friends, not his past or future – only the articles about his life at the airport and a poster advertising *The Terminal* which he proudly hung from a suitcase next to the bench. 'Life is waiting,' went the Hollywood slogan.

Alfred was thrilled about *The Terminal*, though he would never get the chance to see it. Apparently he had received a cheque for several hundred thousand dollars for his life story. (7) ___A___ He was now under the impression that the film company, DreamWorks, was going to get him a passport and take him to California; Steven Spielberg would come to his rescue; Tom Hanks would visit him at the bench. It hasn't happened yet. I wonder how long Alfred will have to wait this time.

3 Read the text again and decide where the sentences belong.

A But Alfred had never cared much about money.

B The picture they painted of him was very different from the Alfred of today.

C It is his bed, living room and office.

D The authorities told him to wait in the airport lounge while they sorted the problem out.

E 'I am famous now,' was the first thing he said.

F He hangs his freshly dry-cleaned clothes from the handle of a suitcase next to his bench.

G He did not aim to please or play on your sympathy.

4 Discuss. How do you feel about a) Alfred's situation and b) the way the film company behaved?

Grammar | *used to/get used to/would*

5 **a** Match examples 1–4 in the Active grammar box to the meanings A–D.

> **Active grammar**
>
> 1 He **used to** sleep on a bench.
> 2 He **is getting used to** sleeping on a bench. *become*
> 3 He **is used to** sleeping on a bench.
> 4 He **would** sleep on a bench.
>
> A He is familiar with sleeping on a bench. It is not strange or difficult for him.
> B Sleeping on a bench is becoming less difficult for him.
> C Sleeping on a bench was part of his typical day/behaviour.
> D In the past, he regularly slept on a bench but now he doesn't.

b Which example above is true for Alfred?

see Reference page 73

6 **a** Choose the correct alternative.

1 I *didn't use/wasn't used* to like jazz very much.
2 I'm getting used to *work/working* from home.
3 I'm *used/used to* living on my own.
4 My family *would/were used to* always go to the same place for their summer holiday.
5 He *would/used to* have a beard.
6 We can't *get/getting* used to the noise.

7 Explain to another student what each sentence means.

When the speaker was younger she didn't really like jazz but now she does.

8 There is one word missing from each of these sentences. Decide what it is and add it.

1 I used play a lot of rugby at school.
2 I can't used to my new boss. She's not very friendly.
3 You use to be so close to your brother when you were children?
4 On Christmas Eve we always go to church.
5 We slowly getting used to living in the country but sometimes it feels a bit isolated.
6 We use to be vegetarian. It's only something we've started doing in the last couple of months.

Person to person

9 Discuss in pairs.

1 Name two or three things you used to enjoy doing when you were younger but no longer do. Why did you stop doing them?
2 How would you typically spend your summer holidays when you were a child?
3 Describe one or two big changes in your life, e.g. moving house/school/job, getting married, etc. What were the most difficult things to get used to?

Lifelong learning

Language learning at school

Did you learn any languages at school? Did you use to have any special or effective ways of learning vocabulary or grammar? What were the best things that your teachers used to do which helped you learn? Try to remember and see if you can use any of them now.

Vocabulary | appearance

[handwritten: Dimples]

10 Put the words/phrases from the box in the appropriate columns in the table.

> ~~straight~~ good-looking (scruffy) ~~muscular~~ a bit overweight
> elegant slim wrinkles clean-shaven curly chubby wavy
> stocky dyed going a bit bald mousy round tanned spiky

[handwritten notes in left margin: (brown colour) mousy, dyed, scruffy (untidy hair)]

[handwritten above table: going a bit bald]

HAIR	FACE	BUILD	GENERAL
straight	wrinkles clean-shaven	muscular a bit overweight	good-looking elegant
curly wavy	round	slim chubby	tanned

[handwritten: scruffy = untidy]

11 Read these descriptions. Correct the mistake in each one.

1 He's got short, black hairs and a small moustache.

2 She's lost a lot of weight recently. She's quite a skinny now.

3 I like having a few of wrinkles. I think it gives your face more character.

4 She's got spiked, blond hair and striking blue eyes. You can't miss her.

5 Simon's changed in the last few years. He's going a bit balding now.

6 She's a terribly elegant and only wears the best designer outfits.

7 His hair used to be very curled when he was a baby.

8 He always looks taned and healthy. I think he spends a lot of time in the Caribbean.

[handwritten: stocky = short, fat]

12 Choose one of the categories below and describe a famous person to other students. See how quickly they can work out who you are describing.

> pop star politician sportsperson TV personality actor

A: *So, what does he or she look like?*

B: *Well, he used to be one of the most famous politicians in the world but he's more or less retired now. He's pretty tall and now has grey hair but he's not going bald at all. He's in his late 50s I think. He's quite well-built but certainly not overweight. He always seems to have a great smile and has very clear blue eyes. His wife is also quite a well-known politician.*

A: *Is it Bill Clinton?*

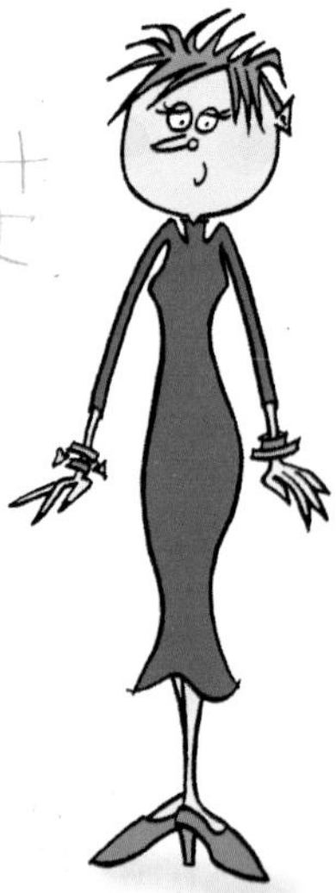

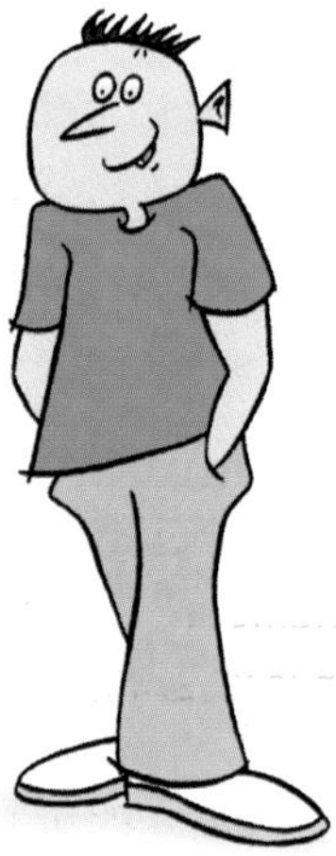

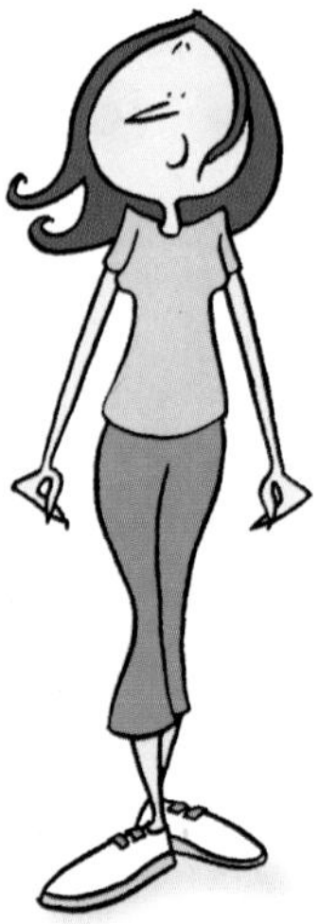

Writing

13 Read this extract from an email. Then look at the pictures and decide which person is being described.

> It's really nice of you to meet me at the airport even though we've never met! Jo's told me so much about you that I actually feel I know you quite well. Anyway, just so you know who to look out for when I get through Passport Control. I'm about 1m 70cm with short, spiky, black hair. I suppose I'm what some people would call stocky. I think that partly comes from going to the gym quite a lot! I'm not sure what I'll be wearing. What's the weather like where you are at the moment?

14 a In pairs, describe the other three people in as much detail as you can.

b Now imagine you have met one of the other people at a party. You got on really well and are hoping to see them again. Write a brief email to a friend telling them what he/she looks like.

grammar	expressing ability
can do	talk about memories

Listening

1 Look at the photo and then read the sentences. Which of the sentences accurately describes the photo? Change the others to make them true.

1 They're sitting on a lawn which is probably in a garden.
2 The woman is looking a bit anxious.
3 There's a Siamese cat just in front of the child.
4 The woman is wearing smart leather boots and a floral dress.
5 It's probably early summer.
6 The child looks as if he'd like to play with the ball.
7 The garden seems well looked after.
8 The woman is probably in her late 20s.
9 You can just make out a wall in the background.

2 **5.2** Listen to the conversation between Simon and his friend Camilla and answer these questions.

1 What is the relationship of the woman to the child?
2 What kind of child does Simon say he was?

3 Listen again. Write questions that are appropriate for these answers.

South London – Where was Simon brought up?

1 Just one floor.
2 Because she wasn't very well.
3 Until he was almost seven.
4 Very good fun.
5 Nine months.
6 Four.

4 **a** Look at the tapescript on page 169. Work in pairs and find the following words/phrases. Discuss what you think they might mean.

1 rambling (l.8)
2 pretty much to ourselves (l.11)
3 haven't changed a bit (l.13)
4 mess around (l.32)
5 a model child (l.37)
6 reasonably well (l.45)
7 apparently (l.46)
8 Shame really. (l.48)

b Use three of the words/phrases above to describe something in your past, e.g. a friendship or your childhood.

Speaking

5 Work with another student. Either refer to a favourite photo that you have or choose one of the photos below. Prepare to describe the photo and explain how it makes you feel. (If you have chosen one of the photos below, make up a story to explain a) where it is, b) who the people are and c) why it is one of your favourite photos.)

Grammar | expressing ability

6 **a** Complete each of the example sentences 1–6 and rules A–D with *can, could, able, manage(d)* or *succeed(ed)*.

> ### Active grammar
>
> 1 I was _able_ to walk by ten months.
> 2 I _could_ play simple tunes on the piano by the age of four.
> 3 Did you _manage_ to find the photos you were looking for?
> 4 Will you be _able_ to come to Sam's birthday dinner on Sunday?
> 5 _Can_ you read the writing on that sign at the end of the road?
> 6 We _succeeded_ in finding the perfect present for my sister.
>
> A Use _can_ to talk about present or 'general' ability.
> B Use *will be* _able_ to talk about future ability.
> C Use _could_ or *was/were* _able_ to talk about past or 'general' ability.
> D Use *was/were* _able_ , _manage_ to or _succeed_ in to talk about ability on a particular occasion.

b Decide which of the sentences below mean approximately the same.

1 She can ski.
2 She could ski really well as a child.
3 She's able to ski quite well.
4 She knows how to ski.
5 She's pretty good at skiing.
6 She's terrible at skiing.
7 She's not very good at skiing. ⇒ she can't ski very well
8 She was great at skiing when she was a child.
9 She can't ski at all well.

see Reference page 73

7 Find the mistake in each of the following sentences and correct it.

1 I can't to tell you when Mr Fozard will be free if I don't know.
2 I was able ~~to~~ drive Sam and Marta to the airport because my uncle lent me his car.
3 Tom and I manage _managed_ to move the piano into the living room this morning.
4 We won't _be_ able to play tennis this weekend unfortunately.
5 He said he knew how to sailing _sail_ but he's never actually been out on a boat!
6 Very few people have succeeded in climb _climbing_ to the very top of that mountain.
7 We haven't _been_ able to find a wedding ring that we both like.
8 I've always been terrible to _at_ remembering names.

8 Complete the sentences using the word(s) in brackets in the correct form and one of the verbs from the box.

> find   drive   meet   get   clean   spend
> beat   swim

1 You _can spend_ the night here if you like. The spare room's free. (can)
2 I _could not drive_ until I was nearly 30. I just never got round to taking my test. (could not)
3 _managed to_ through to someone at your bank and tell them that your credit card had been stolen? (you manage)
4 I'd like to _be able to swim_ but I have problems holding my breath under water. (able)
5 We got lost and so we _couldn't find_ the restaurant you told us about but we did end up going to another one which was really good. (could not)
6 I was surprised that Chris _was able to beat_ Steve at tennis. Steve is a very good player. (able)
7 The sales team have _succeeded in meeting_ all their targets this month and so everyone will get a bonus. (succeed)
8 Fortunately, we _managed to clean_ up the house after the party before our parents got home. (manage)

9 **5.3** Listen to Camilla describing the different things that she and her brother were able to do as children and more recently. Make notes for a) Camilla and b) her brother.

CAMILLA	HER BROTHER
	Could ride a bike on his own at five.

Listening

11 `5.4` Listen to Simon talking about the photo below. Which of the following differences with the first photo (page 65) does he mention?

   1 how he feels about some of the people

   2 how he feels about the place

   3 how he feels about the animals

   4 how he feels about the weather

Person to person

10 Discuss in pairs.

   1 Is there anything you could do well as a child but you can't do so well now? If so, what is it?

   2 Have you ever managed to do something that you really didn't think you would be able to do? If so, what was it?

   3 Is there anything you hope you will be able to do by this time next year, which you can't do at the moment? If so, what is it?

   4 Name one thing you think you're pretty good at, one thing you're not very good at and one thing you're terrible at.

   5 Find out if there is anything that you know how to do which no one else in your class knows how to do.

12 Listen again and then read the summary below. What three mistakes do you notice?

Both of the photos show Simon as a child. This photo shows him with his parents and two friends of theirs. They are staying at their friends' hotel in the north of England. Simon enjoyed staying there because there was lots to do whereas he got bored in the summer when he just stayed at home. There were dogs at the hotel which he liked. They were very friendly, similar to his cat at home. In general, he had a good time and liked going on holiday there.

13 Work with other students.

   1 Describe one or two of your earliest memories of childhood.

   2 Compare the kinds of things you remember. Why do you think you can remember some things but not other things?

Grammar	*although/but/however/nevertheless*
Can do	talk about books

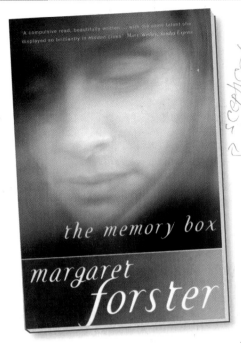

the memory box

margaret **forster**

Vocabulary | feelings

1 **a** Look at the woman in the picture. How do you think she might be feeling?

b **5.5** Listen to these people describing how they are feeling. Match one of the words in the box below to each person.

> confused   suspicious
> uneasy   curious
> annoyed   excited
> uninterested   sceptical
> optimistic   shocked
> relieved

2 Complete each of the following sentences with the most appropriate word from Ex. 1.

1 She's very _relieved_ that the police have dropped all the charges against her.

2 Our children are getting very _excited_ about our trip to Disneyworld next month. They keep asking when we're going.

3 Most of the people interviewed said they felt _uneasy_ about the idea of living near a nuclear power station. *worry.*

4 Sam's _optimistic_ about selling his flat quickly. He's had lots of people come to see it since it went up for sale last week.

5 My sister's _annoyed_ with me because I borrowed her favourite jacket without asking her.

6 When I was learning to ski she gave me so many different pieces of advice that I just ended up totally _confused_.

7 Environmental groups are _sceptical_ that the government is serious about tackling the problem of global warming. *sceptical*

8 I'm very _curious_ to know why Sarah got the job of Marketing Director. She's only been in the company a few months. *curious*

9 I'm afraid I'm fairly _uninterested_ in politics and politicians. They all seem to say the same things these days.

10 The fact that he didn't want to answer the police officer's questions made them _suspicious_.

11 Julie's mother was quite _shocked_ when they told her they were going to get married in June. They've only been together since November. *shocked.*

3 Choose six of the feelings from Ex. 1. Try to remember the last time you had each of them. Tell another student about why you had these feelings.

Reading

4 **a** Look at the cover of the book *The Memory Box* and discuss with other students what you think it might be about.

b Read the extract and decide who Susannah, Charlotte and Catherine are.

5 **a** Read the extract again and answer these questions.

1 'Susannah was apparently perfect, as the dead so often become.' (l.1) What do you think this means?

2 How did Catherine feel about what people said about her mother?

3 'The existence of the memory box may have troubled my father from the beginning.' (l.10) Why do you think this might have been?

4 Catherine thinks she would have reacted differently to the memory box aged ten or fifteen. Do you think this is likely? If so, why?

5 Why do you think Catherine didn't want to think about her real mother as she was growing up?

6 How do you think Catherine felt when she first came across the memory box?

b Find examples in the extract of five of the feelings referred to in Ex. 1. Explain who has the feelings and what causes them.

6 Discuss.

1 What kinds of things do you think Susannah might have left in the 'memory box' for Catherine?

2 What do you think the point of the memory box was?

3 How would you feel about making or being given a memory box?

Susannah was apparently perfect, as the dead so often become. She was, it seemed, perfectly beautiful, perfectly good, and perfectly happy during her comparatively short life. They
5 said she met life with open arms, ever positive and optimistic. I do not believe a word of this. How, after all, could she be happy, knowing she was likely to die soon, when she was a mere thirty-one years old and I, her baby, was hardly six months old?

10 I have a feeling that the existence of the memory box may have troubled my father from the beginning. He didn't give it to me until my twenty-first birthday even though it had been in our house all that time. Charlotte knew about
15 it, of course, but neither she nor my father could bring themselves to mention it. I think they were both afraid of its significance. Also, I was a highly imaginative child and they simply didn't know how to introduce this memory box
20 into my life.

Now, however, their nervousness makes me curious. What exactly were they afraid of? Did they think I might be shocked, and if so why? At any rate, both of them were visibly on edge, almost guilty, when finally on the morning of my twenty-first birthday
25 they told me about it. It was clear they were relieved when I showed little interest in it. I said I didn't want to open it, or even see it.

This was a lie, and yet not a lie. The box did, in fact, make me curious even if I found I wanted to suppress the feeling. Aged ten, I don't think I would have been able to. I'm sure I would have been too excited at the thought that it might contain all sorts of treasures; and then around fifteen I'd have found it irresistibly romantic and
30 would have been ready to weep on discovering dried roses pressed between the pages of meaningful poems. But at twenty-one I was very self-centred; my curiosity was only slight and I could more easily deny it. In fact, I felt a kind of nausea, at the notion of a dying woman choosing what to put in a box for me.

Nevertheless, there was no doubt that it forced me to think of Susannah. Growing up, I could hardly have thought of her less, wanting Charlotte to be my only mother. I was always furious if anyone referred to her as
35 my stepmother. However, Charlotte herself would try to calm me by pointing out that, whether I liked it or not, that was exactly what she was.

After Charlotte died, the hardest thing I had to do was go back into our old home. For a whole month, I was obliged to go there day after day until every bit of furniture, every object, every book and picture, every piece of clothing, every last curtain and cushion was sorted out and ready to be collected by all manner of people. This
40 was, of course, how I found the box, even though I very nearly missed it. My attention might not have been caught if it had not been for an odd-looking pink label attached to the parcel. On the label, written in ink which had faded but which you could
45 still read, was my own name – 'For my darling Catherine Hope, in the future'.

Grammar | although/but/however/nevertheless

7 Look at the pairs of sentences in the Active grammar box. In each pair, one sentence is correct and one is not. Decide which one is not correct and why.

Active grammar

1 a *He didn't give it to me until my 21st birthday. **Although** it had been in our house all that time.*

  b *He didn't give it to me until my 21st birthday, **although** it had been in our house all that time.*

2 a *The ink on the label had faded **but** you could still read my name.*

  b *The ink on the label had faded **but**, you could still read my name.*

3 a ***However** I was always furious if anyone referred to Charlotte as my stepmother, she would always point out that that was exactly what she was.*

  b *I was always furious if anyone referred to Charlotte as my stepmother. **However**, she would always point out that that was exactly what she was.*

4 a *The idea of a dying woman putting things in a special box for me was very strange. **Nevertheless**, it forced me to think about her.*

  b *The idea of a dying woman putting things in a special box for me was very strange **nevertheless** it forced me to think about her.*

---

see Reference page 73

8 Choose the correct alternative.

1 She really liked the shoes *but/nevertheless* they were just too expensive.

2 *Although/However* the jacket was quite cheap, it wasn't exactly the colour she wanted.

3 It is true that Mr Billingham left the shop without paying for the camera. *Nevertheless/Although*, he has been under a lot of stress at work recently.

4 We ran to catch the 8.15a.m. train *but/although* we arrived just after it had gone.

5 They decided to get a dog *however/although* they didn't have a garden.

6 He promised that he would try and find the file. *But/However*, he knew that it had been destroyed.

9 a Complete each of the sentences below in a logical way.

1 The food in the restaurant was extremely good. *However*, ...

2 I like Jane very much *but* she ...

3 I realise that you have worked for this company for many years. *Nevertheless*, ...

4 We decided to buy the house *although* ...

b Now write the sentences again using a different expression of contrast.

Speaking

10 a Think about a book/film that you have read/seen that you can remember quite well.

b Make some notes about:
- the basic plot
- things you particularly liked about it
- any criticisms you had of it

The Memory Box

Plot
Catherine discovers a 'memory box' left by her real mother.

Things I liked
Interesting idea for a story

Criticisms
A bit slow at times

c **5.6** Listen to someone talking about *The Memory Box* and what they thought of it. Were they generally positive or negative?

d Now, tell other students about the book/film you chose. Refer to the plot, things you liked and any criticisms. Use the expressions from Ex. 9 where appropriate.

Lifelong learning

Graded readers

Did you know that you can read many famous and classic novels in a simplified version suitable for your level of English? (See www.penguinreaders.com for more information.)

Idioms describing people

1 **a** Match the <u>underlined</u> expressions 1–8 with the correct meaning a–h.

b Which picture does each expression relate to?

E

1 He's a bit of <u>a cold fish</u>.	**a)** a very kind person who has the right feelings about something important
2 She's <u>as hard as nails</u>.	**b)** very annoying, a nuisance
3 He's <u>a pain in the neck</u>.	**c)** someone who behaves as if they know everything
4 Her <u>heart's in the right place</u>.	**d)** someone who is extremely successful in their job or in school
5 He's <u>an awkward customer</u>.	**e)** someone who prefers to be on their own
6 She's <u>a real know-all</u>.	**f)** unfriendly person who seems to have no strong feelings
7 He's <u>a high-flyer</u>.	**g)** a difficult person to deal with
8 She's a bit of <u>a loner</u>.	**h)** very tough or not caring about the effects of your actions on other people

D

A

B

C

2 Complete the following sentences. Try not to refer to Ex. 1.

1 She loved answering all the questions in class. She thought she was so clever. She was a real _____ .

2 He didn't like going out with friends and he spent most of the time at home in his room on the computer or reading. He was a bit of a _____ really.

3 They say he'll be a partner of the firm by the time he's thirty. He's a real _____ .

4 I wish Caroline would stop coming into my room and borrowing my clothes. She's a pain _____ .

5 Brian's been asking about getting an increase in his salary. Will you talk to him about it? On the subject of money he's a bit of an _____ .

6 I know Steve is a bit loud and insensitive at times but honestly, his heart's _____ .

7 She had to go out to work from the age of fifteen and has had quite a difficult life. As a result she's as hard _____ .

8 He never seemed to get excited about anything. All in all, he was a bit of a cold _____ .

3 **a** Think about people you know who you could describe with five of the expressions in Ex. 1.

b Describe the people to other students. Say how you know them and what they are like. The other students should say which expression from Ex. 1 is appropriate for each person.

4 Discuss. Which of the expressions do you have in your language? Do you have expressions which are different but contain the same idea?

MAKE YOUR
HISTORY!

Imagine someone – a child, a future archaeologist or even an alien being – discovering your time capsule in 100 years, 1000 years or 1,000,000 years from now.

Consider the sensation that it will cause 'Ancient artefacts from the 21st century found in buried time capsule!'.

These future people will study your chosen objects from the past – a crumbling newspaper, a coin, a birthday photo, a piece of technology – and they will learn a little bit more about us.

Leave your mark on the future.

Be a part of history.

Bury a time capsule.

TimeLine Inc.

1   Look at the picture and advert. What are the people putting in the ground and why?

2   **5·7** Listen to someone talking about what she put in a time capsule in 1977. Make a note of five general pieces of advice she gives to other people who want to prepare a time capsule.

3   **a** Work in groups. Choose five things to put in your time capsule. Use the examples below or other ideas. Give reasons to justify each of your ideas.

I think we should include a globe of the world so that they know how the world is divided.

In my opinion, we ought to put a typical piece of clothing like jeans so that they know how we dress.

What about putting in a newspaper so that they know the important things that are happening in the world today?

b Explain your choices to other groups. Which group do you all think had the best time capsule? Why?

Used to/Get used to/Would

Use *used to* to talk about past habits and states that do not happen now.

I used to catch the bus to work but now I go by bike.

I used to have blond hair.

She didn't use to be nearly so ambitious.

Did you use to enjoy travelling for your job?

! In the negative and question forms *use* does not finish with a '*d*'.

Use *would* to also talk about past habits but not past states.

When we were little, we would dress up and pretend to be kings and queens.

We used to live in Manchester. (Not ~~We would live in Manchester.~~)

Use *get used to* to describe the process of becoming accustomed to a new situation.

We're getting used to living in a small village in the country but it's still a little strange.

Use *be used to* to say when you have become accustomed to a new situation.

She's used to being her own boss.

! With *be/get used to*, the spelling is always *used* with a '*d*'.

Expressing ability

Use *can* to talk about present or 'general' ability.

She can speak Russian quite well.

Can you play any musical instruments?

Use *will be able to* to talk about future ability.

She'll be able to run 100m in under 11 seconds by the end of the year.

Use *could* or *was/were able to* to talk about past or 'general' ability.

They could both ski quite well by the time they were seven or eight years old.

She was able to communicate effectively in Arabic after working in Egypt for a year.

Use *was/were able to* or *managed to* or *succeeded in* (+ *-ing*) to say what someone could do on a particular occasion.

They were able to get into the house by forcing open the back door.

She managed to pay off all her debts by working in the evenings and at weekends.

Use *know how to* and *good/bad at*, etc. to describe different levels of ability.

She knows how to count to ten in Japanese.

He's not very good at speaking in public.

Although/But/However/Nevertheless

Use all of these linking words to show that what you are saying is surprising or unexpected in relation to something else you know to be true.

Form *Although* + clause, clause.

Although she was half an hour late, they decided to wait a bit longer.

Form clause, + *although* + clause.

They decided to wait a bit longer, although she was half an hour late.

(*Though* can be used as a shortened form of *although*. It is more common in informal speech.)

Use *even though* to emphasise a contrast.

Even though I was very angry with him, I didn't say anything.

Form sentence. + *However/Nevertheless*, + clause. (*Nevertheless* is formal.)

She was half an hour late. However, they decided to wait a bit longer.

Your work has not been of a very high standard recently. Nevertheless, I am still going to give you a five percent pay increase.

Form clause + *but* + clause. (*But* is not usually used to begin a sentence.)

She was half an hour late but they decided to wait a bit longer.

Key vocabulary

Memory
remember   memory   souvenir   memorable
remind   reminisce   nostalgic   forgetful

Appearance
Hair: straight   curly   wavy   going a bit bald
mousy   spiky   dyed
Face: wrinkles   clean-shaven   chubby   round
Build: muscular   stocky   a bit overweight   slim
General: good-looking   scruffy   elegant   tanned

Feelings
confused   suspicious   uneasy   curious   annoyed
excited   uninterested   sceptical   optimistic
shocked   relieved

Idioms describing people
a cold fish   as hard as nails   a pain in the neck
(someone's) heart is in the right place
an awkward customer   a real know-all   a high-flyer
a bit of a loner

1 Complete the following text with *used to* or *get used to* and the correct form of a verb from the box.

(1) *used to teach*

> have   be   finish   teach   not understand

I recently went back to Cairo where I (1) _____ English as a foreign language in the early 1980s. A lot had changed. The area where I lived (2) _____ very quiet but it's much busier now. There are more modern buildings and bigger roads. I remember when I first arrived that it took a while to (3) _____ most of the shop signs, as they were in Arabic. Now a lot of them are in English too. Every evening we (4) _____ our classes at 9.30p.m. and then all go out to a nearby club which had a great disco. I looked for the club but sadly it had gone. Cairo is a marvellous place and I really missed it when I came back to Britain. It took me ages to (5) _____ a very different style of life.

2 Rewrite the pairs of sentences with correct punctuation, using the words in brackets in the correct place.

It rained a lot. We had a really good time. (although)

Although it rained a lot, we had a really good time.

1 I managed to get a few hours' sleep. The party in the flat upstairs was very noisy. (however)

2 I would say that Charlotte is my best friend. I've only known her for a few months. (although)

3 I wanted to have a party this weekend. My parents weren't happy about the idea. (but)

4 She seems to be in love with him. He is very unreliable. (nevertheless)

5 Sandra is a very good student. She will need to work a bit harder if she wants to pass her exams. (however).

6 I had all the necessary qualifications. I didn't get the job. (although)

7 I enjoyed the film. Some of the acting was awful. (but)

3 Complete the second sentence with the word in **bold** so that it means the same as the first sentence.

She is able to play the piano very well.

can

*She **can play** the piano very well.*

1 Do you think it will be possible for you to finish the presentation by Friday?
able
Do you think you _____ finish the presentation by Friday?

2 They finally succeeded in getting the car out of the mud.
managed
They finally _____ the car out of the mud.

3 I was quite good at drawing as a child.
could
I _____ quite well as a child.

4 He failed to persuade the other employees to go on strike.
able
He _____ persuade the other employees to go on strike.

5 She couldn't make his camera work.
know
She _____ make his camera work.

6 Were you able to speak to Brian before he went home?
manage
Did _____ speak to Brian before he went home?

4 Complete the sentences with one of the words/ phrases from the Key vocabulary section on page 73.

She never says much and always keeps herself to herself. She's a bit of a cold fish.

1 We were all very _____ when she arrived home safely at midnight.

2 What's happened to your beard? I've never seen you _____ before.

3 My sister was always _____ . Even as a child, she never seemed very interested in having friends.

4 Jim has become quite _____ in his arms and legs since he started going to the gym.

5 My little brother is a real _____ . He keeps coming into my room and disturbing me when I'm trying to study.

6 My father said I should go to university but my brother told me it was a waste of time so I was quite _____ about what to do.

→ A dog sleigh.

6 Explore

to dive → with an aqualung   *to snorkel → [☐]*   *to scubadive*

a camel.

Lead-in

1   Discuss.

   1   What can you see in the photos?

   2   Which of the places would you most like to explore? Why?

2   **6.1**   Listen and answer these questions.

   1   What gave the speaker the idea to travel?

   2   Why did she go to Spain?

   3   How did she feel when she first got to Guatemala? Why?

   4   How did she feel later?

3   **a**   **6.2**   Listen again and complete the expressions.

   1   I began *to have _____ feet* and wanted to leave work.

   2   I was a bit worried about *going into uncharted _____* !

   3   I *went as an _____ traveller*, on my own.

   4   I spent a month _____ *around* the town.

   5   I *was bitten by the travel _____* and wanted to explore lots of other places.

   6   The first two months were difficult and I *experienced real _____ shock*.

   b   Check the meanings of the expressions using a dictionary.

4   Discuss.

   1   Why do you think people are bitten by the travel bug?

   2   Has it ever happened to you?

   3   Do you ever have itchy feet?

Bitten by the jungle bug!

Sand flies, sweat bees, eighty-metre high trees ... Hell for most of us, yes, but all in a day's work for Charlotte Uhlenbroek. She moves as elegantly through the lounge of London's Savoy Hotel as she does through the Amazon jungle. But while she loves the adventure, she is also glad to be back in 'civilisation', at least for the moment.

She's just finished filming a TV series called *Jungle* – a gruelling nineteen-week job that involved her exploring the dense jungles of the Congo, the Amazon and Borneo. She says that it was fascinating, but daunting as well. So what was her most challenging experience? 'Definitely climbing an eighty-metre high tree in Borneo, when I'm petrified of heights! I had to keep going up and up, when a voice inside me was saying, "Down! Down!" I kept thinking the ropes were going to break and send me plummeting down below.'

And 'down below' was where the bugs were – clinging, stinging, sucking beasts. Apart from the usual mosquitoes, in the Amazon rainforest, she was plagued by sand fly bites. 'I've had some horrible bites but these really are the itchiest bites I've ever had. At one stage, I counted seventy bites on one arm,' she says. 'Just as annoying were the sweat bees in the Congo. They try to drink the sweat on your face and even the tears from your eyes. The most disgusting thing, though, was trying to pull the slimy leeches off your skin. The more I pulled, the more they stretched and the tighter their jaws clung to my leg. I kept shouting, "Get them off!" and the film crew kept saying, "Just a minute ... this makes a really good shot!"'

Charlotte's journey into the heart of the world's most significant rainforests was an inspiring experience. 'The rainforest really is like a city. Each tree is like an urban tower block with hundreds of residents. If you knock it down, you cause just as much disruption and damage as if those residents were human. The jungle is extraordinary because although it only covers about six percent of the world, it contains over fifty percent of all known animal and plant species, plus lots more that are unknown, too.'

Back in London, what has she been enjoying since her return to 'civilisation'? 'I've been having lots of nice, long showers,' she says. 'In the Congo I was always worried about using up all our water supplies. And I find that when I've been in hot, uncomfortable conditions for a while, the things I look forward to more than anything else are being with my family and enjoying my favourite meal.'

Reading

1 Charlotte Uhlenbroek spent over four months in the jungle. Before you read about her, discuss these questions.

  1 Which things do you think you would find difficult in the jungle?

  2 Which things do you think you would most like to do when you returned to 'civilisation'?

2 Read the text and answer the questions in Ex. 1 about Charlotte.

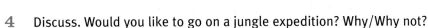
since → specific time
for → period of time

3 Read the text again and decide if the statements are true (T), false (F) or we don't know (DK).

1 Charlotte looks and feels 'out of place' in the Savoy Hotel.
2 She had to climb tall trees without the use of ropes.
3 The mosquito bites she had were the worst bites she's ever had.
4 She cried because she couldn't stand the sweat bees on her face.
5 The film crew helped her to get the leeches off her leg.
6 She compares a tree with a tower block because there are so many living things in each tree.
7 The water she used in the Congo was usually dirty.
8 When she gets home, she loves doing the cooking for her family.

4 Discuss. Would you like to go on a jungle expedition? Why/Why not?

Grammar | Present Perfect Simple and Continuous

5 Match the examples 1–4 with the correct rules A–D in the Active grammar box.

> ### Active grammar
>
> 1 *She's just finished* filming a TV series called 'Jungle' (and is glad to be back in 'civilisation').
>
> 2 *I've had* some horrible bites but these are the itchiest bites I've ever had.
>
> 3 *I've been* in jungles for a total of nineteen weeks and I'm going home today.
>
> 4 What *has she been enjoying* since her return to 'civilisation'? '*I've been having* lots of nice, long showers'.
>
> A Use the **Present Perfect Simple** to talk about an action or experience in the past when the time is not important or not known.
>
> B Use the **Present Perfect Simple** to describe an action that started in the past and continues in the present, when you're focussing on the finished action (or on the number of times the action has been completed up to the time of speaking).
>
> C Use the **Present Perfect Continuous** to describe an action that started in the past and continues in the present, when you're focussing on the activity itself. We often use *for* (length of time)/*since* (starting point) to talk about the duration of the activity.
>
> D Use the **Present Perfect Simple** to describe an action that happened in the past but has the result in the present. We often use *just, yet* or *already* in this case.
>
> • *Just* means a short time ago. It usually comes between *has/have* and the past participle.
>
> • *Already* shows that something happened sooner than expected. It usually comes between *has/have* and the past participle or at the end of the sentence.
>
> • *Yet* shows that the speaker expected something to happen before now. It is used at the end of negatives and questions.

see Reference page 87

6 Correct the mistake in each sentence.

1 I've been to the Brazilian rainforest in 2003.
2 She's bought already her plane tickets.
3 I've been visiting friends in Italy three times this year.
4 What you been doing since I last spoke to you?
5 Have you yet seen that film, *Sahara*?
6 He just has spoken to the tour guide about it.
7 I've been learning Spanish since two months.
8 Have you been knowing each other long?

7 Complete the sentences by using the prompts in brackets. Use the Present Perfect Simple, Present Perfect Continuous or Past Simple.

1 _____ (you/go/ever) to a jungle?
2 _____ (you/decide) where to go for your next holiday?
3 How long _____ (you/study) English?
4 What do you want to do today that _____ (you/not do/yet)?
5 Where _____ (you/go) for your last holiday?
6 How much coffee _____ (you/have/already) today?
7 _____ (you/have/ever) a bad insect bite?
8 Where _____ (you/live) for the last year?

Person to person

8 **a** In pairs, ask and answer the questions in Ex. 7.

b Choose one of the questions you asked and ask your partner more details about it.

Vocabulary | adjectives with -ed/-ing

9 a Find these adjectives in the text on page 76. In pairs, discuss what you think they mean. Use the sentences around the word to help you.

1 fascinating (para. 2) *interesting*
2 daunting (para. 2)
3 challenging (para. 2)
4 petrified (para. 2) → *frtho frightening*
5 annoying (para. 3) → *upset*
6 disgusting (para. 3) → *bad Not pleasant*
7 inspiring (para. 4) → *influency*
8 worried (para. 5)

b Look at the words and their context in the text again and choose the correct alternatives for these rules.

1 Use adjectives ending in -ed/-ing to describe someone's feelings.
2 Use adjectives ending in -ed/-ing to describe a situation.

c Write sentences with adjectives from Ex. 9a.

Pronunciation

10 **6.3** Listen and mark the main stress for each adjective.

1 fascinated, fascinating
2 daunted, daunting
3 challenged, challenging
4 petrified, petrifying
5 annoyed, annoying
6 disgusted, disgusting
7 inspired, inspiring
8 worried, worrying

11 a Complete the dialogues with the most appropriate adjective from Ex. 10.

A: Do you like camping?
B: I can honestly say I hate it! I spent a week camping once and every night I was (1) *petrified* because it was so dark and I kept hearing animals. I even found putting up my tent quite (2) *daunting*. It's quite old and one or two of the bits were missing.
A: Are you scared of heights?
B: Well, no actually. I like being high up. I went up in a small aeroplane a few years ago. I was a little (3) *worried* at first because it was a bit bumpy. But in the end I found the whole experience really (4) _____ . It made me want to do other things – perhaps even go parachuting one day.

A: How do you feel about eating food you've never tried before?
B: I don't usually mind new vegetables and things but I'm not very keen on eating meat I've never tried before. Actually, the other day, a friend of mine persuaded me to try snails. I was (5) *annoyed* with him because he didn't tell me what they were. He pretended they were bits of chicken. Well, when I found out, I was nearly sick! They were really (6) *disgusted disgusted*.
A: How would you feel about a job that involved working with animals?
B: I've just spent the summer holidays working at a monkey sanctuary and I loved it. You might not think monkeys are very interesting but they're (7) *Fasunated* when you get to know them. Some things were difficult – like catching them to give them medicine was pretty (8) *challenging*, but it was all very rewarding.

b **6.4** Listen and check your answers.

12 a Ask and answer the questions in Ex. 11a with other students. Use the adjectives in Ex. 10.

b Who has the most similar feelings to you?

Writing

13 Read the email in the Writing bank on page 162 and do the exercises.

14 Choose one of the situations in Ex. 11a and write an email to a friend telling him/her about your experience. Use Maisie's email and the paragraph plan below to help you.

Paragraph 1: explain where you are and why, and how you feel

Paragraph 2: describe what you've been doing

Paragraph 3: say how you feel about finishing

Reading

1 **a** Look at the photo of Bhutan and discuss.
    1 What do you think life is like there?
    2 Why do you think few tourists go to this country?

  b Read the text quickly and check your ideas.

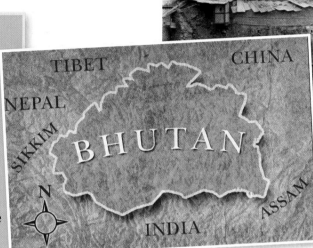

BHUTAN is a country of about 750,000 people in the eastern Himalayas. Visitors may be surprised how much culture, tradition and nature are all flourishing in this very private country. The Bhutanese people believe that all forms of life, human and non-human, are precious and sacred. Because of this attitude, they live in harmony with nature and their environment remains pristine, with an astonishing variety of animals, birds and plants. The people live in harmony with each other too, with no discrimination of any kind.

In order to safeguard this rich natural environment and peaceful culture, Bhutan has adopted a cautious and controlled approach to tourism. In 2003, there were fewer than 6000 tourists and this number is not expected to increase greatly. No independent travellers are permitted in Bhutan; all tourists must go on a pre-planned, prepaid, guided, package tour. However, if you make the effort and manage to get a visa and arrange a trip, you will certainly have a life-changing experience in this magical kingdom.

2 Read the text again. Then, with a partner, summarise the text's main points about a) important beliefs of Bhutanese people, b) nature in Bhutan and c) tourism in Bhutan.

3 Discuss. Would you like to visit Bhutan? Why/Why not? Do you think Bhutanese people would experience culture shock if they visited your country? In what ways?

Vocabulary | weather

4 **6.5** Listen and decide which of these questions each of the three people are talking about:
  A: What's the weather like in your country?
  B: What's your favourite type of weather?

5 **a** Look at the tapescript on page 171 and write the underlined words in the correct place in the table below.

COLD	WARM/HOT	RAIN	WINDY	SKY	WEATHER IN GENERAL
cool		pours		clear	

  b In pairs, explain the differences in meaning between the words in each column in the table. Use a dictionary if necessary.

  c Look at the words again and decide:
  1 if each one is a noun, adjective or verb, e.g. *breeze* = noun
  2 what other forms there are, e.g. *breeze* (n), *breezy* (adj)

6 Match one of the words from Ex. 5 on page 79 to each of the sentences.

It was perfect weather for flying kites. breezy.

1 The weather in Ireland isn't usually very hot or very cold.
2 I got completely soaked even though it was only a five-minute walk.
3 We had to sit in the shade until quite late in the afternoon.
4 The sky was full of clouds and the sun didn't come out all day.
5 It only rained for about ten minutes and then it was fine.
6 It was warm in the day but I was glad I'd taken a jacket for the evenings.
7 I like heavy rain but I can't stand it when it rains gently for hours and hours.
8 We were freezing when we went camping despite having extra-thick sleeping bags.
9 You'll need sun cream and a raincoat. You never know what the weather will be like.
10 It was a lovely place – blue skies and the light was really good for taking photographs.

7 Discuss.

1 How would you describe the weather in your area/country?
2 How would you like the weather where you live to be different?
3 How do you think this would improve your life?
4 Does the weather affect your mood? In what ways?

Listening

8 **a** If you were going on holiday to Bhutan what sort of things would you like to know about in advance, e.g. the weather?

b **6.6** Listen to a question and answer session with an expert on Bhutan and some people who are considering a trip there. In what order do they talk about the things in the box?

> special events/festivals ☐   the ideal time of year to visit ☐
> food ☐   what to do there ☐   what to take ☐   organised trips ☐

9 Listen again and complete the notes below.

TRIP TO BHUTAN

WHEN TO GO:
Spring and autumn are the best seasons to go
Don't go in winter because (1) _____
Don't go in summer because (2) _____

ACTIVITIES:
Trekking is fantastic – amazing views and a lot of different (3) _____

CLOTHES:
Don't forget to take: rain gear and good (4) _____
Also, for the sun: a hat and (5) _____
Don't bring (6) _____ or (7) _____ for trekking (it's all provided)

FOOD:
One of the main ingredients used is (8) _____

FESTIVALS:
The main reason for festivals is for people to (9) _____

FLAGS:
The reason for the flags is for people to (10) _____

10 Discuss. Would you like to go on the organised trekking trips described in the listening? Why/Why not? Have you been to any festivals or celebrations in your country or abroad which you particularly enjoyed? Give details.

Liku *could you tell me what time it is?*

Grammar | questions

11 Complete the questions in the Active grammar box. Then, look at the tapescript on page 171 and check your answers.

Third Person

> ### Active grammar
>
> **Direct questions**
>
> There are two main types of direct questions:
>
> A *Yes/No* questions   (1) _would you need_ *to carry all our equipment?*
>
>   (2) _Do you_ *provide a guide?*
>
> B *Wh-* questions   *What activities* (3) _can_ *you recommend* ?
>
>   *When* (4) _is_ *the best time to go?*
>
> **Subject questions** are used when the question word (e.g. *who*) refers to the subject of the sentence. When a *wh-* word replaces the subject in a question we do not use the auxiliary verb.
>
> *Who* (5) _is / goes_ *with the trekking group?*
>
> **Indirect questions:**
>
> Use indirect questions when you want to be polite (e.g. when you don't know someone). There are different ways of starting indirect questions (e.g. *Do you know ..., Can you tell me ...*).
>
> Use the word order of positive statements. Use *if* or *whether* for indirect *Yes/No* questions.
>
> *Can you tell me what* (6) _I can do_ ?
>
> *Could I ask you what* (7) _Bhutan's_ *like?*
>
> *Do you know* (8) _if I can go_ *any interesting festivals at that time?*
>
> *I'd like to know* (9) _where I should go_ *to take anything special.*

I don't understand what I should do?
would you mind telling me where I can go?

see Reference page 87

Luka Matiz / Luka

12 a Correct the mistake in each question.

You go on holiday every year?

Do you go on holiday every year?

1 Where you are living at the moment? *Where are you living...*
2 He has ever been trekking before? *has he ever...*
3 Who did give you those lovely flowers? *Who gave you...*
4 What time you be here tomorrow? *What time will you be...*
5 You having a holiday soon? *are you having a holiday...*
6 When this company was started? *When was this company started...*

b Change the questions above into indirect questions starting with the words given.

Can I ask you if you go on holiday every year?

1 Can you tell me _where you are living at the moment?_
2 Do you know _if he has? been trekking before?_
3 Can I ask you _who gave? you those lovely flowers?_
4 Can you tell me _what? time you will be here tomorrow?_
5 Do you know _if you? are having a holiday soon?_
6 I'd like to know _when. This company was started?_

Speaking

13 a Find out about two other types of holiday. In A/B groups write questions using the notes below to help you.

Student As write questions about camel trips in Egypt.

Student Bs write questions about bird watching in Mexico.

Think about cost, location, what the area is like, accommodation, food, facilities, activities/ organised tours.

b Student As read the text about bird watching in Mexico on page 150. Prepare to answer your partner's questions.

Student Bs read the text about camel trips in Egypt on page 145. Prepare to answer your partner's questions.

c Work in A/B pairs. Take turns to ask and answer questions.

14 Discuss. Which holiday would you rather go on: bird watching in Mexico, camel riding in Egypt or trekking in Bhutan? Why?

Vocabulary | verb phrases about moving/travelling

1 Work with a partner. Match the underlined verb phrases 1–8 with the correct definitions a–h. Use a dictionary if necessary.

1 My parents are Scottish but they emigrated to Australia.
2 My brother has lived abroad for ten years so I don't see him much.
3 I've just moved house. Here's my new address.
4 My sister left home when she was 18 and went to university in York.
5 I spent a lot of holidays just roaming around the countryside, exploring.
6 After weeks of planning, we finally set off on our round-the-world trip.
7 We all cried when we went to see her off at the airport.
8 I'm off to the shops. Is there anything you need?

a) to live in a foreign country
b) to leave your house and go to live in another one
c) to leave your country and go to live in another country
d) to walk or travel, with no definite purpose
e) when you are ready to go or you're going to go somewhere very soon
f) to leave at the start of a journey (especially an important, exciting or difficult journey)
g) when a young person leaves his/her parents' house and goes to live somewhere else
h) to go to an airport, train station, etc. to say goodbye to someone who is leaving

2 Complete the questions with the correct form of a phrase from Ex. 1.
1 At what age do young people in your country typically _____?
2 Do you like people to come and _____ (you) at the airport?
3 What time did you _____ when you last went on holiday?
4 Which country would you move to if you lived _____?
5 What would you miss if you _____?
6 How many times have you _____ in your life?
7 Where _____ (you) to after class today?
8 When was the last time you went to a new place and just _____ without any clear direction?

3 **a** You are going to ask your partner the questions from Ex. 2. First, predict what you think his/her answers will be.

b Ask the questions. How many did you get right?

Reading

4 **a** Discuss. Do you think the following statements are true (T) or false (F)?

A Over a million British people emigrate every year.
B Spain is a popular destination for British people to emigrate to.
C Most people who emigrate go back home after a year.

b Read the text quickly and check your answers.

5 Read the text again and match each paragraph with the most appropriate summary A–G. Three of the summary sentences cannot be used.

A The appeal of many places is the price of property, better wages and the good weather.
B For most people who emigrate, it's the best thing they've ever done.
C Many people find that the grass is not always as green as they had hoped.
D There is a trend in recent times for increasing numbers of British people to emigrate.
E It's very difficult to get a work permit for popular countries like Australia and Spain.
F Some people go abroad for about three years in order to earn well and save money to go back with.
G Although emigrating can be hard, it can also provide people with greater job satisfaction.

ON THE MOVE!

1 Every day, thousands of people are on the move and, either temporarily or permanently, setting up home abroad. Their move may be job-orientated or perhaps they think the grass is greener somewhere else. Whatever their reasons, it's clear that more and more people are stepping into the unknown and leaving their own country. In Britain alone, over 400,000 people make the move each year. But where do they go and why? And do they 'live happily ever after'?

2 Typically a lot of people move abroad because of their jobs. They may find that their company is moving them overseas but many people make their own decision, believing they will have more successful careers abroad. Paul Derwin is a scientist who used to be based at a prestigious London university. He was dissatisfied, however, with the level of funding and recognition he was getting and decided to explore the possibilities California had to offer. 'Emigration is incredibly difficult, emotionally as well as practically,' he says. 'But after ten years here, I've got a far nicer life than before. I have a fantastic job and the recognition I wanted. People take my work much more seriously here. It would be difficult to give that up now.'

3 The most popular reason for emigrating, however, is the desire for a better quality of life. Destinations that place a greater value on leisure and have a more laid-back lifestyle were the most popular. People also look for places that will give them a sunnier climate and generally hotter weather. Britain is famous for its bad weather especially during the dark and cold winter months. Southern Spain becomes very appealing when you think of the 320 days of sunshine a year. Cheaper property is another reason given for moving abroad. The cost of living in America, for example, is twenty percent lower than in Britain and often salaries are slightly higher. For all these reasons, it's not surprising that the top five most regularly chosen destinations for Britons to emigrate to are: the USA, Australia, New Zealand, Canada and Spain. The fact that most of these are English-speaking countries is obviously also a major factor for British people. Sue Riddell, a thirty-year-old nurse from Birmingham, wants to emigrate to Australia with a group of friends. 'We're fed up of the conditions we work and live in,' she says. 'I went travelling to Australia after I left school and I loved it – the beaches, the fresh air, the sense of space. If I can, I'm going. And I don't know if I'll come back.'

4 Despite the fact that so many Britons move abroad, however, most of them go back home after only about three years. Often living overseas is not as attractive as it first seems. Generally people emigrate because they think life is going to be better. They sometimes want to do this because they get certain feelings on holiday and they romanticise about what it would be like to live there. They tend to focus on the best aspects and think it will be like this all the time when often that is not the case. Making enough money and getting work can be more difficult abroad than at home and people tend to find they miss family, friends and things they took for granted back home.

6 Discuss.

1 What type of person do you think you need to be to emigrate or study abroad?
I think you need to be an independent person.

2 Have you ever lived abroad?
   a If so, where did you go and what was it like? What did you miss?
   b If not, would you ever consider doing so? Why/Why not? Where would you like to go?

3 Is it common for people to emigrate from your country? If so, where do they go and what are their reasons? Do you think they find what they are looking for?

Grammar | making comparisons

7 Complete the rules in the Active grammar box.

> ## Active grammar
>
> 1 A The comparative and superlative of one-syllable adjectives (e.g. *cheap*) and adverbs (e.g. *fast*) are generally made by _er, est_
>
> **Exceptions:**
>
> B Adjectives which end in a vowel plus a consonant (e.g. *hot*). These comparatives and superlatives are made by _Doble consonant_
>
> C Adjectives which end in *-e* (e.g. *nice*). These comparatives and superlatives are made by _R and the end_
>
> 2 A The comparative and superlative of two and three-syllable adjectives (e.g. *popular*) and adverbs (e.g. *carefully*) are generally made by _more, most_
>
> **Exception:**
>
> B Two-syllable adjectives ending in *-y* (e.g. *sunny*). These comparatives and superlatives are made by _er_ .
>
> You can also use (*not*) *as ... as* to make comparisons.
>
> 3 A We use (*not*) *as ... as* to compare things which are _Different_ (e.g. *Often living overseas is not as attractive as it first seems*).
>
> B We use *as ... as* to compare things which are _similar_ (e.g. *The lifestyle in New Zealand is as laid-back as in Australia*).
>
> **Some adjectives and adverbs have irregular forms:**
>
> 4 A good/well → better → _best_ ;
>   B bad/badly → _worse_ → the worst;
>   C much → more → most;
>   D little → less → least;
>   E far → further → furthest
>
> **We can't use *very* to modify comparatives, but:**
>
> 5 A We can use *a bit*, *a little* and *slightly* to show _small_ differences.
>   B We can use *far*, *much* and *a lot* to show _big_ differences.

see Reference page 87 i'm much (er) than
my ___ is a little/a bit more/er than.

8 Complete the second sentence so that it means the same as the first. Use between two and four words (including the word in **bold**).

Spain is sunnier than Britain.

isn't: *Britain isn' t as sunny as Spain.*

1 I find learning foreign languages far more difficult than my sister.
  much: My sister learns foreign languages _____ than me. _much better._

2 I'd prefer to live somewhere drier than this.
  wet: I'd prefer to live somewhere that _isn't_ this. _as wet as_

3 I'm a bit more adventurous now than I was ten years ago.
  slightly: Ten years ago I was _slightly less than_ I am now.

4 At home my life was a lot more complicated than it is abroad.
  much: My life abroad is _less complicated_ than it was at home.

5 I don't think I planned my time on holiday carefully enough.
  carefully: I think I should've planned my time on holiday _more carefully_

6 My lifestyle in Canada now is not better or worse than it was in England.
  as: My lifestyle here in Canada is _as good as / the same as_ it was in England.

Person to person

9 **a** Write six sentences about yourself using comparatives and superlatives. You can use the ideas in Ex. 8 to help you. Four of the sentences should be true and two should be false.

I'm more adventurous than I used to be.

b Say your sentences to another student. Can he/she guess which two are false?

Lina Matiz.

? which one are you going for?

1 Match the expressions with *go* in **bold** with the correct definitions a–j.

1 We're **going away** for two weeks to stay with my cousin. *j*

2 There's a lot of shouting next door. I wonder what's **going on**? *a*

3 Which course have you decided to **go for**? *d*

4 I totally trust Danielle. She would never **go back on** her word. *h*

5 He **went down with** terrible flu the day before his interview. *b*

6 I've never been skiing before but I'd like to **have a go**. *e*

7 He's decided to **make a go** of the new business for at least a year. *i*

8 I've been **on the go** all day and I'm exhausted. *g*

9 It **goes without saying** that we'll all support you. *f*

10 They **went to great lengths** to make the party a success. *c*

a) to happen

b) to catch an illness

c) to take a lot of time and effort

d) to choose a particular thing

e) to attempt to do something → *to decide*

f) to be clear without being said

g) to be very busy or working all the time

h) to not do what you've promised or agreed to do

i) to make something (e.g. a business or a marriage) successful *important.*

j) to leave your home and go to another place for a few days or weeks

2 Work in pairs. Say one of the definitions in Ex. 1. Your partner should say the correct expression.

A: *to be clear without being said*

B: *it goes without saying*

3 Choose the correct alternatives.

1 When I'm abroad I always *make/have* a go at speaking the language.

2 We're going *away/out* for the weekend. Could you look after our cat?

3 Don't worry. It goes without *saying/talking* that I'll meet you at the airport.

4 There's something going *down/on* in the city centre. It's full of people.

5 Although they argue a lot, they want to *make/have* a go of their marriage.

6 I promise I won't go back *with/on* what I've said.

7 Can you help with dinner please? I've been *on/off* the go all day.

8 Your teacher can't be here today. She's gone *off/down* with a bad cold.

9 I couldn't decide which kitten to go *away/for*. They were all gorgeous.

10 He went to *great/long* lengths to make sure he was totally prepared for the interview.

4 a **6.7** Listen and check your answers.

b Listen again and underline the part of the expression with *go* which has the main stress. Then repeat the sentences.

When I'm abroad I always have a go at speaking the language.

5 a In pairs, prepare to tell a story using five of the expressions in Ex. 1. Your story should include one of the sentences below.

One day I decided that I wanted a bit more adventure in my life.

I'd always been fascinated by the idea of exploring caves.

I'd never considered myself much of an explorer before.

b Listen to other students' stories. Which did you think was the most exciting? How far were the stories based on true feelings/events?

make a go at doing sth of something

Shounyudou

6 Communication

Travelling companions

1 **Discuss in pairs.**

  1 Which of the holidays in the photos appeals to you most? Why?

  2 What is the best holiday you've ever been on? Why?

2 **Do the quiz with as many different students as possible. When you're asking the questions, make notes about the other students' answers. When you're answering the questions, use the ideas in the quiz and your own ideas.**

3 **a** Look at the notes you made about other students and read the descriptions on page 147.

  • Which one do you think you are most like?

  • Which one do you think each person you questioned is most like?

  b Which students do you think would be the best travelling companion for you? Why? Which would be the worst? Why?

Lifelong learning

Travelling is learning

Travelling time is good learning time. Brainstorm all the ways to continue learning while travelling.

• watch English films on a plane

• listen to your coursebook CDs on a bus

• talk to English-speaking people you meet on a train

Who's your **ideal** **travelling** companion?

Are you an intrepid adventurer who loves sleeping under the stars or someone who prefers a home from home and all life's luxuries? Who is your ideal travelling companion? And who is your travelling companion from hell?

Do the quiz and find out.

① What would your ideal summer holiday be?
package holiday/beach/pool   independent travel
alone/with friends   camping   exploring jungle/desert, etc.
sports/activities (e.g. skiing, scuba diving, etc.)

② What would you definitely pack in your suitcase?
romantic 'easy-reading' novels   serious novels
magazines   guidebooks   study/work books   first aid kit
sun cream   sleeping bag   penknife

③ How would you spend your ideal evening on holiday?
in the hotel restaurant   in your tent
in local restaurants trying different food
in various bars and nightclubs

④ How long do you like your holidays to be?
not more than a week   two weeks
at least three or four weeks   open-ended

⑤ What do you dread most about your holiday?
missing favourite TV programmes   missing friends/family
being bored   spiders, mosquitoes, etc.
toilets that don't work properly
being on a beach with only people of my nationality
not being able to speak the language
getting robbed

⑥ What are you most likely to bring home?
cheap cigarettes and perfume   lots of photos
souvenirs from the airport   a tropical disease
a fantastic suntan   arts and crafts made by the locals

Present Perfect Simple and Continuous

Use the Present Perfect Simple to talk about an action or experience in the past when the time is not important or not known.

I've visited several countries in South America.

Use the Present Perfect Simple to describe an action that started in the past and continues in the present, when you're focussing on the finished action or on the number of times the action has been completed up to the time of speaking.

I've lived here since last January.

Contrast with Present Perfect Continuous. Use the Present Perfect Continuous to describe an action that started in the past and continues in the present, when you're focussing on the activity itself.

He's been playing tennis for three hours.

Use the Present Perfect Simple to describe an action that happened in the past but has the result in the present.

The post has come. There's a letter for you.

just, *yet* and *already*

Just means a short time ago. It usually comes between *has/have* and the past participle.

I've just seen Mariana.

Already shows that something happened sooner than expected. It usually comes between *has/have* and the past participle or at the end of the sentence.

I've already done the shopping.

Yet shows that the speaker expected something to happen before now. It is used at the end of negatives and questions.

Have you finished that email yet?

She hasn't replied to the invitation yet.

Questions

Direct questions:

There are two main types of direct questions:

Yes/No questions

Are you going to Danka's party on Saturday?

Wh- questions

Where did she learn to speak such good Spanish?

Subject questions are used when the question word (e.g. *who*) refers to the subject of the sentence. When a *wh-* word replaces the subject in a question we do not use the auxiliary verb.

The teacher told us to go. → Who told you to go?

Indirect questions:

Use indirect questions when you want to be polite (e.g. when you don't know someone).

Use the word order of positive statements.

Use *if* or *whether* for indirect *Yes/No* questions.

Can you tell me where the nearest bank is?

I'd like to know whether this bus goes to Oxford.

Making comparisons

Add *-er* and *-est* to form the comparatives and superlatives of:

one-syllable adjectives and adverbs

two-syllable adjectives and adverbs ending in *y*

Use *more* and *most* to form the comparatives and superlatives of two or more syllable adjectives and adverbs.

You can also use (*not*) *as ... as* to make comparisons.

I can't play the piano as well as Michael.

We can't use *very* to modify comparatives, but we can use the following:

for a small difference – *a bit, a little, slightly*

for a larger difference – *far, much, very much, a lot, quite a lot*

I'm feeling quite a lot better today.

Key vocabulary

Exploring

to have itchy feet   to be bitten by the travel bug
to go as an independent traveller   to experience culture shock   to go/be taken into uncharted territory   to wander around

Adjectives with *-ed* and *-ing* endings

fascinated/fascinating   daunted/daunting
challenged/challenging   petrified/petrifying
annoyed/annoying   disgusted/disgusting
inspired/inspiring   worried/worrying

Weather

cool   chilly   subzero temperatures   mild
scorching   to pour   to drizzle/drizzle   shower/
showery   breeze/breezy   clear   overcast   bright
changeable

Verb phrases about moving/travelling

to emigrate   to live abroad   to move house
to leave home   to roam around   to set off
to see someone off   to be off

Expressions with *go*

to go away   to go on   to go for   to go back on
to go down with   to have a go at   to make a go of
to be on the go   to go without saying
to go to great lengths

6 Review and practice

1 Choose the correct alternatives.

Thanks for the party last week. I've really enjoyed/really enjoyed it.

1 I've *written/'ve been writing* eight emails all morning.
2 I've *seen/saw* a really awful film yesterday.
3 My brother is in France. He's been there *for/ since* a week.
4 She's very well travelled. She's *been/gone* to more than twenty countries.
5 Billy's the nicest person I've *ever/already* met.
6 I live in a flat in London. I've *lived/lived* here for three years.
7 He's *worked/been working* in the garden for hours and he's exhausted.
8 Would you like some coffee? I've *yet/just* made some.

2 Write sentences using the prompts. Use the Past Simple, Present Perfect Simple or Continuous.

I/stand/at this bus stop/forty minutes

I've been standing at this bus stop for forty minutes.

1 He/already/phone me/three times today.
2 We/go/to India/three weeks last summer.
3 I/just/see/a really fantastic musical.
4 You/hear/the news/yet?
5 I/decorate/the living room/all day.
6 I/know/my best friend/primary school.
7 You/ever/read/the *Lord of the Rings* books?
8 How long/you/study/English?

3 Complete the direct questions for the underlined answers.

Where did you go on holiday last year?

I went to Sardinia.

1 _____ your motorbike?
   I've had my motorbike for a week and a half.
2 _____ at university?
   She's going to study engineering at university.
3 _____ ?
   I think I'm about 1 metre 70 centimetres tall.
4 _____ that box on the top shelf for me?
   No, sorry, I can't reach it. I can only reach the second shelf.

4 Write indirect questions for the underlined answers starting with the words given and using the words in brackets.

Can I ask you where you went on holiday last year? (you go on holiday last year)

I went to Rio de Janeiro for carnival.

1 Can _____ ? (this shop)
   It closes at half past five.
2 I'd _____ (can buy/theatre tickets here)
   Yes, you can.
3 Would _____ ? (you/finish your homework)
   I'll definitely finish it by 12.00.
4 Can _____ ? (the most interesting country/you ever visit)?
   I'm not sure – either Japan or Russia.

5 Choose the correct alternatives.

I want to get to work earlier than/as yesterday.

1 My suitcase is *much/more* heavier than yours.
2 Tania got the *worse/worst* maths results in the whole class.
3 The exam wasn't as difficult *than/as* I'd expected.
4 You're the *most/more* helpful person I know.
5 You need to speak *quite/quiet* a lot louder than that.
6 People are far more *friendly/friendlier* here than in my country.
7 This one is *a/the* little more expensive than that one.
8 Which actor is the *better/best*: Brad Pitt or Leonardo DiCaprio?

6 One word is wrong in each sentence. Find the word and correct it.

1 We'll need an alarm because we're putting off very early in the morning.
2 He's desperate to go travelling. He's got really scratchy feet.
3 I'd really love to make a go with drama lessons.
4 I think I'm going down of a sore throat.
5 I'll give you a lift. That goes without speaking.
6 I experienced country shock at first and found it hard to get used to living in a new place.
7 I can't believe she went back to her word.
8 It was lovely having so many people to see me away at the station.

7 Excess

[handwritten: to much / Too much]

Lead-in

[handwritten: He always has an excess of alcohol]
[handwritten: excess → verb]
[handwritten: excessive. / adjective]

1 Discuss.

  1 What can you see in each picture?
  2 In what ways do you think they represent 'excess'?
  3 In what other ways might people's lifestyles be described as 'excessive'?

2 **7.1** Listen to three lifestyle descriptions. Do you think the things described are 'excessive'? Why/Why not?

3 a In pairs, discuss the meaning of the words in **bold**.

  1 When was the last time you bought something really **extravagant**?
  2 Do you think spending €100 on one meal is **excessive**?
  3 If you could take one **luxury** to a 'desert island', what would it be?
  4 Do you ever order **extra-large** portions in restaurants?
  5 Do you think you were **spoilt** as a child? Why/Why not?
  6 When was the last time you bought something you thought was **overpriced**?
  7 Do you think the idea of having a 'self-cleaning' house in the near future is **far-fetched**?
  8 Do you know anyone who would go on a **spending spree** to cheer him/herself up?

  b Ask and answer the questions with a partner. How many of his/her answers are similar to yours?

[handwritten: He has a excess of fat]
[handwritten: It's excessive]

Reading

1 Look at the photo and discuss.

1 How does the picture make you feel?

2 Do you eat a lot of fast food? Why/Why not? Do you think that the amount of fast food you eat is healthy?

2 a Read the text quickly and answer this question. According to the film-maker, what is the main message of the film?

SUPER SIZE ME

Three trips to McDonald's a day might be every little boy's dream. But the reality was a nightmare for Morgan Spurlock whose
5 film *Super Size Me* documents his one-month existence on fast food and its disastrous consequences. So, if it was so awful, why did he do it? And
10 does it work as a film?

The main basis of the film is that Spurlock promises to eat three McDonald's meals a day, every day, for a month. He must only eat food
15 from McDonald's and every time an employee asks if he would like to 'super size' the meal, he must agree. 'Super sizing' refers to the fact that with this type of meal you
20 get a considerably larger portion of everything. Instead of the normal burger, fries and a drink, you get an extra-large burger, extra-large fries, and an extra-large drink for
25 only a very small price increase.

Spurlock admitted that the whole experiment ignored any sensible eating plan. He knew that by eating three McDonald's meals a day, he
30 would be consuming more calories, fat, salt and sugar per meal than he needed. Before he started, three doctors certified that Spurlock was 183cm tall, weighed about 84kg
35 and was in good health. Although both Spurlock and his doctors knew this diet was unhealthy, none of them were quite prepared for just how unhealthy it turned out to
40 be. The changes in his body were

horrifying. In the first week, he put on 4.5 kilos in weight and by the end of the thirty days he had gained nearly 14 kilos, bringing his
45 total weight to a massive 98kg.

Weight gain was only one of the negative effects, however. When all three doctors saw the severe damage to his liver, they
50 all recommended stopping the experiment after twenty days. Spurlock continued to follow the diet, however, because he wanted to show people what this kind of
55 diet can do to you. And you begin to realise that the film could be a fast-forward picture of your life: in thirty days you get to see what could happen to you over twenty or
60 thirty years of over consumption. You're on a path to heart disease, liver failure, high blood pressure, diabetes, depression and more.

'I think we need to take
65 responsibility for ourselves,' says Spurlock. 'There also has to be some responsibility on the part of the fast food companies. McDonald's alone feeds 46 million
70 people every day. They have an obligation to give their consumers information about exactly what they're eating.' Spurlock also focusses on the advertising and
75 marketing of fast food products, especially to children. McDonald's markets to children through Happy Meals (a children's meal in a box including a free toy) and
80 playgrounds in the restaurants.

'The playgrounds aren't there just for kids to come and play,' he says. 'You're only allowed into the playground when you've bought a
85 burger or some fries or a Coke. It's an effective way of establishing a positive association in children's minds.'

It's the humour above all that
90 makes this film work. Even towards the end of the month, when he admitted to feeling lethargic, depressed and smelly, the audience remain entertained by his
95 sense of humour and upbeat style. Spurlock says that he hopes that the film is entertaining, but he also hopes that it encourages them to take better care of themselves. He
100 says, 'I'd love people to walk out of the movie and say, "Next time I'm not going to 'super size'. Maybe I'm not going to go there at all. I'm going to sit down and eat dinner
105 with my kids, with the TV off, so that we can eat healthy food, talk about what we're eating and have a relationship with each other."' Judging by critics and audiences
110 alike, the film certainly does seem to work. Food for thought indeed.

in my country, we have many different food. → countable and uncountable

b Read the text again and explain what each of these phrases means in its context.

1 'the reality was a nightmare' (l.3)
2 'to "super size" the meal' (l.17)
3 'ignored any sensible eating plan' (l.27)
4 'just how unhealthy it turned out to be' (l.39)
5 'recommended stopping the experiment' (l.50)
6 'a fast-forward picture of your life:' (l.57)
7 'an obligation to give their consumers information' (l.71)
8 'a positive association in children's minds' (l.87)
9 'his sense of humour and upbeat style' (l.95)
10 'have a relationship with each other' (l.108)

3 Discuss. Have you seen this film? What did you think of it? Would you like to see it? Why/Why not?

Grammar | countable and uncountable nouns

4 **a** Look at the underlined words in the examples in the Active grammar box. Is each one countable or uncountable?

b Divide the words in the box into three groups: countable, uncountable and those which can be both.

c For the words that can be both, discuss what the difference in meaning is.

You can say 'a coffee' when you're talking about a cup of coffee and you can say 'some coffee' when you're not saying exactly how much.

Active grammar

1 *He ate three McDonald's meals a day, every day, for a month.*
2 *He must only eat food from McDonald's.*
3 *I'll have sausage, beans and a black coffee, please.*
4 *If I drink coffee in the evenings, I can't sleep properly.*

food   meal   coffee   diet   burger
meat   sugar   salt   chicken   bread
chocolate   fruit   cake   weather
luggage   paper   trip   travel
equipment   advice   iron   furniture
business   hair   information   news

COUNTABLE	UNCOUNTABLE	BOTH
diet meat burger	meat salt sugar bread cereal	food coffee chocolate

see Reference page 101

5 What is the difference in meaning between *few/a few* and *little/a little* in these sentences?

1 a He's lucky. He's got *few* problems to worry about. *(not many)*
  b Things aren't going well. He's got *a few* problems. *(some)*
2 a We must go. There's *little* time before the train leaves. *(not much)*
  b Stay and have a drink. We've got *a little* time before the show starts. *(much/some)*

6 Complete the sentences with the correct word/phrase from the box.

much   many   a little   a few   lots   lot
some   a great deal of   piece   slice

1 You haven't eaten *many* fries.
2 I only have *a little* sugar in my coffee nowadays.
3 There is too *much* traffic in the city centre.
4 She gave me a *piece* of paper with her address written on it.
5 He gave me *some* really good advice.
6 I've got *lots* of bags to carry. Can you help me?
7 He's very lazy. He spends *great deal* time doing nothing.
8 I'll just have one *slice* of toast please.
9 There were only *a few* shops still open when I went out.
10 I've spent a *lot* of time working with children.

7 Find the mistakes in eight of the sentences and correct them.

1 Do you spend *a* lot of time doing exercise?
2 Have you given anyone *some* a good advice recently?
3 How *much* many sugar do you have in your coffee?
4 When was the last time you had piece of cake?
5 How often do you watch the news on TV?
6 How *much* many fruits do you usually eat every day?
7 Do you like *a* very hot weather?
8 Do you ever use the Internet to get *some* information?
9 When did you last go on an interesting *trip* travel?
10 When did you last buy some new furniture?

Person to person

8 Ask and answer the questions in Ex. 7 with a partner.

Vocabulary | food and cooking

9 **a** Put these words into the correct place in the word map below.

> a saucepan   an oven   sweet   to bake
> a cooker   beef   to scramble   bitter
> a frying pan   salty   to fry   a peach
> to roast   cabbage   to boil   sour
> a wooden spoon   to grill   savoury
> parsley   a plate

Food and cooking

- Food
- Ways of cooking
- Kitchen equipment
- Taste

b What is the difference between:

1 a cook/a cooker
2 a vegetable/a vegetarian
3 a recipe/a dish
4 rare/raw
5 to stir/to beat
6 to slice/to chop/to grate

c Work in pairs. Add at least two more words to each group of words in the word map.

10 **a** Choose the correct alternatives.

1 Sushi is a Japanese dish made with *raw*/*rare* fish.
2 *Beat*/*Stir* the mixture slowly every five minutes.
3 Ugh! This soup is much too *savoury*/*salty*.
4 First, you *slice*/*chop* the onion into small squares.
5 I don't eat many cakes and biscuits. I find them too *sweet*/*sour*.
6 Fill a large saucepan with water and *bake*/*boil* the pasta for ten minutes.
7 Macaroni cheese is my favourite *dish*/*plate*.
8 The *cook*/*cooker* has broken. I need to buy a new one.
9 In Britain at Christmas, it's traditional to *bake*/ *roast* a turkey in the oven.
10 Which vegetable shall we have today: *cabbage*/*parsley* or broccoli?

Pronunciation

11 **a** [7.2] With a partner, decide which syllable in each of the words below has the main stress. Then listen and check your ideas.

cooker

1 saucepan
2 oven
3 vegetable
4 vegetarian
5 bitter
6 savoury
7 carrot
8 sugar

b Now decide which syllable(s) in each of the words above you think is pronounced as a weak form /ə/. Listen again and check your ideas.

Speaking

12 [7.3] Listen to someone talking about a traditional British Christmas dinner. Do you think you would enjoy this meal?

13 **a** Choose one of the things in the list below. Think about how it is prepared and cooked.

1 your favourite dish
2 the last meal you made for visitors
3 a traditional dish in your country
4 a dish you used to love as a child

b Tell other students what the dish is and how to prepare/cook it.

c Which of the meals you heard about would you like to eat most?

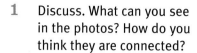

Grammar	passives
Can do	write a formal letter of complaint

Listening

1 Discuss. What can you see in the photos? How do you think they are connected?

2 [7·4] Listen and check your ideas.

3 Listen again and decide if these statements are true (T), false (F) or we don't know (DK).

1 A friend of Andress found the bikini in her attic.

2 Andress said it was a difficult decision to sell the bikini.

3 Someone bought the bikini for $6100.

4 Six stormtrooper helmets were auctioned in London.

5 The owner made a profit of nearly $25,000.

6 Someone sold Britney Spears' chewing gum at a traditional auction.

7 The gum came with a guarantee to prove it was real.

8 Thousands of people put in bids for the gum.

9 One man in Texas bought his sons Christmas presents on eBay.

10 When he sold the presents again, he made $1000 profit.

4 Discuss.

1 Do you know anyone who collects things (e.g. pop memorabilia, old magazines, stamps, etc.)? What do you think of this kind of hobby?

2 What do you think of what the Texan father did?

3 Have you ever visited eBay or a traditional auction? What do you think of these ways of buying and selling things?

Vocabulary | verb phrases about money

5 What is the difference in meaning between the verb phrases in *italics* in each pair of sentences?

1 a Lots of people *bid* for the chewing gum on eBay.
  b That bag is very expensive. Why don't you try and *haggle* for it?

2 a These boots were only £30. I think I *got a bargain*.
  b I'd like to buy this T-shirt but it's slightly marked. Could I *get a discount*?

3 a You can *get a refund* within twenty-eight days if you are not completely satisfied.
  b *Get a receipt* just in case you want to take the CDs back.

4 a I'd love to get a new camera but I *can't afford* it at the moment.
  b It'll cost £10 to take a taxi – it's *not worth it*. Let's walk instead.

6 a Read the sentences and decide which of the phrases in Ex. 5 you could use for each one.

1 One man offered to pay £5000 for a small antique chair at an auction.

2 Ten CDs for only £50 – that's really cheap!

3 I asked if I could pay less, but the shop assistant said no.

4 I'd like to buy a motorbike but I haven't got enough money.

5 This DVD player broke after only a week. I'd like my money back, please.

6 I always try and negotiate a lower price with market traders.

7 The rent on that tiny flat is much too expensive.

8 Don't forget to keep the paper they give you when you buy something.

b Rewrite the sentences using the correct form of the verb phrase.

c [7·5] Listen and check your ideas.

93

Grammar | passives

7 **a** Look at the example sentences in the Active grammar box and answer these questions.

1 Which of the <u>underlined</u> verbs are active and which are passive?

2 For each pair of sentences, why would we choose to use the passive (not the active)?

b Check your answers by reading the rules of meaning A and B.

Active grammar

1 **a** *The bikini <u>was bought</u> for $61,000.*

  b *Someone <u>bought</u> the bikini for $61,000.*

2 **a** *The bikini <u>was bought</u> by the American, Robert Earl, co-founder of Planet Hollywood.*

  b *The American, Robert Earl, co-founder of Planet Hollywood, <u>bought</u> the bikini.*

Meaning

Use the passive when you want:

A to talk about actions, events and processes when who or what causes the action, event or process is unknown or unimportant. This is often the case in writing (or more formal speech)

B to put new information or longer expressions later in the sentence

Form

verb *to be* + past participle

---

c Read the rule of form in the box and complete the passive sentences below using the correct verb forms (in brackets).

Thousands of things <u>are bought</u> (buy) on eBay every day. (Present Simple Passive)

1 The car _____ (clean) at the moment. (Present Continuous Passive)

2 The stormtrooper helmet _____ (find) by chance at a second-hand sale. (Past Simple Passive)

3 The painting _____ (display) when I arrived at the auction. (Past Continuous Passive)

4 Some items _____ (buy) at auctions for absurdly high prices. (Present Perfect Simple Passive)

5 It was a piece of chewing gum which _____ (spit) out by Britney Spears. (Past Perfect Simple Passive)

6 Ridiculously high prices _____ (pay) for completely useless items. (Future Simple Passive with *will*)

7 The new shop _____ (open) by the mayor. (Future with *going to*)

8 It seems that almost anything _____ (buy). (Modals in the passive, e.g. *can*)

see Reference page 101

8 Complete the email with an appropriate active or passive form of the verbs in brackets.

Hi John

Just a quick message to tell you about an auction I was *taken* (take) to in London last week. I (1) _____ (persuade) to go by some friends of mine and although I wasn't very keen at first, I ended up having a great time. When we first got there we (2) _____ (give) a list of all the items in the auction and then we (3) _____ (have) some time to look at everything. Most of it was rock-and-roll memorabilia and there were some old records and things. I was a bit nervous about bidding for things at first, but soon got into it.

Anyway, to cut a long story short, I (4) _____ (buy) a large jukebox. It's really fantastic – and a real bargain I think. It (5) _____ (deliver) next week. But can I ask you a huge favour? You see, they said it (6) _____ (could/not/send) abroad to my house so I (7) _____ (give) them your address in London. I hope that's OK! I (8) _____ (arrange) for my uncle to pick it up from your place very soon, I promise. Then he'll look after it until I'm in London again in the summer. Don't worry, when it arrives, you (9) _____ (ask) to sign something but you won't have to pay anything. All the payment (10) _____ (sort) out already.

I'll phone soon to let you know the exact time of delivery.

All the best

Guiseppe

Speaking

9 Discuss with a partner what you would do in each of the situations below and why.

1 You have just been served a meal in a restaurant which is cold and very late to arrive.

2 You realise that you bought four CDs in a shop yesterday but you were charged for five.

3 You have just arrived at your hotel on holiday. The brochure said there was a swimming pool but it hasn't been finished.

4 Your new washing machine is broken and some wet clothes are stuck inside it.

10 a **7.6** Listen to the conversation and answer the questions.

1 Which of the situations in Ex. 9 is it?

2 How does the customer feel?

3 What solution is offered?

b Listen again and complete the How to box.

<table>
<tr><td rowspan="6">HOW TO …</td><td colspan="2">**complain in a shop, restaurant, hotel, etc**</td></tr>
<tr><td>Customer asks to speak to someone</td><td>*I'd like to speak to the* (1) _____ , *please.*
Could I speak to Customer Services, please?</td></tr>
<tr><td>Manager/ Assistant asks what problem is</td><td>*Can I help you?*
Can I be of any (2) _____?
What (3) _____ *to be the problem?*</td></tr>
<tr><td>Customer says what problem is</td><td>*My washing machine has stopped completely and there's a load of washing stuck inside.*
Your computers were down and I couldn't get through.
We have been waiting for over an hour for our main course.</td></tr>
<tr><td>Manager/ Assistant apologises and offers a solution</td><td>*Oh, I'm very sorry about that, madam.*
I can only (4) _____ .
We'll provide a (5) _____ *free of any extra charge.*
Would you like a refund?</td></tr>
</table>

c Add one sentence to each section in the How to box.

11 In pairs, choose one of the situations in Ex. 9. Do a roleplay in which the customer complains about the situation. Use the language in the How to box to help you.

Writing

12 Read the letter in the Writing bank on page 163 and do the exercises.

13 Choose one of the situations in Ex. 9 or one of your own ideas and write a formal letter of complaint. Use the paragraph plan to help you.

Paragraph 1: state briefly what you're complaining about

Paragraph 2: give details about your complaint

Paragraph 3: give further details about your complaint (if necessary)

Paragraph 4: say what you would like them to do

Reading

1   Discuss.

1   Do you have any pets? Did you use to have any pets when you were a child? If so, which ones? If not, why not?

2   What do you think are the main reasons why people keep pets? Do you think it is a good idea for children to have pets? Why/Why not?

3   What can you see in the photos?

2   Read the text quickly. Which of the things in the photos are mentioned?

Pet heaven?

In some parts of Europe and the USA, many pet owners see their cat or dog as a member of the family. In the UK, owners spend an amazing €4 billion annually on keeping their pets fit, well and entertained. In one survey, it was found that up to forty percent of owners said they bought gifts for their pets, including Christmas and birthday presents. Owners happily pamper their pets with increasingly lavish lifestyles, including toys, furniture, accessories and 'gourmet' food. There are also pet psychologists for those with problems, pet passports for those who want to travel and a whole range of services on offer. There are hundreds of retail outlets offering owners a vast array of products. But many pets have everything they could ever ask for (or bark for?). The question for many owners now is: what do you give to the pet that has everything? We asked some owners what their pet got for his or her last birthday …

Marion Dowdeswell and 'Pixie': Marion lives on her own in Edinburgh, UK with her dog, Pixie. 'Pixie really is my best friend,' says Marion. 'He's such a lovely dog and my constant companion. I'd be lost without him, so I think I just treat him like I'd treat anyone I love.' For his last birthday, Marion bought Pixie a bed costing over €300. She admits that it was too much money to spend on an animal. 'I know it's a bit over-the-top,' she says, 'but he does love it!' Marion says she doesn't only indulge him on his birthday. Last week, she got a set of 'doggie boots' to keep Pixie's paws warm and stop him from slipping on wet ground. 'Probably a luxury, but why not occasionally?'

Sylvia and Brad Phillips and family and 'Beauty': The Phillips family from California, USA, acquired Beauty three years ago when some friends emigrated. 'We didn't really know much about dogs then, and at first we didn't know how it would work out,' says Sylvia. 'But right from the start, she just made our family complete and the kids adore her. They're always finding new things to buy for her. She probably is spoilt but it's fun.' Last year, they got her a present they were

really excited about: a necklace made of fake pearls which cost about €70. 'She doesn't really wear it because it seems to irritate her, but we took some great photos!' says Sylvia.

Claudette and Pierre Leroi and 'Mignon': Claudette and Pierre live in Paris with their Yorkshire terrier, Mignon. Because Mignon is a longhaired dog, Claudette says that it's necessary to take her to the hairdresser regularly. 'I take her to the beauty parlour once a week to have her fur done. I don't think it's a luxury really.' Mignon has it washed and brushed and sometimes cut and even curled. On special occasions, like her last birthday, for example, Mignon had the fur from the top of the head pulled back and tied as a ponytail, while the rest of her fur was cut short. 'She looked so cute – like a little Barbie doll,' says Claudette. She gets the dog anaesthetised to do these things so that she stands still for long enough, but Claudette thinks it's worth it.

So, is all this pet indulgence gone mad? Or is it simply spoiling a valued member of the family?

3 a Read the first paragraph again and decide if these statements are true (T), false (F) or we don't know (DK).

1 British owners spend €4 billion on their pets every year.

2 One quarter of owners buy their pets presents.

3 More pets than before have psychological problems.

4 Some owners have a problem knowing what to buy for their pets.

b Read the rest of the text. Which of the following apply to which pet or pets (or none of them)?

1 his/her owner buys him/her clothes

2 his/her owner wants to make him/her look nice

3 he/she provides friendly company for his/her owner

4 his/her owner takes him/her on expensive holidays

5 his/her owner knows he/she is overindulgent

6 his/her owner takes him/her to the hairdresser

7 his/her owner buys him/her toys and dolls

8 his/her owner was ignorant about pets initially

4 Discuss. Do you think pets should be treated like a member of the family? In general, what is the attitude to pets in your country?

Grammar | *have/get something done*

5 a Complete examples A–C in the Active grammar box using *had*, *have* and *gets*. Then look at the text again to check your answers.

Active grammar

A *I take her to the beauty parlour to (1) _____ her fur done.*

B *On her last birthday, Mignon (2) _____ the fur from the top of the head pulled back and tied as a ponytail.*

C *She (3) _____ the dog anaesthetised so that she stands still at the hairdresser.*

Form *have* (or *get*) + object + _____

Meanings

1 In examples A–C, is this structure (with *have* or *get*) used to talk about a) doing something ourselves or b) arranging for something to be done by somebody else?

We can also use this structure:

2 with *have* or *get*, to talk about things that happen to us, and

3 with *get* only (not *have*), to mean 'finish doing something'.

D *I had my bag stolen on my way home from work.*

E *She got her fingers caught in the car door.*

F *As soon as I get this essay written, I'll take the dog out.*

---

b Complete the rule of form with the correct part of speech.

c Look at rule 1 and answer the question.

d Look at rules 2 and 3. Then match each rule with the correct examples D–F.

see Reference page 101

6 Find the mistakes in six of the sentences and correct them.

1 I've never had my hair dye.

2 I've had my house broken into several times.

3 I never my house have decorated – I do it myself.

4 I haven't had my eyes testing for ages.

5 I've got a lot of things to get doing by this weekend.

6 I have dry-cleaned some of my clothes every month.

7 I really need to have my hair cut soon.

8 I'd like to get my photo took by a professional photographer.

Person to person

7 Discuss.

1 Are any of the sentences in Ex. 6 true for you? Tell another student and change the others so that they are true.

It's true I haven't had my eyes tested for ages. I think I should have it done soon because my eyes hurt when I use a computer.

2 What things do you have done regularly? Why? What things can you have done in your neighbourhood?

I have my car cleaned inside and out once a month! I know it's extravagant but I hate doing it myself.

HAND CAR WASH

Vocabulary | animal expressions

8 **a** With a partner, divide the animals in the box below into six groups.

eagle, duck = birds

> ~~eagle~~ horse dog whale spider bull
> fish bat fly ~~duck~~ cat bear

b Add at least three more words to each of your groups.

9 **a** **7.7** Label the parts of the animals in the pictures using the words in the box. Then listen and check your answers.

> f<u>u</u>r f<u>ea</u>thers p<u>a</u>ws h<u>oo</u>ves cl<u>a</u>ws t<u>ai</u>l
> w<u>i</u>ngs wh<u>i</u>skers f<u>i</u>ns h<u>o</u>rns b<u>ea</u>k

b Which of the <u>underlined</u> vowel sounds in the words in the box have the same sounds as each other? Listen again and check.

c In pairs, describe an animal using the words in the box. Your partner should guess which animal it is.

A: *This animal's body is covered in fur. It has four paws and it wags its tail when it's happy.*

B: *A dog!*

10 **a** Complete the expressions in *italics* by writing the name of one animal in each.

1 It's true she paid over £300 for one pair of shoes. I didn't just hear it from someone else – she told me herself. It was *straight from the _____'s mouth*.

2 It's my job to tell him he's failed his exam. I've got to tell him but I feel really bad about it. I'll just have to *take the _____ by the horns* and do it.

3 My eyesight has got much worse. I can't read this price label at all. I need glasses for most things nowadays. *I'm as blind as a _____* without them!

4 My boss was in a bad mood with everyone yesterday. He shouted at anyone who went near him. He *was like a _____ with a sore head*.

b **7.8** Listen and check your answers.

11 **a** What do you think the expressions mean? Read the sentences again and discuss in pairs.

b Match the expressions 1–4 in Ex.10a with the correct definition a–d below.

a) to have very bad eyesight

b) to be in a bad temper and extremely irritable

c) 'first hand' information from the original source

d) to confidently deal with a difficult or dangerous situation

c Choose two of the expressions and tell other students about a person or situation using them.

d Do you have similar expressions in your language?

7 | Vocabulary

Prefixes

1 **a** [7.9] Listen and match the people with items A–D. One of them cannot be used.

A Someone annoying
B Someone completely 'over-the-top'
C Something to be proud of
D Something embarrassing

b Listen again and make brief notes about each story.

c Retell each story with your partner.

2 **a** Look at the tapescript on page 172 and find a word to match with each definition below.

Story 1

1 to sleep more than you had intended
– *oversleep*

2 to think or guess something is less than it is

3 a former employer

Story 2

4 to go back to studying again and learn new skills

5 to be able to speak two languages equally well

6 describing a company that has offices, factories, etc. in many different countries

Story 3

7 not usual or normal

8 very big

9 describing a way of speaking that sounds uninterested because it's on one note

b Look at the words from Ex. 2a and write the appropriate prefixes in the table.

	PREFIXES	MEANINGS	EXAMPLES
1	*mono*	one/single	*monolingual*
2		twice/two/every two	
3		many	
4		more than	
5		less than	
6		former	
7		again	
8		very	
9		not	

c Read the rule about hyphens. Then write one more example of your own for each prefix in the table above.

> **Hyphens:** We use hyphens (-) with some prefixes, including *extra-* and *ex-*. Check in a dictionary if you are unsure.

3 **a** Complete the sentences below with the most appropriate word from the box. Not all the words can be used.

> monologue   monolingual   bicycle
> biannual   multimedia   multipurpose
> overtired   overworked   undercooked
> underpaid   ex-girlfriend   ex-husband
> reheat   rewrite   extra-small
> extra-strong   uncomfortable   unnecessary

I always feel slightly uncomfortable and silly wearing a hat.

1 The company holds a big _____ conference, so the next one will be in six months' time.

2 When you go camping, what you need is a good _____ knife that does everything.

3 You'll need to use some _____ packaging so that it doesn't get torn in the post.

4 Be careful that the food is hot all the way through and never eat _____ meat.

5 I think nurses are _____ especially considering the amount they get paid.

6 I've only studied English in my own country where the classes are all _____ .

7 The teacher has asked me to _____ my essay because I misunderstood the question the first time.

8 I still get on well with my _____ even though I don't see her much nowadays.

b [7.10] Listen and check your answers.

4 **a** Work with a partner. Choose something to talk about from the list in Ex. 1a. Prepare to tell your story using as many of the words in Exs. 2a and 3a as you can.

b Listen to other students' stories. Which of the items in the list do you think each of the stories you heard was about?

1 a In pairs, complete the word maps for each of the places in the pictures. Include as many words as you can which are related to each place.

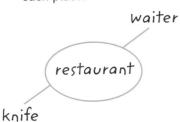

waiter

restaurant

knife

clothes shop/ shoe shop

fitting room

hairdresser

scissors

b Compare your words with other students.

2 a Which of the sentences would you expect to hear in a) a restaurant, b) a shoe shop, c) a hairdresser?

1 I'd like to try these on, please.
2 I'll have the grilled tuna, please.
3 Just a cut and blow-dry?
4 I've got black in size 38, but not in 39.
5 Rare, please.
6 I'd also like some highlights done.
7 A bottle of the house red, please.
8 They look really nice on you. How do they feel?
9 I'd like to book an appointment.
10 We're offering all customers an Indian head massage.
11 We booked a table for two in the name of Morrison.

b [7.11] Listen to three conversations and number the sentences in the order you hear them.

3 a In pairs, choose one of the situations from the listening. Look at the tapescript on page 172 and underline any important phrases.

b Roleplay the situation using the ideas from the listening and your own ideas.

4 a Look at the table and note down some more things that people complain about in the three places.

RESTAURANT	SHOE/CLOTHES SHOP	HAIRDRESSER
Food is undercooked	*Shoes are dirty*	*Cut too short*
Service is slow	*Button is missing*	*Dyed wrong colour*

b In pairs, choose a different place and decide on one or two things to complain about. Roleplay the situation.

7 Reference

Countable and uncountable nouns

Countable nouns are words like *banana*, *hotel*. They can use a singular or plural form of the verb.

That's a lovely hotel!

Uncountable nouns are words like *food*, *information*, *equipment*. They use a singular form of the verb.

There isn't much food left.

Common uncountable nouns:

accommodation, advice, behaviour, bread, equipment, food, furniture, health, information, knowledge, luggage, news, research, salt, spaghetti, traffic, travel, trouble, water, weather, work

Common nouns which can be countable or uncountable:

chicken, chocolate, coffee, egg, glass, hair, iron, paper, room, space, time, wine

You can use: *a/an*, *few*, *a few*, *some*, *any*, *many*, *a lot of*, *lots of*, before countable nouns.

I haven't roasted any potatoes.

You can use: *little*, *a little*, *some*, *any*, *much*, *a lot of*, *lots of*, before uncountable nouns.

There wasn't much traffic this morning.

few/a few and *little/a little*:

Few and *little* (without '*a*') are used to talk about negative ideas.

She's got few friends and is quite lonely.

He's got little money and can't afford a new car.

A few and *a little* are used to talk about more positive ideas.

I've got a few biscuits left. Would you like one?

Could I have tea with a little milk, please?

Passives

We can use active constructions when the subject is the person or thing that does the action.

I bought a really fantastic party dress on eBay.

We can use passive constructions:

when who or what causes the action is unknown or unimportant

when we want to put new information or longer expressions later in the sentence

We often use passive constructions in writing or in more formal speech. The passive is common in news stories, scientific and academic writing.

The dog was found three days after it went missing.

Also use the passive when the object of the active sentence is the main focus. Use *by* to say who did the action.

A Picasso painting was sold by a wealthy businessman last week.

We can use the passive in any tense and with modal verbs.

Form verb *to be* + past participle

We haven't been given the exam results yet.

have/get something done

Form *have* (or *get*) + object + past participle

Use the structure *to have* (or *get*) *something done*:

to talk about arranging for something to be done by someone else

I have my hair dyed once every six months.

to talk about things that happen to us or to describe an 'experience'

I had my bike stolen last week.

There is another use of *get* + object + past participle (NOT *have*) which is used to mean 'finish doing something'.

I need to get my homework done.

Key vocabulary

Excess

extravagant excessive a luxury extra-large
to spoil someone overpriced far-fetched
to go on a spending spree

Food and cooking

a saucepan a frying pan a wooden spoon
an oven a cooker a cook a plate a dish
a recipe sweet savoury bitter salty sour
rare raw to bake to roast to scramble to fry
to grill to boil to stir to beat to slice
to chop to grate beef cabbage parsley
a peach a vegetable a vegetarian

Verb phrases about money

to bid for something to haggle for something
to get a bargain to get a discount
to get a refund to get a receipt
to be able to afford something to be worth it

Animals and animal expressions

dog cat bull horse bear bat fish whale
duck eagle fly spider fur feathers paws
hooves claws tail wings whiskers fin horns
beak straight from the horse's mouth
to be as blind as a bat
to be like a bear with a sore head
to take the bull by the horns

Prefixes

oversleep undercooked ex-boss retrain
bilingual multinational unusual extra-large
monotonous

1 Choose the correct alternatives.

Is there a/(any) bread in the cupboard?

1 Could you give me *an/some* information about train times please?

2 I've got two large pieces of *luggage/luggages*.

3 How *many/much* furniture have you got in your living room?

4 The news *is/are* always so depressing.

5 He's been doing *a/some* research into global warming.

6 There were only *few/a few* people there when I arrived.

7 I'd like *a/some* slice of toast with jam and an orange juice, please.

8 Can I give you *an/some* advice about revising for your exam?

2 Complete the sentences using the correct tense of a verb from the box in the passive form.

> catch charge deliver employ include
> open repair send

1 Service _____ in the bill so you don't need to leave a tip.

2 I _____ some flowers yesterday but I don't know who they're from.

3 The goods that you ordered _____ next Friday.

4 My car broke down last week. It _____ at the moment.

5 Don't use the medicine if the packet _____ already.

6 It's unlikely that the robbers _____ .

7 I was annoyed because we _____ for a bottle of wine we didn't have.

8 She was sacked after she _____ by that company for over fifteen years.

3 Look at part of Tilly's diary and imagine that today is Tuesday and it's 1.30p.m. Write sentences about what she *had done*, *is having done* and *will have done*.

She had her living room decorated yesterday.

1 _____

2 _____

3 _____

4 _____

5 _____

6 _____

7 _____

8 _____

Monday

10.30a.m. Decorator (living room)
Pick car up from garage (fit new tyres)
Delivery of new cooker (after 5p.m.)

Tuesday

Haircut (& highlights) 9.15a.m.
Carpet fitters (living room) – between 1 and 2p.m.
Take watch to repair shop – don't forget!

Wednesday

Eye test (optician on High Street) 10.00a.m.
Window cleaner (a.m.)
Don't forget to take coat to dry-cleaners

4 Choose the correct alternative.

1 I don't really like cooked carrots. I much prefer them *rare/raw/roast*.

2 I've decided to bid *from/for/at* that table I told you about.

3 £60 is too much for that bag. It's really not *value/afford/worth* it.

4 I won't believe he's got the job until I hear it straight from the *cat's/bull's/horse's* mouth.

5 I'm taking my dog to the vet because he cut his *hoof/paw/claw* on some broken glass.

6 The sound on this CD is really strange. Take it back and get a *discount/refund/receipt*.

7 Before you roast potatoes, you should *bake/beat/boil* them for ten minutes.

8 She's like a *bat/bear/bull* with a sore head today. She's already shouted at me twice.

5 Complete the words with the most appropriate prefix.

1 The children need an early night. They are ____tired and rather irritable.

2 It all took a lot longer than I expected. I ____ estimated the time by several hours.

3 She talks in such a boring and ____tonous voice that I just fell asleep.

4 I've been a teacher for ten years but I've decided to ____train as a computer technician.

5 We've decided to have a school reunion every two years and make it a ____ennial event.

6 The classrooms are extremely modern and have all the latest ____media equipment.

7 When you ____heat food, you need to make sure that you get it hot enough.

8 She's got a very ____usual name. I wonder where it comes from.

8 Success

Lead-in

1 In pairs, describe the photos and answer the questions.

　1 What do you think the people all have in common?

　2 What do you think they had to do to achieve their success?

2 **a** Complete the sentences with the words/phrases from the box in the correct form. Use a dictionary if necessary.

> best-seller　succeed　go under　have had their day　have a go
> give up　up to scratch

　1 If the business doesn't start making money by the end of the year, it will probably _____ and have to close.

　2 His book's been an instant _____ . Everybody's talking about it.

　3 Just because you failed this exam doesn't mean you should _____ . You can always re-take it in October.

　4 I think these reality TV shows _____ . No one's very interested in them anymore.

　5 You know what they say: 'If at first you don't _____ – try, try, try again!'

　6 I'm afraid the work you've done on the house really isn't _____ . You'll have to redo a lot of it.

　7 I'm not sure that pushing the car will help start it, but you can ___ .

b **8.1** Listen and check your answers.

3 Tell another student about the last time you felt you achieved something special.

Reading

1 Discuss.

1 Is leadership a natural-born talent or a learned skill?

2 What qualities does a successful leader need?

3 In what different situations do people need to work together as a group?

4 Does every group need a leader? Why/Why not?

2 Read the text quickly and match the questions above with the correct paragraphs.

3 Read the text again. Are these statements true (T), false (F) or we don't know (DK).

1 Being able to work in a group is one of the most important life skills.

2 Groups of people doing social activities generally don't need leaders.

3 Members of leaderless groups often stop attending.

4 Antonio Carluccio thinks he is a natural-born leader.

5 Good leaders are often slightly afraid of their role.

6 Good leaders should do more work than the other group members.

Are YOU a successful leader?

The Successful Leadership Trust – our company specialises in training you to be a successful leader for whatever situation you're in.

A ...?

Almost nothing we do in this world is done in isolation. At work or at play, you'll find yourself in groups, working with other people: your team at work, a meeting with colleagues, your family, a holiday with friends, a group of students working together, a day out walking in the mountains, a group of neighbours wanting to make changes. It is now recognised that being able to work successfully with other people is one of the major keys to success, partly because we need to do it so often.

B ...?

In almost every situation where you're in a group, you will need a skilled leader. All groups need leaders and all successful groups have good leaders. Groups without leaders or with weak leaders almost always break down. Members of a leaderless group often begin to feel dissatisfied and frustrated. Time is wasted and the tasks are not achieved. There are often arguments and tensions between people as there is nobody to keep the goals clear. Some personalities dominate and others disappear. Often group members begin not to come to meetings in order to avoid more disharmony.

C ...?

Some people are natural leaders. The celebrity chef, Antonio Carluccio says, 'True leaders are born and you can spot them in kitchens. They're people who combine toughness, fairness and humour.' Although a lot of people agree that there are some natural-born leaders, most people now recognise that leadership can also be taught. Our professional and experienced staff can train almost anyone how to be a successful leader. Good leaders don't make people do things in a bossy, controlling way. You can learn how to involve everyone, encouraging the whole group to work towards a common goal.

D ...?

Our training courses use activities and techniques to develop a range of qualities which are necessary to be a good leader. Self-confidence is vital and being able to overcome your own fears about being a leader. Successful leaders also need to be calm and intelligent. They need to be able to work out good strategies and make sound judgements under pressure. Lastly, and probably most importantly, good leaders need to be sensitive, sociable and be able to get on with a wide range of people. Good leadership is essentially the ability to influence others and good leaders allow all members of the group to contribute.

4   Discuss. Do you agree with the quotes? Why/Why not?

> 'The art of leadership is saying no, not yes. It is very easy to say yes.' Tony Blair

> 'The most important thing about successful leadership is knowing how to get on with people.' Teddy Roosevelt

> 'Don't tell people how to do things, tell them what to do and let them surprise you with their results' George S. Patton

Grammar | *It's time/I'd rather/I'd better*

5   **8.2** Listen to the work appraisal interview and decide which of the sentences best summarises the main points.

1   He's doing well in his role of team leader but would like some more training

2   He's finding his role of team leader difficult and thinks he needs some training

3   He's interested in becoming a team leader but would like some training first

6   **a**   **8.3** Complete sentences 1–4 in the Active grammar box. Then listen and check your answers.

Active grammar

1   *I feel that it's _____ I moved on now.*

2   *I think I _____ you did the first course.*

3   *I _____ not wait for two months.*

4   *I _____ get your name on the list immediately.*

A   **Form** *It's time* + subject + _____

   Meaning to talk about when you should have done something already or at least started it

B   **Form** subject + *would rather* + object + _____ (+ *than ...*)

   Meaning to talk about what you'd prefer someone else to do

C   **Form** subject + *would rather* + _____ (+ *than ...*)

   Meaning to talk about what you'd prefer to do

D   **Form** subject + *had better* + _____

   Meaning to talk about something when it is advisable to do it (in the present or future)

---

b   Complete the rules of form by writing *past tense* or *infinitive*.

c   Look at the sentences 1–4 again and explain what each one means. Read the rules about meaning to help you.

see Reference page 115

7   **a**   Complete the dialogue. Use *It's time, 'd rather* or *'d better* and the correct form of the verb in brackets.

   Anna: Hi, Will. How did your appraisal go?

   Will: It went well, thanks. My boss thinks (1) _____ (have) more responsibility and maybe became a team leader.

   Anna: Oh that's good. How do you feel about that?

   Will: I'm pleased because I was thinking of looking for a better job in another company, but (2) _____ (stay) here if I can.

   Anna: It would be great if you were our team leader. (3) _____ (be) in charge than someone we don't know.

   Will: Thanks. Anyway, (4) _____ (go) because I've got a meeting in five minutes. See you later.

   b   **8.4** Listen and check your answers.

Person to person

8   **a**   Write three sentences about you starting with *It's time ...*

   It's time I tidied up the living room.

   It's time I got in touch with my brother.

   It's time I changed my job.

   b   In pairs, compare your sentences with another student. Ask your partner to tell you more details about his/her sentences. Try and include *I'd better* and *I'd rather* in your answers.

Vocabulary | describing personality

9 **a** Work in A/B groups. Use a dictionary to find out the meanings and pronunciation of the five adjectives in your group below.

GROUP A	GROUP B
outgoing	easy-going
open	selfish
proactive	witty
opinionated	manipulative
single-minded	headstrong

b Work in A/B pairs.

1 Tell each other about the meaning and pronunciation of the five words in your group.

2 Add some adjectives which have a) opposite meanings and b) similar meanings to the ones in the box.

open → reserved (opposite)

headstrong → determined (similar)

c Compare the adjectives you added with other students.

10 **8.5** Listen to ten people describing different people they know. For each one write an adjective from Ex. 9 which you think describes him/her best.

1 *easy-going*

11 **a** Think of three people you know who you can describe using some of the adjectives in Ex. 9.

b Tell your partner about each person, giving examples of how he/she behaves which show why you've chosen those adjectives.

My sister is a very headstrong person. She really wanted to travel around South America on her own. Everyone tried to persuade her not to because it was dangerous but she decided to do it anyway and …

c Which of the qualities from Ex. 9 do you think successful people usually have, and which can stop you being successful? Give reasons.

I think that most successful people are very determined and single-minded but if you are too headstrong it could go against you because …

12 **a** Match the expressions in the box with the correct picture. In pairs, say what you think each one means.

> be the centre of attention   be a party animal
> be a complete doormat   be down-to-earth
> be really high maintenance

b Do you have any similar expressions in your language?

13 **a** Talk about yourself and the different sides of your personality. First, think about how you behave in different situations using the ideas in the box and your own ideas.

> leading a discussion at work or school
> giving a presentation at work
> making a complaint in a shop or restaurant
> talking about yourself in a job interview
> performing on stage
> being in a crowd of people at a party
> cooking for a small group of friends
> playing a team game (e.g. football)
> organising a group of children

b Work in pairs and tell each other about the different sides of your personality in different situations.

I think I'm generally an outgoing person in social situations like a party. I like being the centre of attention and I'm quite witty sometimes! I can be shy too, though, especially at work if I have to speak in public or chair a meeting – I just clam up.

Listening

1   Discuss.

1   Match each photo above with the most appropriate feeling in the box below. What do you think is happening/has happened in each case?

> completely ecstatic
> absolutely devastated
> totally single-minded

2   Can you remember any sporting moments that you've watched (or been involved in) when someone has felt in similar ways?

2   **8.6** Listen to part of a radio programme and answer the questions.

1   What proportion of sportspeople use sports psychologists to help them with their mental attitude?

2   What are the main purposes of the Haka war dance used by the New Zealand All Blacks rugby team?

3   Listen again and write one sentence summarising the speaker's main points about each of the following:

1   self-belief
2   negative thoughts
3   personal lucky 'routines'

4   Discuss. Do you (or does anyone you know) have lucky routines, superstitions or lucky charms for things like sport, exams, special events, travelling, etc.?

Vocabulary | adjectives and intensifiers

5   **a** Look at the <u>underlined</u> adjectives in the table. What is the difference in meaning between gradable and non-gradable adjectives?

Gradable adjectives	He missed an <u>important</u> goal.
	He is a <u>big</u> success as a racing driver.
Non-gradable adjectives	He missed a <u>vital</u> goal.
	He is a <u>huge</u> success as a racing driver.

b Match the gradable adjectives in 1–4 with the correct non-gradable adjectives a–d. Use a dictionary if necessary.

1   happy   a) starving
2   upset   b) ecstatic
3   hungry   c) exhausted
4   tired   d) devastated

6   **a** Read the rules A and B. Then look at the sentences and decide if one or both intensifiers are correct.

A   We can use intensifiers *very, really* and *extremely* with gradable adjectives to make the meaning stronger.

B   We can use intensifiers *really* and *absolutely* with non-gradable adjectives to make the meaning stronger.

1   Kelly Holmes must be *really/absolutely* ecstatic about her success.

2   A(n) *extremely/very* big sports centre near here has just opened.

3   If you want to get to the top in athletics, it's *really/extremely* vital to get yourself a professional trainer.

4   Whenever he plays football, he comes back *really/absolutely* filthy.

5   She was *absolutely/extremely* exhausted at the end of the race.

6   I love running. I'd be *really/very* devastated if I had to give it up.

b **8.7** Listen and check your answers.

7   Think of a true story about you that relates to one of the phrases in the box in Ex. 1. Tell your partner what happened.

I couldn't believe it when I won the prize for best actor. I was completely ecstatic!

Grammar | reported speech

8 a **8.8** Listen and complete the sentences and questions.

Direct speech

1 _____ to be the last player onto the pitch.

2 _____ the race easily.

3 _____ to train _____ .

4 _____ do it by thinking about something different.

5 Why _____ so negative?

6 _____ help _____ ?

b Compare the reported speech in the Active grammar box with the direct speech above. Find examples of the changes 1–6 and write them in the box.

Active grammar

Reported speech

Andy Cole said (that) he <u>wanted</u> to be the last player onto the pitch.

She said (that) she <u>had won</u> the race easily.

He told me (that) he <u>wasn't going</u> to train that day.

I told him (that) he <u>could</u> do it by thinking about something different.

I asked him why he was <u>feeling</u> so negative.

She asked me if I <u>would</u> help her the following day.

1 Tense changes, e.g. *go → went*: <u>want → wanted</u>

2 Modal verb changes, e.g. *can → could*: _____

3 Subject pronoun changes, e.g. *I → he*: _____

4 Object pronoun changes, e.g. *me → him*: _____

5 Time reference changes, e.g. *now → then*: _____

6 Word order changes, e.g. *were they going → they were going*: _____

Rules

A We can use *that* after both *say* and *tell*, but it isn't necessary.

B We don't use an object after *say*.

C We must use an object after *tell*.

D We use a question word when reporting *Wh-* questions.

E We use if when reporting *Yes/No* questions.

F We sometimes ignore the rule that changes the tense or modal verb back. This can happen if the situation is still true, or for dramatic effect when telling a story.

---

see Reference page 115.

9 Read the rules A–F in the box and decide if these sentences are correct or not. Correct the ones which are wrong.

1 He said that he was totally devastated about the result.

2 She told me that she couldn't come to training this evening.

3 He told me he's training three times a week at the moment.

4 She said him she had taken up basketball the previous January.

5 I told them I was going to be late and that they should start without me.

6 I asked her she wanted to come round and watch the tennis.

7 He asked me why I went to a sports psychologist.

8 She told me she wants to move away from sport and further her career elsewhere now.

10 a Check you understand the meanings of the verbs in **bold** in the sentences below.

*Nobody needed to **remind** him to focus on the goal.*

*She **admitted** feeling totally out of control.*

*He **explained** that he wanted to compete in the Olympics.*

*I **promise** to go swimming at least three times a week.*

*I **suggested** talking to a sports psychologist.*

*They **decided** to buy tickets for the football match.*

*My trainer **warned** me that the training would be very hard.*

b Write the verbs in **bold** from Ex. 10a in the correct place in the table.

VERBS	CONSTRUCTIONS
say,	verb + (*that*)
tell,	verb + object + (*that*)
ask,	verb + object + infinitive
	verb + infinitive
	verb + gerund

11 Report these statements starting with the words given.

1 'I broke the window yesterday when I kicked a ball through it by mistake.'
He admitted ...

2 'Why don't we try the new Italian restaurant when we go out on Friday?'
He suggested ...

3 'I think I'll stay in tonight because I'm completely exhausted.'
She decided ...

4 'I'm going to buy my girlfriend some flowers as a way of saying sorry.'
He told ...

5 'Are you going to book tickets for the cinema or are you going to just turn up?'
She asked ...

6 'You really mustn't be late for your interview this afternoon.'
She warned ...

7 'Please all bring your homework to me by 9.00 on Monday morning.'
The teacher reminded ...

8 'I'll pay you back all the money I owe you by tomorrow.'
He promised ...

Person to person

12 Choose A or B below and follow the instructions.

A

1 Write notes about three things that you've seen or heard in the news in the last week. Make notes about when and where you saw or heard each story and details of each story.
TV news /yesterday/interest rates up by one percent ...

2 Then tell your partner details of the news stories you've seen or heard.
'On the news yesterday, they said that interest rates were going to go up by one percent ...'

B

1 Write notes about three things that three different people have said to you in the last twenty-four hours. Make notes about the time, the person and his/her actual words.
10.30 this morning/Marianne/'Why don't we go out for lunch today?'

2 Then tell your partner what the three people said, giving details.
'At 10.30 this morning, Marianne suggested going out for lunch today.'

Speaking

13 a Look at the photos. Discuss what you think is happening in each one.

b Think about someone who has helped you to succeed in something. Make notes using the questions below to help you.

1 What were you trying to do? And when?
2 Who helped you?
3 What did he/she suggest that really helped?
4 What did you learn from this person?
5 How did you feel when you succeeded?

14 a Tell other students about the person who helped you succeed. Make short notes about other students' experiences.

b Report back to the class about the most interesting story you heard about.

Lifelong learning

Successful language learning

A successful language learner is generally someone who:

- is willing to make mistakes
- wants to get his/her message across
- finds as many opportunities to practise as possible
- doesn't worry about words he/she doesn't understand

1 Which of the characteristics above apply to you?
2 Do you know anyone who is a very successful language learner? What kind of person is he/she?

Reading

1 Look at the photo. Discuss.

1 At what age should children learn how to use computers?

2 How do you feel about how much children use computers in your country?

2 Read the article. What does Dr Ryde think the advantage of sending children to his school is?

TOT.COM

Every week, a group of British pupils file into class to start their lessons, turn on their computers and obediently follow their teacher's instructions. For an hour, they are taught
5 mouse techniques, keyboard skills, and reading and writing, using the computer. However, these are toddlers, hardly out of nappies. (A) _____ .

At Ryde College they take the idea that 'It's never too young to start' very seriously indeed. Since the
10 college opened in 1982, more than a thousand pupils have achieved exam results at an earlier than usual age.

The college was founded by Dr Ronald Ryde, a former university lecturer, now aged seventy.
15 (B) _____ . Word spread around the neighbourhood and Dr Ryde soon had to move to a special centre to cope with the demand for his services. To the man who happily puts seven-year-olds in for GCSEs, the 'Technology for Toddlers' classes were
20 the next logical step. (C) _____ . Aside from the actual lessons, parents are also encouraged to get the children to practise their new skills at home.

The parents of these young computer whiz kids have no qualms about giving their children a head
25 start. Kevin Mills, forty-four, enrolled his son, Piers, a year ago, just before his second birthday, after he showed an interest in playing with a computer at home.

Elick Harding, a marketing manager and father of
30 Safiya, another of the toddler students, admits his daughter is not always in the mood to sit still and learn but says her vocabulary and reading skills are now streets ahead of other children her age. (D) _____ .

35 Whereas toddlers are tutored during the day, the older children attend either in the evenings until as late as 9p.m. or at weekends. So, there is an issue about when they get to run around and climb trees like their friends. (E) _____ . Last year parents
40 Teeta and Kaushik Radia, whose son, Krishnan, became the youngest child ever to get a GCSE in Information Technology, aged just six, complained that Ryde College pushed young children into sitting exams for the publicity.

45 Dr Ryde remains unrepentant. 'I would argue that it's a crime to hold children back. (F) _____ . All of us here are committed to education, not publicity.' Dr Ryde sees his college not as a hothouse for brilliance – he claims there is no great secret to their
50 success other than small class sizes and traditional schooling methods – but rather as a way to make up for the time wasted in normal state secondary schools. 'All too often the first years in secondary are lost years and teachers waste them getting all
55 the children up to the same level.'

> **Glossary**
> GCSE = General Certificate of Secondary Education.
> National exams in all subjects, usually taken at age sixteen.

3 **a** Each of the sentences 1–6 comes from the article. Read the article again and decide where each one should go.

1 'She can count up to thirty, has an excellent vocabulary and has gained so much confidence through her classes.'

2 Introduced last year, they are aimed at giving the eighteen-month to three-year-old pupils a head start in writing, reading and communication using the computer.

3 There is also the question of why these children need to take additional exams, especially at such a young age.

4 Next term, they will move up a class to begin instruction in computer science, just months after they have celebrated their fourth birthdays.

5 The only thing we are exploiting is their ability to learn.

6 He started offering home classes after he helped his son, Mike to pass a computer GCSE at the age of fourteen, rather than the normal sixteen.

b Read the text again through from beginning to end, to check your answers.

4 Find these words in the article. Write a short definition for each one. To help you a) decide if they are nouns, verbs or adjectives, b) look at them in the context of the words before and after them.

file (l.1) – verb: to walk in line

1 nappies (l.7)   5 qualms (l.24)
2 former (l.14)   6 head start (l.24)
3 spread (l.15)   7 mood (l.31)
4 cope (l.17)   8 hothouse (l.48)

5 Discuss. What are the advantages and disadvantages of pushing children to study intensively and take exams early?

Grammar | *hard* and *hardly*

6 **a** Look at examples 1–3 in the box and decide if the words in **bold** are adjectives or adverbs.

> **Active grammar**
>
> 1 *Studying every weekend for my exams was **hard** work.*
> 2 *The children are encouraged to work **hard** for their exams.*
> 3 *The pupils in the college are **hardly** out of nappies.*
>
> *Hardly* means almost not or very little. It is often used with *any(thing/one/where*, etc.) and *ever*. It is not used with negative words (~~I hardly never eat chocolate~~).
>
> 4 *I'm very tired this morning. I hardly slept last night.*
> 5 *I have hardly any money. I must go to the bank.*
> 6 *She hardly ever comes to visit us. Just once or twice a year.*

b Look at examples 4–6 in the box . Explain the meaning of each one in other words (not using *hardly*).

see Reference page 115

7 Complete each of these sentences with *hardly* and a verb from the box in the correct form.

> know say believe
> walk change have

1 I'm very busy at the moment. I _____ any time to go to the gym.

2 Are you ok? You _____ a word during dinner.

3 Doesn't Tom look amazing? He's _____ at all since we were at school.

4 I don't understand why that woman from the office was so friendly. I _____ her.

5 Her leg is hurting her a lot. She says she can _____ at the moment.

6 I was shocked when she told me he had left. I could _____ it.

8 Decide if each of the sentences is correct. If not, correct it.

1 I can hardly hear you. Could you speak up, please?

2 She needs to study hard if she is going to pass her exam.

3 He's eaten anything hardly all day.

4 We tried very hard to finish the report but there wasn't enough time.

5 Hardly anybody I know is going to Sarah's party.

6 We've got hard any milk left.

Person to person

9 Complete the sentences so they are true for you. Compare your answers in pairs.

1 The last time I studied hard …

2 At school/work, I hardly ever …

3 Recently, I've hardly been to any …

Speaking

10 Read the questions below and make a note of your answers.

1. What are the three most important things that help children to do well at school?
2. Which three subjects should children spend most time studying at school?
3. What are the most important qualities of a good teacher?
4. What are the three most important things that help people to do well at work?
5. Which three things should people get most training in for work?
6. What are the most important qualities of a good manager?

11 a Look at the How to box. Add one more way of giving opinions and one more way of justifying opinions.

Give your opinion

Give your opinion	*I believe* small class sizes are crucial …
	As far as I'm concerned maths is the most important subject …
Justify your opinion	… *because* the teacher can spend more time with each child.
	… *for several reasons; firstly,* you need maths for lots of things in everyday life …
	If a teacher is approachable, *then* children will feel able to ask questions.

b Ask other students the questions in Ex. 10 and note their responses. When answering, use the How to box to help you.

c Make notes of the main findings of your survey.

1 a good teacher
  small classes
  modern technology

2 Maths
  English
  I.T.

3 caring
  knowledgeable
  keep control

4 feeling appreciated
  good environment
  good salary

5

6

Writing

12 Look at the report in the Writing bank on page 164 and do the exercises.

13 Discuss with other students which words or phrases in the report might be useful in other similar reports.

14 Write a report on one of the topics in Ex. 10 in 120–140 words. Divide it into separate paragraphs.

8 | Vocabulary

Phrasal verbs with three parts

1 Match the phrasal verbs in *italics* with the correct meanings a–j below.

1 We'll never *catch up with* them. They're too far ahead.

2 They stole £1m and *got away with* it.

3 Don't walk so fast! I can't *keep up with* you.

4 They're *putting* her *in for* her Grade 8 piano exam this year.

5 Have you *come up with* any new ideas for the advertising campaign?

6 I'd like us to *cut down on* the amount of TV we watch.

7 I've always *looked up to* my grandmother. She's an amazing person.

8 I'm *looking forward to* seeing my sister's new baby at the weekend.

9 How do you *put up with* the noise of the traffic outside your bedroom window?

10 We want to *make up for* all the time she wasted in her first year at secondary school.

a) to think of, suggest

b) to think you will enjoy

c) to move at the same speed

d) to formally apply to do something

e) to tolerate

f) to reduce

g) to respect, admire

h) to reach the same place

i) to compensate for

j) to escape punishment

2 **a** Complete the sentences with one of the phrasal verbs from Ex. 1 in the correct form.

1 You need to _____ how much salt you have in your food.

2 If none of us says anything to the police, we'll probably _____ it.

3 We're really _____ moving back to New Zealand. It'll be especially great to see all our friends.

4 I can't _____ his constant criticism anymore. I've decided to move out.

5 The increase in salaries isn't _____ the rise in the cost of living. People's disposable income is getting less and less.

6 She's _____ a transfer to the London office to be nearer her parents.

7 I think I've _____ a rather good solution to our problem.

8 The delicious food more than _____ the slow service.

9 All her students _____ her. She's an amazing teacher.

10 I had to run to _____ you. You walk incredibly fast!

b 8.9 Listen and check your answers.

c Listen again and decide which part of each phrasal verb is stressed.

3 **a** Which of the following sentences are correct?

1 You won't catch up with them.

2 You won't catch up them with.

3 You won't catch them up with.

4 I'm looking my holiday forward to.

5 I'm looking forward my holiday to.

6 I'm looking forward to my holiday.

b What does this tell you about the grammar of this kind of phrasal verb?

4 Discuss.

1 Is there anything you are really looking forward to doing over the next few weeks? If so, what?

2 Is there anything you are trying to cut down on at the moment? If so, what and why?

3 Are there any things in everyday life that you find difficult to put up with, e.g. mobile phones? If so, what?

4 Is there anyone that you really look up to? If so, who and why?

5 Are there any kinds of crime that you think are easy to get away with? If so, which and why?

8 Communication

Radio phone-in

1 Discuss.

1 What can you see in the picture above?
2 How often do you listen to the radio?
3 What different kinds of radio programmes do you know?

2 **a** **8.10** Listen to the extracts from a radio phone-in. What is the reason for each person's call?

b Listen again and decide what advice you would give each caller and why.

3 Discuss.

1 Do you ever listen to this kind of radio programme? Why/Why not?
2 Who/Where do you usually go to for advice about problems?

4 **a** Work in A/B groups. Decide on some interesting problems for a radio phone-in.

b In A/B pairs, take it in turns to roleplay phoning a radio phone-in programme and asking for advice.

It's time/I'd rather/I'd better

It's time ...

Form *It's time* + subject + past tense

Meaning 'It's time I did something' is used to mean 'I should have done something already or at least started it'.

It's time you did your homework.

I'd rather ...

Form subject + *would rather* + object + past tense (+ *than* ...)

Meaning 'I'd rather you did/didn't do something' is used to talk about what you'd prefer someone else to do.

I'd rather you didn't smoke in here.

Form subject + *would rather* + infinitive (+ *than* ...)

Meaning 'I'd rather do/not do something' is used to talk about what you'd prefer to do.

I'd rather not spend all day lying on the beach.

I'd better ...

Form subject + *had better* + infinitive

Meaning 'I'd better do/not do something' is used to talk about something when it is advisable to do it (in the present or future).

I'd better mend that window as soon as I can.

Reported speech

Use 'reported' or 'indirect' speech to tell people what somebody said or thought.

Make the tense of the verb one 'step' further back into the past.

'I want to go out.' → *She said (that) she wanted to go out.*

Modal verbs also change.

'Can you help me paint the kitchen?' → *She asked me if I could help her paint the kitchen.*

Subject and object pronouns change.

'I will give it to you soon.' → *He said he would give it to me soon.*

References to particular times change, e.g.

'The books will be delivered tomorrow.' → *She said the books would be delivered the next day.*

Word order changes, e.g.

'What are you doing at the weekend.' → *He asked me what we were doing at the weekend.*

Use *if* (or *whether*) when reporting *Yes/No* questions, e.g.

'Did you enjoy the film?' → *He asked me if I had enjoyed the film.*

Reporting verbs

Say and *explain* are followed by verb + (*that*).

She explained that John was ill and couldn't come.

Tell is followed by verb + object + (*that*).

He told us we needed to show identification.

Ask, remind and *warn* are followed by verb + object + infinitive.

We reminded him to post the letter.

Promise and *decide* are followed by verb + infinitive, e.g.

We decided to stay at home and watch TV.

Admit and *suggest* are followed by verb + gerund.

He admitted liking her a lot.

Hard and hardly

Hard as an adjective means firm and difficult to cut or break.

The mattress is quite hard.

These plums are too hard to eat.

Hard as an adverb means using a lot of effort or force, e.g.

She's been working hard all day.

Hardly is an adverb which means *almost not* or *very little*.

I hardly know the people in my class.

Hardly is often used with *any*(*thing/one/where*, etc.) and *ever*.

We hardly ever go out in the evening.

Key vocabulary

Success

best-seller   succeed   go under   have a go
have had their day   give up   be up to scratch

Personality

proactive   headstrong   opinionated   manipulative
selfish   single-minded   open   easy-going   witty
outgoing   to be the centre of attention
to be a party animal   to be a complete doormat
to be really high maintenance   to be down-to-earth

Adjectives/Intensifiers

happy – ecstatic   important – vital   big – huge
upset – devastated   hungry – starving
tired – exhausted   very   really   extremely
absolutely

Phrasal verbs with three parts

catch up with   get away with   keep up with
put in for   come up with   cut down on   look up to
look forward to   put up with   make up for

1 Find the mistakes in six of the sentences and correct them.

I'd better <u>wrote</u> your phone number down before I forget it. → *write*

1   I'd better went to the shops before they close.
2   Had you rather I didn't say anything to your boss?
3   Isn't it time you told him how you really feel?
4   I'd rather not working this weekend if at all possible.
5   Would you better take a raincoat in case it rains?
6   I'd rather you paid me back in cash than by cheque if that's OK.
7   What's that smell? I think it's time you get the cake out of the oven.
8   I'd rather took just hand luggage on the plane than a large suitcase.

2 Complete the sentences using the past.

Zoe/say/can't remember/where/leave/keys. → *Zoe said she couldn't remember where she had left the keys.*

1   Tony/ask/I like/play/tennis/this weekend.
2   They/tell/best time/visit Egypt/be/in January or February.
3   Helen/say/not know/what time/firework display/start.
4   He ask/me when/I want/go/see/the London Eye.
5   My boss/tell/I have to/make/presentation/at sales conference/in March.
6   The newspaper/say/one/our athletes/fail/ drugs test.

3 Choose the correct alternative in each case.

He told (me)/to me that he was going to be at least twenty minutes late.

1   She promised *to do/doing* all her homework before she went out to see her friend.
2   Can you explain *me/to me* exactly how this DVD recorder works?
3   They decided *to sell/selling* their house and move to the country.
4   My doctor suggested *taking/to take* a week off work.
5   They warned *us/to us* that the weather conditions would make walking in the mountains quite dangerous.
6   Will you remind me *to go/going* to the post office this afternoon?
7   He admitted *being/be* wrong about the time of the train.

4 Complete each of the following gaps with *hard* or *hardly*.

1   I'm going to work really _____ on my maths from now until the end of term.
2   We _____ have any time to see friends at the moment. Life is just too busy!
3   I could _____ believe it when she said they were going to get married!
4   It will be a long, _____ climb to the top of that hill.
5   _____ anyone came to opening night of the restaurant. It was very disappointing.
6   If you look _____ , you can just see Michael on the other side of the car park.

5 Unjumble each of the words in *italics* in the sentences below.

1   She loves being the centre of *nnaoiettt*. She wants everyone to be talking about her.
2   He's terribly *doopitninae*. He really thinks that his own opinions are the only ones which are worth listening to!
3   Tara got all As in her final school exams. She's absolutely *ccttiase*!
4   She finally *ducdecees* in persuading him to go to the police.
5   We're really looking *rrwfdoa* to visiting my brother in Australia. It'll be the first time we've been out there.
6   My brother's very *goginuto*. He really enjoys being with friends and meeting new people.
7   He's spent a lot of money getting his new car up to *hctsacr* before the big race.
8   I told her not to take her driving test yet but she's very *narthesdog* and insisted on doing what she wanted.

9 Crime

Lead-in

1 a How are the photos connected to the topic of 'crime'?

b Think of words and expressions connected with crime and the law. Write them in the appropriate columns.

LAW COURT	CRIME	CRIMINAL	EVIDENCE	PUNISHMENT
a judge	robbery	thief	fingerprints	community service

2 Explain these newspaper headlines. Use a dictionary if necessary.

1 Local MP stopped for speeding

2 **Cyber crime up by 50%**

3 **Overcrowded prisons slammed in new report**

4 **Chaos in fraud case after witness intimidation**

5 Suspended sentence for teacher in road rage incident

6 **Keen cop gives out record number of fines**

3 Do you think crime is increasing or decreasing where you live? Are there any particular types of crime which are a special problem in your area?

Vocabulary | law and insurance

1 Match the words/phrases 1–10 to the appropriate definitions a–j.

1	insurance	a)	officially decide in a court of law that someone is guilty of a crime.
2	premium	b)	an amount of money that you pay for insurance
3	fraud	c)	when you pay a company money and they pay the costs if you are ill, have a car accident, etc.
4	to file (a claim)	d)	give a legal punishment to someone who is guilty of a crime
5	to sue (someone)	e)	the crime of deliberately making something burn, especially a building
6	to guarantee	f)	start a legal process to get money from someone who has harmed you in some way
7	an appeal	g)	make an official statement that you are going to do something, especially in a court
8	arson	h)	promise that something will happen or be done
9	to convict (someone of)	i)	when someone deceives people to get money
10	to sentence (someone to)	j)	when someone asks a higher court to change the decision of a lower court

2 **a** Complete the sentences with the words/phrases from Ex. 1 in the correct form.

1 She plans to _____ the hospital after they gave her the wrong operation.
2 Bailey was _____ to three years in prison for his part in the robbery.
3 We lost the case this time but there's going to be an _____ . We will never give up.
4 I'm afraid that the cost of the annual _____ has gone up again. They say it's because of the number of claims last year.
5 My neighbour has been _____ of shoplifting but luckily he doesn't have to go to prison.
6 Does this _____ plan cover things that are stolen from me while I'm on holiday?
7 Can you _____ that this TV will be delivered before Christmas? It's very important.
8 They don't think the fire was an accident. They think it was _____ .
9 Ted's wife has _____ for divorce. He's very upset about it.
10 He's been arrested and charged with _____ . Apparently, he pretended that an expensive painting had been stolen to get the insurance money.

b **9.1** Listen and check your answers.

3 Discuss.

1 Imagine someone buys a coffee in a fast food restaurant. They then spill the hot coffee on themselves and are burned. Should they sue the fast food company?
2 What different things do people insure? Have you ever heard about anyone insuring something strange?
3 Do you know any famous cases of fraud? If so, what happened?

Listening

4 a You are going to listen to a story about a crime involving cigars. Before you listen, suggest what the story might be using as many of the words in Ex. 1 as possible.

b **9.2** Listen to the story and compare your ideas.

5 Listen again. Put these sentences in the order in which they happen in the story.

1 The lawyer is arrested.
2 The insurance company refuses to pay.
3 He makes a claim against the insurance company.
4 The lawyer is sentenced to jail.
5 He smokes the cigars.
6 The insurance company pays the lawyer.
7 He insures the cigars against fire.
8 The lawyer sues the insurance company.
9 A lawyer buys some rare cigars.

6 a Listen to the story again. Which of the following expressions do you hear?

1 Go on ...
2 The way it goes is that ...
3 Fancy that.
4 Fair enough.
5 What on earth for?
6 Pull the other one.
7 You're kidding!
8 Cross my heart.

b Find the expressions in the tapescript on page 174. Discuss in groups what you think each expression means.

Grammar | sequencing devices

7 a Look at the examples in the Active grammar box. Then, complete the structures A and B by writing the correct part of speech for each one.

> ### Active grammar
>
> *Having cashed the cheque, the lawyer was arrested.*
>
> *After cashing the cheque, the lawyer was arrested.*
>
> Use the following two forms to describe the order of events in a story.
>
> | (Clause 1) | (Clause 2) |
> |---|---|
> | A: *Having* + ___ , | Past Simple |
> | B: *After* + ___ , | Past Simple |

see Reference page 129

b Which clause comes first in the order of events?

8 Complete the sentences by writing the correct form of a verb from the box.

> stay   read   promise   do   go   win

1 After _____ to the bank a number of times, the robbers felt they understood all the security systems.
2 Having _____ to pick his friend up from the police station, Terry completely forgot.
3 After _____ extremely well in his first year exams, we were very surprised when he said he wanted to stop studying law.
4 Having _____ some excellent reviews of the new P.D. James murder mystery, I wanted to get a copy to take on holiday with me.
5 Having successfully _____ her case against her old employer for wrongful dismissal, she decided to go out and celebrate.
6 After _____ at the office until midnight to prepare her report for the judge, she decided to give herself the next day off.

9 a Think about three things that happened to you last week and what you did after each one.

b Tell another student the first thing and see if they can guess what you did next. Then, tell them if they were right or not.

A: *After doing my English homework ...*

B: *... you watched a film on TV?*

A: *No. I collapsed on the sofa and fell asleep!*

Speaking and reading

10 Work in pairs. Student As look at the pictures for Story 1 below. Student Bs look at the pictures for Story 2 on page 151. The pictures make a story. With another student, work out the story.

Story 1

11 Check your ideas by reading the story. (Story 1 is on page 149, Story 2 is below).

Story 2

An ambitious burglar broke into a vast mansion on millionaires' row at Bel Air, Los Angeles. He went through the house room by room, putting anything of value that he could see and carry in the large bag he'd brought with him. Having completely filled his bag, he decided it was time to leave.

He started to realise that he wasn't sure of the way out but moved on quickly, through a large dining-room, past an indoor gym and through another room filled with exotic parrots. By now he was beginning to panic. Then, having run through a large library and a small room full of art, he began to get quite desperate.

He ran up a small circular staircase to what seemed to be a large bedroom. He knocked on the door and went in. The owners of the house had been asleep in bed but sat up in fright only to find a traumatised burglar desperate to find his way out of the maze of rooms. After giving him detailed directions, they phoned the police, who arrived minutes later and escorted the relieved burglar to the safety of a nearby police station.

12 a Prepare to tell another student your story using the expressions in the How to box.

HOW TO ...	tell a funny story	
	Check you remember all the important information.	*A lawyer bought some rare cigars.* *He insured them against fire.*
	Check you know the key vocabulary	*cigar, to insure*
	Introduce the story	*Did you hear the story about the man who stole a parrot?* *Have you heard the one about the robber who fell asleep?*
	Keep the funny part until the very end.	*... and so can you believe it? He was sentenced to twenty-four months in jail and a $24,000 fine.*

b In A/B pairs, show your partner your pictures and tell him or her the story. Include the structures *Having* + past participle and *After* + present participle as appropriate.

9.2 | It's a mystery!

Grammar | past modals of deduction *must/might/can't have done*
Can do | speculate about past events

Grammar | *must/might/can't have*

1 Look at the pictures. What do you think the person is doing?

2 **9.3** Listen to the conversation. What do the people say is happening in the photos?

3 Read the examples 1–3 below, then complete the rules A–C.

> **Active grammar**
>
> 1 *He must have fixed up some kind of security camera.*
> 2 *He might have done it before.*
> 3 *He can't have realised he was being caught on camera.*
>
> A Use _____ _____ + past participle to say that you think something is possible in the past.
> B Use _____ _____ + past participle to say that you think something is not possible in the past.
> C Use _____ _____ + past participle to say that you are certain about something in the past.

see Reference page 129

4 Choose the correct alternative in each sentence.
  1 They *must/might/can't* have got into the house through a window. They were all locked.
  2 He *must/might/can't* have told my parents that I was caught shoplifting but I hope he didn't.
  3 The judge *must/might/can't* have liked you. It's unusual to only get a suspended sentence in this kind of case.
  4 They *must/might/can't* have sacked him because he was lazy. He was one of the hardest working people in the company!
  5 Don't be negative. She *must/might/can't* have passed her English test. We will only know when we get the results.
  6 She *must/might/can't* have left very quietly. I didn't hear her go.
  7 She *must/might/can't* have had a bad meeting with the Marketing Director. She's been in a terrible mood ever since.
  8 He *must/might/can't* have arrived yet because he promised to phone us the minute the plane landed.

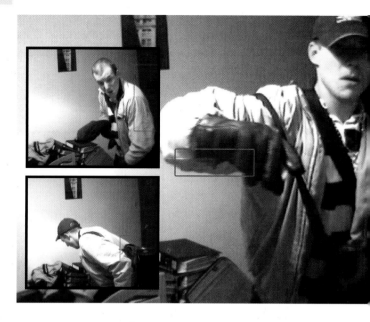

5 **a** Complete the sentences using *must/might/can't have* and an appropriate verb from the box.

> go   forgot   drop   tell   finish   be   leave
> spend

  1 We don't know who took the money. There were lots of people in the office during the day and it _____ any of them.
  2 I wonder why Pete didn't turn up to do his community service. He _____ about it. I reminded him yesterday.
  3 I'm not sure where Jo is. She _____ round to Sally's. They're working on a school project together.
  4 How did you know about the surprise party? Someone _____ you!
  5 You _____ all your birthday money already. You got nearly £100!
  6 I _____ my keys at home. I remember feeling them in my jacket pocket when I got on the bus.
  7 She _____ her homework yet. She only started it at 9 o'clock.
  8 I've lost one of my gloves. I _____ it on the way to work.

b **9.4** Listen and check your answers. Pay attention to the pronunciation of *must/might/can't have*. How is *have* pronounced each time?

6 **9.5** Listen to the extract from a radio news programme. How did the police find the photos from Ex. 1?

Vocabulary | compound adjectives

7 Combine a word from column A below with a word from column B to make compound adjectives. Check in a dictionary if necessary.

1 *single-minded*

A	B
1 single-	a) minute
2 one-	b) aged
3 middle-	c) time
4 left-	d) called
5 home-	e) minded
6 last-	f) made
7 part-	g) new
8 so-	h) consuming
9 time-	i) way
10 brand-	j) handed

8 a Complete the sentences with the compound adjectives from Ex. 7.

1 Apparently, she said that the computer and TV that were stolen were _____ when in fact they were several years old.

2 They arrested a _____ man for joy-riding last night. It's surprising because joy-riders are usually in their teens.

3 In his interview for inspector he came across as very _____ which is exactly what we want. We need someone who will get things done.

4 He said he just wanted a _____ ticket to Alicante which is what made me a little suspicious.

5 I'm doing some voluntary work with young offenders. I really like it but it's quite _____ . It's taking up most of my weekends at the moment.

6 It was a _____ decision to go to Paris but I'm really glad we did. After all the hassle of the court case we needed a break.

7 The fact that the thief was _____ was a vital clue that helped the police catch him. They found some specially designed scissors in his flat.

8 The _____ expert for the defence was very vague in his answers. I'm not sure it was really his specialist area.

9 I'm starting work as a _____ community police officer in January. It's Monday and Friday mornings which is perfect for me.

10 You must try a piece of this _____ chocolate cake. One of the prisoners made it in the cookery class.

9 Discuss.

1 Do you consider yourself to be a single-minded person? Why/Why not?

2 When is someone 'middle-aged' do you think?

3 What things in your life are particularly time-consuming? Can you do anything about this?

4 Are you a 'last-minute' kind of person? If so, give some examples.

5 Have you ever had a part-time job? If so, what was it? Did you enjoy it?

6 Do you think home-made cooking is always the best?

Reading

10 Work in pairs. How many different ways can you think of to steal $200,000?

11 Read the article and briefly summarise how D.B. Cooper managed to steal $200,000.

D.B. Cooper

At 2p.m. on 24th November 1971, a middle-aged man of average height, dressed in a dark suit, white shirt, dark glasses and a black tie, handed a $20 note to a clerk at the Portland airport, asked for a one-way ticket and then boarded Flight 305 for Seattle. Identifying himself as Dan Cooper, he carried only a briefcase. Just before take-off, he handed the flight attendant a note. Watching her put the note in her pocket, he said quietly, 'Miss, you'd better look at that note. I have a bomb.' The message demanded $200,000 and four parachutes – by 5p.m. To remove any final doubts, Cooper opened his briefcase and showed the flight attendant sticks of dynamite, attached to wire and a battery. As the plane circled over Seattle, the pilot, William Rataczak, quickly learned he was not dealing with an amateur. This man was totally single-minded. With the confidence of an army commander, Cooper told Rataczak that after the money and parachutes had been delivered, he wanted him to head south from Seattle, fly no higher than 10,000 feet and leave the rear door open.

The plane landed in Seattle and by 7p.m, it had refuelled and the parachutes and money were on board. The plane took off again a few minutes after 7.30p.m. Then Cooper carefully collected all his cigarette ends, made sure he had all his handwritten notes and strapped the money bag to his body using cords he cut from one of the parachutes.

At 8.12p.m, 'we felt a little bump and the air pressure changed,' Rataczak said. And that was the last fix on D. B. Cooper. The Air Force had sent up two F-106 fighter planes to chase the Boeing 727 and try to keep Cooper's parachute in sight but they were too fast and had to keep making giant S-curves in the sky. For the next few weeks, hundreds of federal agents, helped by Army troops, searched around the area under where Cooper jumped. A small submarine also searched nearby Lake Merwin. But they found nothing. In fact there was no concrete evidence of any kind until February 1980 when an Oklahoma boy, having a picnic with his family on the shore of the Columbia River, came across a waterlogged bag containing 294 mouldy $20 notes. The serial numbers matched those on the notes given to D.B. Cooper. This find got the FBI's attention. Helicopters flew over the area, squads of agents dug up the shore, searching for more notes, Cooper's body or parachute but again, nothing.

D.B. Cooper entered the history books as an authentic American legend. 'There's a good reason for this,' says Larry Goldfine, a Seattle lawyer who was sitting on Flight 305 that day. 'It was the first skyjacking for money and then the skyjacker disappeared without a trace. No one was hurt and it all happened right under the noses of the FBI'. Most people think D.B. got away with it. The Cooper of the legend has the coolness of a Steve McQueen or Clint Eastwood. In the end, no one has ever worked out just who he was – or is. In his enduring anonymity, he has inspired three books, a play, a film, a song and thousands of D.B. Cooper bars and restaurants. Perhaps the ultimate tribute is the annual 'D.B. Cooper Days' festival in the tiny Washington town over which Cooper was thought to have parachuted. There's a D.B. Cooper look-alike contest (lots of forty-ish men in dark suits and dark glasses), and half-a-dozen parachutists make a jump.

12 Read the article again and answer these questions.

1 What did D.B. Cooper take with him onto the plane?

2 What did he want?

3 How did Rataczak realise he was not dealing with an amateur?

4 At what time did the plane take off for the second time?

5 At what time did D.B. Cooper jump from the plane?

6 Why couldn't the fighter planes follow D.B. Cooper?

7 Who took part in the official search for D.B. Cooper?

8 What single clue did they get?

9 Why has the case of D.B. Cooper captured the popular imagination?

10 What different things have been done to commemorate what D.B. Cooper did?

13 Find three examples of compound adjectives in the text.

14 Discuss.

1 What do you think of what D.B. Cooper did?

2 How do you think he got away with it?

3 Do you understand why some people admire what he did?

4 Do you know any stories about famous criminals from your country?

Grammar	relative clauses
Can do	write an article

Reading

1 **a** Discuss with other students.

   1 What do you know about Sherlock Holmes?

   2 Was he a real person?

   3 Why and when was he famous?

  b Now read the text and check your ideas.

The Real Sherlock Holmes

A SIGHT TO SHATTER THE NERVES! A STORY TO STUN THE SENSES!

The
Hound
OF THE **Baskervilles**

PETER CUSHING · ANDRE MORELL · CHRISTOPHER LEE · BASED ON THE NOVEL BY SIR ARTHUR CONAN DOYLE
It's Ten Times The Terror in
TECHNICOLOR!

Was Sherlock Holmes a real person? Not exactly, but Dr Joseph Bell, the man who inspired the character of Sherlock Holmes, shared many qualities with the famous detective. Arthur Conan Doyle, the writer and creator of Holmes, met Dr Bell in 1877 at the University of Edinburgh Medical School. Conan Doyle was studying to be a doctor and Bell was one of his professors.

Bell was thirty-nine years old when Conan Doyle first attended one of his lectures. He is said to have walked with great energy. His nose and chin were angular and his eyes twinkled with intelligent humour. Bell, who was a brilliant doctor, liked writing poetry, playing sport and bird-watching.

By the end of Conan Doyle's second year Bell had selected him to serve as his assistant. Being on a ward with Bell, where he had plenty of opportunity to observe, only increased Conan Doyle's admiration for the great doctor. Amongst other things he was able to witness Dr Bell's remarkable ability to quickly deduce a great deal about the patient.

Dr Bell observed the way a person moved. The walk of a sailor, who had spent many years at sea, varied greatly from that of a soldier. If he identified a person as a sailor, he would look for any tattoos that might assist him in knowing where their travels had taken them. He trained himself to listen for small differences in his patients' accents to help him identify where they were from. Bell studied the hands of his patients because calluses or other marks could help him determine their occupation.

Conan Doyle published the first Holmes story in 1887. His innovation in creating a character that would appear over and over in a series of self-contained stories meant that Holmes's popularity grew with each instalment. Soon the character was so beloved that people refused to believe he wasn't a real person; letters addressed to 'Sherlock Holmes, Consulting Detective' arrived daily at Baker Street and Scotland Yard, each begging him to take on a real case.

2 Read the text again and complete the notes.

> **The Real Sherlock Holmes**
> Person who Sherlock Holmes was based on: *Dr Joseph Bell*
> Relationship to Conan Doyle: (1) _____
> Where/When met Conan Doyle: (2) _____ , (3) _____
> Dr Bell's hobbies: poetry, (4) _____ , (5) _____
> Things Dr Bell observed about patients: the way they moved, (6) _____ , their accents, (7) _____
> Date first Holmes story published: (8) _____
> Letters for Sherlock Holmes sent to: (9) _____

3 Read the text again and find words that mean:

1 to give someone the idea for something (para. 1)
2 very good, intelligent, skilful (para. 2)
3 part of a hospital where patients stay (para. 3)
4 new idea, method, etc. that is used for the first time (para. 5)
5 to ask for something in an urgent or anxious way (para. 5)

4 Discuss.

1 What new information have you learned about Sherlock Holmes?
2 Do you think you are observant like Dr Bell? Would you be a good witness in a crime situation?
3 Would you be interested in being a police detective? Why/Why not?

Grammar | relative clauses

5 Read the information in the Active grammar box and decide which of the examples 1–5 contain 'defining relative clauses' and which contain 'non-defining relative clauses'.

Active grammar

1 *Dr Joseph Bell was the man <u>who inspired the character of Sherlock Holmes</u>.*
2 *Bell, <u>who was a brilliant doctor</u>, liked writing poetry, playing sport and bird-watching.*
3 *Bell was thirty-nine years old <u>when Conan Doyle first attended one of his lectures</u>.*
4 *Being on a ward with Bell, <u>where he had plenty of opportunity to observe</u>, only increased Conan Doyle's admiration for the great doctor.*
5 *Conan Doyle, <u>whose Sherlock Holmes novels were enormously popular</u>, died in 1930.*

Defining relative clauses

The underlined part of the sentence is essential to the meaning of the sentence.

Commas are not used to separate the clauses.

Who and *which* can both be replaced by *that*.

Non-defining relative clauses

The underlined part of the sentence gives us extra information. This clause can be removed without affecting the central meaning of the sentence.

Use commas at the beginning and end of these clauses unless they end the sentence.

Who and *which* cannot be replaced by *that*.

---

6 Join these pairs of sentences to make one sentence.

The police still haven't found the man. He stole my bag.

The police still haven't found the man who stole my bag.

1 John's been my best friend since school. He's helping me start a new business.
2 My current flat needs redecorating. I've been in it for a couple of years.
3 Tamsin's going to Australia for the winter. Her parents emigrated there last year.
4 My neighbour has given me his old computer. I've always liked him.
5 The family at the end of the road are thinking of moving. Their dog barks constantly.
6 Tina's car is up for sale. She's had it for years.

7 Complete the sentences in a way that makes sense.

1 Where are the jeans which … ?
2 That's the pop star who …
3 She's the little girl whose …
4 I'd like to find a place where …
5 I think that's the couple whose …
6 We went to a shop where …
7 Wasn't it your father who … ?
8 She bought the mobile phone which …

Person to person

8 Tell another student three interesting things about you. Begin like this:

Libya is the place where I was born. My mother was an English teacher there.

1 X is the place where …
2 Y is the person who …
3 Z was the time when …

see Reference page 129

Listening

9 **a** **9.6** Listen to an interview with an ordinary American whose name is 'Sherlock Holmes'. First, discuss with another student:

1 Why do you think he has this name?

2 What do you think are the possible consequences of having a name like this?

b Listen and check your ideas.

10 Listen again and explain the significance of the following things in the interview:

1 This is what the American Sherlock Holmes likes to be called.

1 The name 'Holmes'

2 The original Conan Doyle stories

3 A favourite literary figure

4 The question 'Where's Dr Watson?'

5 TV magicians

6 The mother of an old family friend

7 $7000

8 His torch and magnifying glass

11 Discuss.

1 How do you feel about your name? Does it mean something? Were you named after someone in your family or someone famous? If so, who and why?

2 What reasons do people have for changing their names? Do you know anyone who has changed his/her name? If so, why did he/she do it?

3 In Britain, women often take their husband's surname when they get married? What do you think about this?

Writing

12 Read the article in the Writing bank on page 164 and do the exercises.

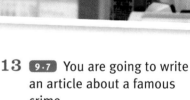

13 **9.7** You are going to write an article about a famous crime.

1 Listen and make notes from this description of how Nick Leeson broke the Barings investment bank.

2 Decide on the main points for your article.

3 Organise your ideas into paragraphs.

4 Write your article in 100–150 words. (Check the important points about writing articles from Ex. 12.)

5 Read your article through. Is it interesting and easy to read? Make any necessary changes.

9 Vocabulary
Newspaper headlines

Hollywood star in bank drama

Riddle of PM's missing diary

1 Discuss.

1 Do you ever read English newspapers?
2 What is the purpose of a headline?
3 Do you ever have problems understanding headlines? Why?

2 **a** Match the words 1–12, with the meanings a–l. Use a dictionary if necessary.

A	B
1 aid	a) strong request
2 axe	b) affect badly
3 back	c) explosion
4 bid	d) leave, resign
5 blast	e) essential, vital
6 blaze	f) cut, remove
7 quit	g) dispute, conflict
8 clash	h) attempt
9 drama	i) tense situation
10 hit	j) support
11 key	k) help
12 plea	l) serious fire

b In pairs, discuss what you think the two headlines above might mean.

3 Choose the most likely alternative in each headline.

1 *Key/Plea* witness receives death threat
2 IBM *axes/bids* top managers
3 Guests escape hotel *clash/blaze*
4 School governors *back/quit* teacher
5 Chat show host fight *drama/key*
6 Police and students *clash/hit*
7 BT *bids/pleas* for US communications network
8 General *quits/aids* top job

4 Discuss. Would you be interested in reading articles with the following headlines? Why/Why not? What do you think each one might be about?

1 **Interest rate cut boosts exports**

2 **Prince and model to wed**

3 **Leading bank in sex discrimination case**

4 **Man. Utd. crash to defeat in Cup match**

5 **MP spy drama**

6 **Riddle of 2nd Van Gogh painting**

7 **Butler quits the Palace**

8 **Cape Town bids for Olympics**

9 **Bomb blast in northern India**

10 **Votes scandal in California**

5 Discuss.

1 Do you read newspapers/magazines often? If so, which ones? Why do you like them?
2 Do you read the whole paper/magazine or just certain parts? If so, which parts?
3 Do you think newspapers are the best way of getting the news in your country?
4 Which are the most popular newspapers in your country? What are the main differences between them?

9 | Communication

Mind benders

1 A police officer was sitting on his motorcycle at a red traffic light when two teenagers in a sports car drove by him at 50 mph. He did not chase them or try to apprehend them. **Why not?**

2 A man was driving alone in his car when he came off the road at high speed. He crashed through a fence and went down a steep slope before the car plunged into a fast flowing river. As the car slowly settled in the river, the man realised that his arm was broken and that he could not release his seat belt and get out of the car. He was trapped in the car. Rescuers arrived two hours later, yet they found him alive. **How come?**

3 A man rode into town on Friday. He stayed for three nights and then left on Friday. **How come?**

4 Bobby lives with his parents in London. Last week, while his parents were out, Bobby's neighbour Susie came round to spend the evening. At 8 o'clock precisely she went out to buy some cigarettes from the corner shop five minutes walk away. One minute after she left, two men burst into the house and, ignoring Bobby, took the TV set, the stereo and a computer. Bobby had never seen the men before and they had no legal right to remove the equipment – yet he did nothing to stop them. In fact, he didn't even act surprised by their behaviour. **How come?**

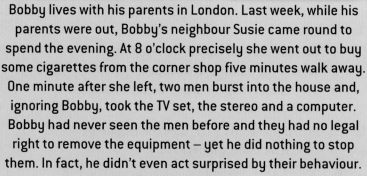

5 A man leaves hospital and begins to walk home. On his journey he passes a phone box which begins to ring. Instead of answering it he punches the air and runs all the way home cheering. **Why?**

6 When a fire broke out in an airplane, a panicking passenger opened the emergency hatch and threw himself out, even though he had no parachute. **How was it that when the rescue services found him, he was alive and well and without injury?**

1 Try and solve the lateral thinking problems above. Follow these instructions:

1 Read each of them and make a note of any vocabulary which stops you understanding them.
2 Ask other students and/or check in a dictionary to find out the meaning of the unknown vocabulary.
3 Work with another student. Discuss ideas you have to explain each of the problems.

2 Now choose the one you are most interested in and read the explanation for it. (1 page 149; 2 page 145; 3 page 147; 4 page 148; 5 page 150; 6 page 151).

1 Make two *Yes/No* questions to ask about each of the other problems.
   Was the policeman asleep? Were the teenagers invisible in some way?
2 Ask other students who know the explanations for the other problems your questions.
3 With the additional information, suggest explanations for each of the other problems.
   The teenagers might have been the policeman's children.

Sequencing devices

Use *Having* + past participle or *After* + present participle to show the order of events when telling a story or describing a series of events.

Having discussed the problem for several hours, we decided to go out for something to eat.

After explaining to her boss why she needed a raise, she told him that she was thinking of leaving the company.

Other examples with a similar structure include:

Before painting the room, she had to strip off the old wallpaper.

On entering the room, he noticed that all the windows were open.

While cleaning the room, she discovered a locked diary.

Must/Might/Can't have

Use *must* to say that you believe something is certain.

Use *might* to say something is a possibility.

Use *can't* to say that you believe something is not possible.

For the past, use *must/might/can't have* + past participle. This is the same for *I/you/he/we/they*.

You must have enjoyed your holiday in Australia.

I think I might have left my wallet in that shop.

She hasn't phoned me so she can't have got my message.

You can use *may* instead of *might* and *couldn't* instead of *can't*.

She may have stopped to get some petrol

They couldn't have gone swimming. They didn't take any towels.

May/might have + past participle can also refer to the present or future.

I'll give him a call but he may have left by now.

By this time next year I might have moved to Brussels.

Relative clauses
Defining relative clauses

Defining relative clauses define or identify the person, thing, time, place or reason. They cannot be left out.

Tim is the teacher who I told you about.

That's the street where I grew up.

No commas are used before and after the defining relative clause.

That can be used instead of *who* or *which*.

The woman that/who I share an office with has been in the company for years.

The relative pronoun can be left out if it is the object of the verb in the relative clause.

Simon bought the jacket (that/which) we saw when we went shopping last weekend.

Non-defining relative clauses

Non-defining relative clauses give extra information which can be left out.

Commas are used before and after non-defining relative clauses unless they end a sentence.

Who and *which* cannot be replaced by *that*.

I've lent my new bike, which I really like, to my brother.

Cairo, where I lived for several years, is a fascinating city.

Key vocabulary

Crime
robbery   thief   fingerprints   community service
speeding   fraud   witness   intimidation   road rage

Law and insurance
premium   fraud   to file (a claim)   to sue (someone)
to guarantee   appeal   arson
to convict (someone of)   to sentence (someone to)

Conversational expressions
Go on ...   The way it goes is that ...   Fancy that.
Fair enough.   What on earth for?
Pull the other one.   You're kidding!   Cross my heart.

Compound adjectives
middle-aged   one-way   single-minded
left-handed   home-made   last-minute   part-time
so-called   time-consuming   brand-new

Newspaper headlines
aid   axe   back   bid   blast   blaze   quit   clash
drama   hit   key   plea

---

1 Join the following pairs of sentences. Use *After* + present participle or *Having* + past participle.

She arrived at the office early. She worked hard and fast all morning.

Having arrived at the office early, she worked hard and fast all morning.

1 She travelled for hours to get to the village. She thought she should stay there for at least a couple of days.

2 He saw his neighbour struggling with a lot of heavy bags. He offered to help her.

3 She came first in her university exams. She was approached by a top firm of lawyers.

4 She took home an injured cat she had found by the side of the road. She felt she had to keep it.

5 He saw a young man take a CD without paying. He told the security staff.

6 He spoke to his father. He told his boss he wanted a raise.

7 They got a long letter from their cousin. They decided to go and see him.

2 Complete the second sentences so that they mean the same as the first. Use *must/might/can't* with the verb in brackets.

I don't believe she got an 'A' in her exam.
She _____ . (get)

She can't have got an 'A' in her exam.

1 It is possible he stayed late at the office.
He _____ . (stay)

2 There's no chance that I left my gloves in the car.
I _____ . (leave)

3 I'm sure she's shown me her holiday photos at least ten times.
She _____ . (show)

4 It's not possible that she's finished all her homework already.
She _____ . (finish)

5 I have no doubt that they were really pleased to win the competition.
They _____ . (be)

6 There's a chance my letter got lost in the post.
My letter _____ . (got)

3 Add commas as necessary to the sentences.

David Gray who wrote the song *White Ladder* is performing in Paris this weekend.

David Gray, who wrote the song White Ladder, is performing in Paris this weekend.

1 I'm afraid I lost the book which she lent me.

2 I'm going to spend a few days in Seville where I first met Raquel.

3 These are the apples which I picked from the tree in my garden.

4 The young man who I spoke to has promised to give me a refund.

5 We decided to stay at the Regina Hotel which some friends had recommended to us.

6 Tim whose job involves a lot of travelling has offered to let us use his flat for a few weeks.

4 Find the mistakes in four of the sentences and correct them.

1 Steve works for a small company makes kitchen equipment.

2 I think the name of the film that I'd like to see is *Collateral*.

3 Did you hear exactly that he said?

4 The demonstration, had been going on for several days, is finally over.

5 Isn't that the place where you grew up?

6 My sister, that speaks French and Italian fluently, wants to be an interpreter.

5 Complete the sentences with one of the words from the Key vocabulary section on page 129.

I'm going to get a <u>part-time</u> job working in a local newsagents. It's just three days a week.

1 I remember being forced to write with my right hand as a child even though I was obviously _____ .

2 Government _____ gives boost to troubled steel industry.

3 They say I have to pay a fine for travelling without a ticket but I'm going to _____

4 We're going to try and get a _____ deal with a local travel agent. Apparently there are some real bargains.

5 **A:** If you come to my place, I'll cook dinner.
B: _____ enough. Shall I bring some wine?

6 Can you believe it? My DVD recorder stops working after thirteen months and the _____ is for one year!

7 Mystery _____ at chemicals factory injures three workers. Arson suspected.

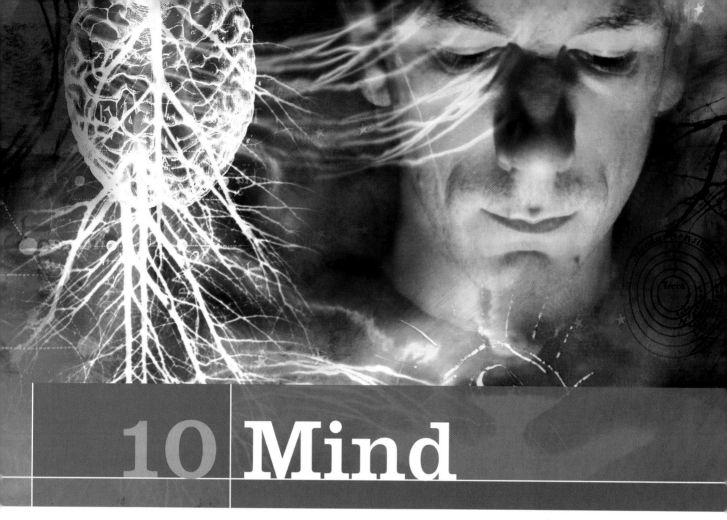

10 Mind

Lead-in

1   Discuss.

What is happening in each photo? How are they connected?

2   **a** In pairs, match the quotes below with pictures 1–3 and explain what you think the phrases in *italics* mean.

'Walking on hot coals is a question of *mind over matter*.'

'Politicians often rely on the *power of persuasion* to make people vote for them.'

'I gave up eating all sweet things using nothing but *willpower*.'

b In what situations have you used a) mind over matter, b) the power of persuasion and c) willpower?

3   **a** **10.1** Listen to six people answering questions 1–6. Make brief notes about their answers.

1   Do you ever *have premonitions*? Do you take them seriously?
2   Have you ever *had a feeling of déjà vu*? What happened?
3   Are you someone who is usually able to *trust your intuition*?
4   Do you know anyone who uses *his/her sixth sense* a lot?
5   Have you ever *been unconscious*? What happened?
6   Do you think you have any *subconscious fears*?

b In pairs, write a short definition for each of the phrases in *italics* in the questions above. Then, compare your definitions with the definitions in an English–English dictionary.

c Ask and answer the questions with a partner.

Reading

1 a Discuss.

What sort of problems do hypnotists help people with?

b Read the text quickly and answer the questions .

1 What problems are mentioned in the text?

2 How do you think the writer feels about the hypnotist Paul McKenna: sceptical, impressed, indifferent or nervous?

Their lives in his hands

He is a modern-day guru. The rich and famous all turn to him when they are in need of help. Christa D'Souza meets Paul McKenna, the hypnotist with hidden powers.

It is early in the afternoon in West London and the office of Paul McKenna Productions is bustling with activity. McKenna himself is a small, mousy man and when I arrive he is talking animatedly on the phone. On the shelves around the office, I notice boxes marked 'smoking', 'motivation' and 'flying' amongst others. McKenna eventually puts the phone down, apologises and then, noticing me looking at the boxes, politely wonders whether I am frightened of flying. 'Yes, that's why I'm here,' I admit. Already, I feel in awe of this man.

Paul McKenna has an eclectic band of followers, who come to him with a wide range of problems and phobias, from fear of flying to depression. He has worked with many famous people, including actors, rock stars, sportspeople and even royalty. He doesn't charge his clients for their treatment, but asks them to make a donation to a charity of his choice. Besides, he doesn't need to charge them; he has his incredibly successful TV career, with programmes like *The Hypnotic World of Paul McKenna*. His two-year contract with one television station is said to be worth about £2.5 million.

McKenna is more than just a hypnotist, however. He has become a new-style guru and many of his clients now turn to him instead of their doctor or psychiatrist. He is fascinated by phobias and is constantly getting clients with problems that their doctors just can't do anything about. Recently he saw a woman who thought her fingernails were turning into knives. Her doctors were completely at a loss to know what to do but amazingly McKenna cured her with just one half-hour session. 'I can see why people come to me,' he says. 'If you use the traditional approach, it sometimes takes six months.'

This is how it works. When the client gets there, McKenna sits them in the chair I'm sitting in. He will then hypnotise the client by having him or her fix on a point on the ceiling. After a while the 'natural relaxation of trance' sets in, the eyes close and McKenna then talks to the client. One exercise that he uses on sportspeople involves them resisting pressure from his arm. You hold your arm out straight and try to keep it there while McKenna pushes it downwards. First, you do it while thinking about something nasty (like a bad day at the dentist) and then while thinking about something nice (like a relaxing holiday you had). Oddly, it's thinking the nice thoughts that makes you stronger. I tried it, and it really works. The difference really is amazing.

I asked McKenna to put me into a trance. Initially I resisted and resisted, rather as you do just before being given a general anaesthetic, but soon found myself, not exactly 'under', but completely relaxed. One of his clients said of McKenna, 'He hypnotised me down the telephone. It gave me a really good feeling, like when you've done strenuous exercise and you feel great.' I know exactly what she means. And I'll definitely be back.

2 a Read the text again and decide if these statements are true (T), false (F) or we don't know (DK).

1 The writer is frightened of flying.

2 His clients give money to a charity that McKenna specifies.

3 Some clients go and talk to McKenna every week.

4 He hypnotises people by looking into their eyes.

5 The writer enjoyed being hypnotised by McKenna.

b Write a paragraph of about 75 words summarising the main points from the text.

c Read your partner's paragraph. Did you include the same points?

3 Discuss.

1 What is your reaction to Paul McKenna and what he does?

2 Have you (or has anyone you know) had any experience of being hypnotised? Give details.

3 Would you like to be hypnotised? Why/Why not?

4 If you were going to be hypnotised, what would you ask for help with?

Grammar | reflexive pronouns

4 Complete the reflexive pronouns 1–6 in the Active grammar box.

Active grammar

	SUBJECT PRONOUNS	REFLEXIVE PRONOUNS
Singular	I	(1) _____
	you	*yourself*
	he	(2) _____
	she	*herself*
	it	(3) _____
Plural	we	(4) _____
	you	(5) _____
	they	(6) _____

A A common use of reflexive pronouns is to talk about actions where the subject and object are the same person. The reflexive pronoun is essential to the grammar of the sentence.

He started to <u>teach himself</u> to be a hypnotist.

B We can also use reflexive pronouns for emphasis, when we mean 'that person or thing, and nobody or nothing else'. The reflexive pronoun is not essential to the grammar of the sentence, but is added for emphasis.

McKenna <u>himself</u> is a small, mousy man with glasses.

5 **a** Match the examples 1–6 with the correct rule A or B in the Active grammar box.

1 I cut myself while I was cooking.

2 Emily herself said she's not very good at maths.

3 They blamed themselves for the accident.

4 I spoke to the boss himself.

5 You should put yourself in my position and try to understand.

6 She didn't go to the hairdresser; she cut her hair herself.

b Which one of these sentences is grammatically incorrect and what do the other two sentences mean?

1 We taught ourselves how to play tennis.

2 We taught each other how to play tennis.

3 We taught us how to play tennis.

see Reference on page 143

6 Complete these sentences with *each other*, reflexive pronoun (*myself, themselves*, etc.) or object pronoun (*him, us*, etc.).

1 I _____ have never been hypnotised but I know people who have.

2 My best friend and I often know what _____ are thinking.

3 A friend gave _____ a book about acupuncture for my birthday.

4 I'm so forgetful – I'm always locking _____ out of my house.

5 People in Britain usually give _____ presents at Christmas.

6 I'd like to speak to the doctor _____ , not the receptionist.

7 The teacher taught _____ to meditate by thinking about our breathing.

8 The people in my family talk to _____ a lot.

Person to person

7 **a** Do you agree with these statements? Make brief notes about your views.

1 Most people can cure themselves of a phobia (e.g. fear of spiders) or an addiction (e.g. smoking) without getting help from a professional.

2 One of the best ways of learning is being with other students and teaching each other.

3 Parents should be punished for persistent child truancy, as well as the children themselves.

b Compare your views with other students. Do you agree with each other?

Listening

8 **10.2** Listen to three people talking about Paul McKenna and hypnosis. Which statement best summarises each person's opinion. One statement cannot be used.

1 He/She has benefited personally from hypnosis.
2 He/She admires McKenna for what he has achieved.
3 He/She thinks that going to hypnotists is often a waste of money.
4 He/She thinks it's good but doesn't understand how it works.

9 **a** Listen again and complete these verb phrases about belief and opinion.

1 I _reckon_ he's probably genuine myself.
2 I'm in _____ of just accepting it if it works for you.
3 I've always _____ that people like Paul McKenna are just good showmen.
4 I have my _____ about how much he can actually do for people in the long-term.
5 I'm _____ that hypnosis has any effect at all.
6 I'm _____ people paying for a service and getting nothing real in return.
7 I _____ hypnosis actually works for anyone.
8 I'm _____ that it was the hypnosis that helped me.
9 I _____ I would've left my job by now.

b Answer the questions about the meaning of the verb phrases.

1 Which two verb phrases mean: I feel almost certain that something is true?
2 Which three verb phrases mean: I think that something may not be true or is unlikely to happen?
3 Which two verb phrases mean: I think something is true or is likely to happen?
4 Which one verb phrase means: I agree with and support a plan, idea or system?
5 Which one verb phrase means: I disagree with and am opposed to a plan, idea or system?

Pronunciation

10 Listen again and repeat the sentences paying special attention to the pronunciation of the phrases in Ex. 9a.

11 Rewrite the sentences using the words in brackets.

1 My view has always been that there is life on other planets. (believed)
2 I think that ghosts don't really exist at all. (doubt)
3 I had a very strong feeling that I knew what she was thinking. (convinced)
4 I agree with people trying all sorts of different treatments. (favour)
5 I think that some people have supernatural powers. (reckon)
6 I am not sure about the existence of UFOs. (doubts)
7 I disagree with paying someone for a service I don't understand. (against)
8 I think it's unlikely that anyone can predict the future. (sceptical)

Speaking

12 In pairs, discuss your views about some of the topics in the box. Use the How to box and the verb phrases in Ex. 9.

> hypnosis   vegetarianism   marriage
> military service   smoking in public places
> ghosts   telepathy   Internet chat rooms

HOW TO …

ask about other people's views

What are your views on …?

What do you think of …?

Are you for or against …?

How do you feel about …?

Do you have any strong feelings about …?

13 **a** Choose a topic from Ex. 12. Prepare to talk for one minute about your views. Use the notes below to help you.

1 Say what experience you have of the topic and/or why it interests you
2 Say arguments in favour or any positive points about the topic
3 Say arguments against or any negative points
4 Say your conclusion and/or summarise your personal views

b Listen to other students give their talks. Which of the views you heard were similar to yours?

Grammar	gerunds and infinitives
Can do	write the arguments for and against a point of view

Listening

1 Discuss.

1 What are the people in each picture doing?

2 What do you think their aim is in each case?

3 What different techniques are they using to achieve their aim?

2 **10.3** Listen to an extract from a radio programme and decide which two of these things are being discussed: a) advertising, b) politicians, c) supermarkets.

3 Listen again and complete the notes.

> **Persuasion**
>
> 1 Where persuasion takes place: *television*, ... _____
>
> 2 Large amounts of money spent on: _____
>
> **Supermarkets**
>
> 3 Two ways to relax customers: _____
>
> 4 Why reward cards are good for supermarkets: _____
>
> **Advertising**
>
> 5 Two types of advert: _____
>
> 6 Adverts for cleaning products: _____
>
> 7 Most powerful adverts: _____
>
> 8 Adverts for luxury cars: _____
>
> 9 Adverts which use famous people: _____

4 Discuss.

1 What do you think about the ways that supermarkets persuade you to buy more things or visit more frequently?

2 How much do you think you are influenced by advertising?

3 Can you describe an advert that you particularly like or that has stuck in your mind? Why do you like it or why do you think you've remembered it?

Vocabulary | advertising

5 Choose the correct alternatives.

1 Have you got any favourite *advertising/advertisements*?

2 What are three of the best-known *target markets/makes* of clothing in your country?

3 Would you like to work in *commercial break/marketing*?

4 Do you think you would be good at thinking up *commercial breaks/slogans*?

5 What do you usually do during *commercial breaks/marketing* on TV?

6 Have you ever bought anything through a *target market/classified* ad?

7 Which film has had a lot of *classified ads/hype* recently?

8 What do you think the *hype/target market* is for eight-seater 'people-carrier' vehicles?

Pronunciation

6 a **10.4** Listen to these three words and mark where the main stress is. Is it on the same syllable or not?

1 advertising

2 advertisement

3 advert

b Choose four of the questions in Ex. 5 to ask and answer with a partner.

Grammar | gerunds and infinitives

7   a Look at the verbs in **bold** in sentences 1–5 in the Active grammar box and choose the correct alternatives.

   b **10.5** Listen and check your answers.

   c Write the verbs in **bold** in the correct place in the Active grammar box.

Active grammar

1 They **persuade** us *buying/to buy* things we may not want.
2 We **carry on** *using/to use* reward cards at the same supermarket.
3 Adverts for clothes often **want** *making/to make* us feel that we belong.
4 I **try** *resisting/to resist* buying expensive designer clothes but it's difficult!
5 You could **try** *leaving/to leave* your credit card at home if you don't want to spend so much.

verb + gerund	*carry on*
verb + infinitive	
verb + object + infinitive	
verb + gerund OR verb + infinitive with a different meaning	

---

8   a Check the meaning of the verbs in the box. Then, write them in the correct place in the Active grammar box. Use a dictionary if necessary.

> advise   agree   allow   arrange   avoid   encourage   hope
> practise   regret   remember   stop   suggest

   b Look at these pairs of sentences. What is the difference in meaning between the underlined parts in each pair?

1 a The TV remote control wouldn't work so I <u>tried changing</u> the batteries.
   b I <u>tried to change</u> the batteries in the remote control but I couldn't open it.

2 a Did you <u>remember to buy</u> some shampoo when you were out?
   b I <u>remember buying</u> some more shampoo but now I can't find it.

3 a I <u>regret to tell</u> you that you failed your final exam.
   b I <u>regret telling</u> her that I failed my final exam.

4 a The news was on but we <u>stopped watching</u> when the adverts came on.
   b We were having lunch but we <u>stopped to watch</u> the news.

see Reference page 143

---

9 Complete the second sentence in each pair, so it has the same meaning as the first. Use between two and four words including the word in **bold**.

As a rehearsal, I gave the speech in front of a mirror.
practised
I practised giving the speech in front of a mirror.

1 'Why don't we go to the cinema?' he said.
   suggested
   He _____ to the cinema.

2 'You really should get a job in advertising,' she said to me.
   encouraged
   She _____ a job in advertising.

3 I made an attempt to speak to her on the phone but she was out.
   tried
   I _____ to her on the phone but she was out.

4 'OK. I'll give you a lift to the airport,' he said.
   agreed
   He _____ me a lift to the airport.

5 I used to come here when I was a child.
   remember
   I _____ here when I was a child.

6 'If I were you, I'd see a doctor,' he said.
   advised
   He _____ see a doctor.

7 We drove the long way so we wouldn't get stuck in traffic.
   avoid
   We drove the long way to _____ stuck in traffic.

8 'Go on! Buy the jeans and the boots! They're so cheap,' she said to me.
   persuaded
   She _____ the jeans and the boots.

Person to person

10 Talk to different students in the class and find someone who …

- … was allowed to watch as much TV as he/she wanted as a child
- … regrets not learning to play a musical instrument as a child
- … has arranged to do something exciting this weekend
- … hopes to travel to a different continent next year
- … remembers what they were doing on 31st December 1999
- … has tried to give up smoking

Writing

11 a Discuss the statement in pairs. Do you agree? Why/Why not?

Advertising on TV during children's programmes should not be allowed.

b The sentences in the box are taken from an essay. Complete the table with the correct paragraph number 1–4.

Paragraph 1: Introduction – general statement about the issue
Paragraph 2: Arguments in favour of the statement
Paragraph 3: Arguments against the statement
Paragraph 4: Conclusion – briefly summarise your opinion

Paragraph 2	A Firstly, companies know that children can be persuaded to want things very easily.
	B Finally, it is important to remember that many children enjoy watching advertisements and finding out what is available in the shops.
	C In conclusion, I think it is the parents' responsibility to control how much television their children watch.
	D In this essay, I will consider the question of whether companies should be allowed to advertise to children on television.
	E On the other hand, it is not only the companies who have responsibility for what children watch.
	F On balance, I am convinced that companies should be banned from advertising to children, especially on television.
	G Another reason why they should not be allowed to advertise to children is that they are using children to make their parents spend more.
	H This is an important issue and there are strong feelings on both sides of the argument.

12 Choose a topic for your essay using one of the statements below or something else you feel strongly about. Write down arguments in favour and against your statement.

1 teenagers should not be allowed to wear designer clothes or shoes at school

2 small, local shops are better for the community than large supermarkets

3 background music and TV screens should be banned in public places, e.g. cafés, waiting rooms, shops, etc.

13 a Write an essay about your statement. Use the plan and the language in the table in Ex. 11b and your notes to help you.

b Read another student's essay. Do you agree with his/her final conclusion? Why/Why not?

Grammar	*if* structures (2)
Can do	talk about your regrets and resolutions

Reading

1 Read the short text below and answer the questions.

   1 What is the matter with Bernard Marx?

   2 Why is this a problem for him in his world?

2 Read the extract and answer this question: What are the babies learning while they are asleep?

   1 what different types of work they could choose to do in the future

   2 how to get on well with other children

   3 how to be happy with their future role in society

Aldous Huxley wrote *Brave New World* in 1932. It remains one of the most powerful science fiction stories ever.

It is set in a future where peace and good health are compulsory but love and parenthood are obsolete. Thinking for yourself, being an individual and being unhappy are not allowed. Babies are produced and 'brought up' scientifically in 'Hatchery and Conditioning Centres'.

But one of the main characters, Bernard Marx, refuses to be happy and to fit in. He is haunted by the feeling that there must be more to his life than this.

'Silence, silence,' whispered a loud speaker. 'Silence, silence,' repeated other loudspeakers at intervals along the corridor. The students and even the Director himself, without thinking, obeyed the voices and walked on the tips of their toes. They were Alphas, of course, but even Alphas have been well conditioned. 'Silence, silence.' The air of the fourteenth floor was heavy with the whispered command.

The Director carefully opened a door. They entered a room where the light was very low. Eighty little beds stood in a row against the wall. All that could be heard was light regular breathing and a continuous hum like the sound of very faint voices speaking softly at a great distance.

A nurse stood up as they entered. 'What's the lesson this afternoon?' the Director asked quietly. 'Elementary Class Consciousness,' she answered. The Director walked slowly down the long line of beds. In each one lay a child asleep. Eighty little boys and girls with pink, healthy faces lay there softly breathing. There was a whisper under every bedcover. 'Elementary Class Consciousness, did you say? Let's have it repeated a little louder by the loudspeaker.'

At the end of the room a loud speaker hung on the wall. The Director walked up to it and pressed a switch.

'... all wear green,' said a soft but very distinct voice, beginning in the middle of a sentence, 'and Delta Children wear light brown. Oh no, I don't want to play with Delta children. And Epsilons are even worse. They're too stupid to be able to read or write. Besides, they wear black, which is such an ugly colour. I'm so glad I'm a Beta.'

There was a pause, then the voice began again.

'Alpha children wear grey. They work much harder than we do, because they're so clever. I'm really very glad I'm a Beta, because I don't work so hard. And then we are much better than the Gammas and Deltas. Gammas are stupid. They all wear green, and Delta children wear light brown. Oh no, I don't want to play with Delta children. And Epsilons are even worse.'

The Director pushed back the switch. The voice sank to the faintest of whispers which could just be heard from beneath the eighty bedcovers.

'They'll have that repeated a hundred and twenty times three times a week for thirty months while they are sleeping, then they go on to a more advanced lesson. Sleep-teaching is the most powerful force of all time in social education. The child's mind becomes these suggestions and the total of these suggestions is the child's mind. And not only the child's mind. The adult's mind too, all his life long. The mind that thinks and desires and decides. But all these suggestions are our suggestions!' The Director almost shouted in his enthusiasm. 'Suggestions from the State.

(Extract from: *Brave New World* by Aldous Huxley, Penguin Readers, Level 6)

3 Read the text again and write the question for each of these answers.

1 Because the loudspeakers were whispering 'Silence'.

   Why were the students walking quietly along the corridor?

2 They heard children breathing and the sound of quiet voices talking.

3 They looked healthy with pink faces.

4 Because he wanted the students to be able to hear what the loudspeakers were saying to the children.

5 Epsilons.

6 Betas.

7 360 times.

8 When they're thirty months old.

9 It means that the child learns to think in exactly the way he/she is taught.

10 The fact that the suggestions are all controlled by him and the State.

4 Discuss.

1 What do you think of the extract? How does it make you feel?

2 What kind of world does the book describe? Do you know of any other books or films that depict futuristic worlds?

3 Do you think that people in our world are conditioned to do certain things?

Vocabulary | ways of speaking

5 **a** Work in A/B groups. Look at the words/ phrases in the table. Using a dictionary, find the following: a) the meaning, b) the pronunciation, c) an example sentence.

GROUP A	GROUP B
to whisper	to mumble
to shriek	to interrupt
to blurt out	to speak your mind
to be lost for words	to have a word with

b In A/B pairs, tell each other the meaning, pronunciation and example sentence for each word/phrase.

6 **a** Complete the quotes with the correct form of the words/phrases from Ex.5.

1 'I told a colleague that I'd been using one of those self-help CDs to help deal with my stress. Then, in the middle of a meeting with some other colleagues, he suddenly _____ everything I'd told him. Honestly, I _____ – I was so shocked I didn't know what to say.'

2 'I went to the cinema last weekend and the people behind me were _____ to each other throughout the whole film. They didn't seem to notice that they were annoying everyone else. In the end, my friend _____ them and they stopped, but by that time the film was nearly over.'

3 'My cousin has been staying with me for the last week. I must say she's quite irritating. She's really loud and every time I say anything she _____ with laughter. The other thing she does is constantly _____ people when they're in the middle of a conversation. I don't mean to be horrible but I'll be really glad when she goes!'

4 'I did my first presentation at work yesterday and it was OK. But at the end one of my colleagues told me that I had been _____ and he couldn't really hear me. He's the kind of person who isn't afraid to _____ and I was a bit upset at first. I suppose it's useful feedback though.'

b **10.6** Listen and check your answers.

7 Choose three of the words/phrases from Ex. 5a. Tell your partner about different situations in which you or someone else spoke in each of these ways.

Grammar | *if* structures (2)

8 **a** Match the examples 1–3 with the correct uses A–C in the Active grammar box.

1 *If parents always speak two languages to their children, they become bilingual.*

2 *If she works really hard, she'll pass her exams.*

3 *If I won a lot of money, I'd give up my job.*

b Now match examples 4–6 with the correct meanings D–F.

4 *If she had studied harder, she would be at university now.*

5 *If she didn't study as hard as she does, she would have failed the test.*

6 *If he had memorised his verbs, he wouldn't have failed the test.*

Active grammar

Uses

A First conditional: to talk about future possibility

B Second conditional: to talk about present or future unreal or imagined situations

C Zero conditional: to talk about things that always happen

D Third conditional: to talk about past unreal situations with a past result

E A mixed conditional: with an '*if* clause', referring to the past and a main clause referring to the present/future

F A mixed conditional: with an '*if* clause', referring to the present/future and a main clause referring to the past

Modal verbs (*can*, *could*, *might*, etc.) can be used in First, Second, Third and mixed conditionals instead of *will* and *would*.

Form:

a) *First conditional* = *If* + Present Simple, *will* + infinitive

b) _____ = *If* + Past Simple, *would* + infinitive

c) _____ = *If* + Past Perfect, *would have* + past participle

d) _____ = *If* + Present Simple, Present Simple

e) _____ = *If* + Past Perfect, *would* + infinitive OR *If* + Past Simple, *would have* + past participle

---

9 **a** Look at the rules of form a–e in the Active grammar box and write the correct type of conditional next to each one.

b Look at the examples and choose the correct alternatives from rules 1 and 2 below.

If you talk to babies a lot, they will learn to speak quickly.

Provided you talk to babies a lot, they will learn to speak quickly.

Unless you talk to babies a lot, they won't learn to speak quickly.

1 *unless/provided* has a similar meaning to *if*.

2 *unless/provided* means *if not*.

see Reference page 143

10 What type of conditional is each sentence? Correct the grammar mistake in each one.

1 If I had more time, I'll go and study English abroad.

2 If parents shouted at their children, they become aggressive.

3 I speak English fluently now if I'd learned it as a child.

4 I usually remember vocabulary, provided I'll write it down.

5 If you'll repeat a word enough times, you'll probably remember it.

6 If I'd attended more lessons, I would passed my exams.

7 I'd have a better job if I passed my exam.

8 If a student reads books in English, his/her vocabulary improved.

Person to person

11 Which of the sentences in Ex. 10 apply to you or do you think are true? Tell a partner.

Speaking

12 **a** Look at the sentences in Ex. 10. Which of them could be:

1 regrets

2 resolutions

b Think about your language learning or your school/work life. Make a note of one or two of your regrets and your resolutions using *if* structures.

c Compare your lists with a partner. Have you got any of the same resolutions?

Commonly misspelt words

1 a Discuss these questions.

1 How many basic spelling rules do you think there are in English?

a twenty-five

b sixty

c ninety

2 How many different ways do you think there are for spelling the sound /iː/?

a at least five

b at least eight

c at least twelve

3 What do you think the *Spelling Society* in Britain wants to do?

a simplify English spelling

b encourage correct spelling

c go back to old spelling rules

b Read the text and check your answers.

There are ninety basic spelling rules in English and eighty-four of these have exceptions! For some sounds, there are no clear rules at all and identical sounds can be spelt in several different ways. For example, the sound /iː/ can be spelt as in: seem, team, theme; sardine, protein, thief, people, he, key, ski, debris, quay.

The Spelling Society in Britain thinks that the English spelling system should be simplified. They say, for example, that we should spell the sound /iː/ simply as 'ee', e.g. peeple, and save learners a lot of time and effort. Until then, however, it's just a question of lots of learning and testing!

2 Choose the correct spelling for each pair of words?

1 beleive/believe

2 intelligence/intelligance

3 subconscious/subconsious

4 psychologist/pyschologist

5 dout/doubt

6 existance/existence

7 successful/successfull

8 responsability/responsibility

3 a Find the 18 common spelling mistakes in the email and correct them.

Dear Emine

Hi. How are you? I'm having a grate time. All the people I've met have been very genrous. Of course, I'm still a foriener here and it felt wierd at first, but I'm begining to feel more at home now. The wether is definately very changable – and it rains a lot! So that feels like home!

I've now got my accomodation sorted out. I'm living in an intresting part of town with lots of restraunts and a good libarry round the corner. Everything is very close so it's not really nessasry to go to school by bus. I usally walk, although I occasionly get a lift with some freinds in there car.

I'm going to send a seperate email to Mum and Dad. But say 'hi' to Murat from me. I'll write again soon.

Lots of love, Melisa

b Compare with a partner. Do you agree?

4 a **10.7** Listen and say which of these questions the student does NOT talk about.

1 Why is it important to spell accurately?

2 Why is it difficult to spell accurately in English?

3 Are there any words that you particularly like or dislike the spelling of?

4 What are some of the ways you use to remember how to spell words?

b Discuss the questions with other students.

Lifelong learning

Spelling test

Can you add any more tips to this list?

- use a dictionary to check spelling
- keep a notebook of words you find difficult to spell
- choose ten words to learn how to spell every week. Ask a friend to test you.
- use a computer spell-check

10 Communication

How does your mind work?

William Shakespeare

Albert Einstein   Madonna   Nelson Mandela   Buddha

1 Discuss.

  1 What do you know about each of the people in the photos?

  2 Whose approach to life do you think is most similar to yours? In what ways?

2 **a** Do the quiz and make notes about your own answers. Use the ideas in the boxes and your own ideas.

  b Now do the quiz with your partner and make a note of his/her answers.

  1 What would you most like to spend your time doing when you're on holiday?

> playing sports   doing nothing
> reading a good book   doing a puzzle book
> talking to local people

  2 When you're learning a language, which of these appeals to you most?

> analysing grammatical rules
> speaking without worrying about mistakes
> immersing yourself totally in the country where the language is spoken

  3 Which one of these would you be most keen on doing as part of your work?

> working together in a team
> writing a story or poem
> doing scientific research
> doing something practical   being outdoors

  4 When you're in a group, which one of these are you most likely to do?

> wonder what other people are thinking
> be the 'entertainer' who keeps the mood high
> speak on behalf of the group
> take control of any money or number issues
> keep the group focussed on reaching its goal

  5 Do any of these statements describe you? If not, write one which does.

> I enjoy dancing.
> I like trying to figure people out.
> I like telling stories.
> I'm interested in science.
> I enjoy a good discussion.

  6 Which of these jobs would you like to do most?

> politician   artist   journalist   lawyer
> psychologist   teacher   astronaut   nurse

3 Compare your notes with the descriptions on page 150. Then discuss these questions.

  1 Which description do you think you are most like?

  2 Which description do you think your partner is most like?

  3 Do you and your partner think/learn in a similar or a different way?

Reflexive pronouns

Singular: *myself/yourself/himself/herself/itself*
Plural: *ourselves/yourselves/themselves*

We use reflexive pronouns to talk about actions where the subject and object are the same person. The reflexive pronoun is essential to the grammar of the sentence and would not make sense without it.

I cut myself while I was cooking.

We can also use reflexive pronouns for emphasis, when we mean 'that person or thing, and nobody or nothing else'. In this case, the reflexive pronoun is not essential to the grammar of the sentence, but is added for emphasis.

They built that house themselves.

Gerunds and infinitives

Some verbs are followed by particular structures. The following verbs are some of the most common ones for each structure.

Verb + gerund: enjoy, avoid, imagine, consider, finish, miss, practise, involve, carry on, suggest

Does the job involve working in the evenings?

Verb + infinitive: want, seem, offer, decide, hope, afford, agree, arrange, promise, refuse, manage

He offered to give me a lift into town.

Verb + object + infinitive: persuade, convince, encourage, allow, advise

I encouraged her to work as hard as she could.

Verb + gerund OR verb + infinitive – with a different meaning: remember, regret, try, stop, go on

I stopped talking to Sam. (I was talking to Sam and then I stopped)

I stopped to talk to Sam. (I stopped what I was doing and started talking to Sam)

If structures (2)

If structures or conditional sentences generally have two clauses. The '*if* clause' can come first or second. When the '*if* clause' is first, we need a comma at the end of the clause.

Use the First Conditional to talk about future possibility.

If + Present Simple or Present Continuous or Present Perfect, *will/could/should/might/may/going to* + verb or Present Continuous or Imperative

If you're going to the party tomorrow, I'll see you there.

Use the Second Conditional to talk about present or future unreal or imagined situations.

If + Past Simple/Past Continuous, *would/could/ should/might* + infinitive

He'd be much more healthy if he didn't smoke.

Use the Third Conditional to talk about past unreal situations with a past result.

If + Past Perfect, *would have/could have/should have/might have* + past participle

If you hadn't been so rude, he wouldn't have walked out.

Use the Zero Conditional to talk about things that always happen.

If + Present Simple, Present Simple

If you heat ice, it melts.

Use Mixed Conditionals:

with an '*if* clause' referring to the past and a main clause referring to the present/future

If + Past Perfect, *would* (or *'d*) + infinitive

If we hadn't missed the plane, we'd be in Spain now.

with an '*if* clause' referring to the present/future and a main clause referring to the past

If you didn't want to come to the theatre tomorrow, I wouldn't have bothered getting you a ticket.

We can use modals in the First, Second, Third and Mixed Conditionals.

If you see James, you should invite him to the party.

If I had studied harder, I might have passed my exam.

Key vocabulary

The power of the mind
willpower, mind over matter, the power of persuasion, to have a premonition, to have a feeling of déjà vu, to trust your intuition, your sixth sense, to be unconscious, subconscious (fears)

Belief and opinion
to reckon, to suspect, to doubt, to have your doubts about, to be sceptical that, to have always believed that, to be convinced, to be in favour of, to be against

Advertising
advertisement, classified ad, commercial break, advertising, marketing, target market, slogan, make, hype

Speaking
to whisper, to shriek, to mumble, to blurt out, to interrupt, to speak your mind, to have a word with, to be lost for words

Commonly misspelt words
accommodation, beginning, believe, changeable, definitely, doubt, existence, friend, foreigner, great/grate, generous, intelligence, interesting, library, necessary, occasionally, psychologist, responsibility, restaurants, separate, subconscious, successful, there/their/they're, usually, weird, weather/whether

1 Complete each sentence using the correct form of a verb from the box. Use a reflexive pronoun where necessary.

> relax   feel   ~~blame~~   enjoy   express   meet
> hurt   concentrate   burn

They are blaming themselves for the accident, but it wasn't their fault.

1 Don't touch the iron. You'll _____ .
2 I _____ very disappointed when I found out I'd failed my driving test.
3 She's a good speaker. She _____ very clearly.
4 You've worked hard today. You should sit down and _____ now.
5 Jack's gone to the doctor because he _____ while he was playing football this morning.
6 My boss and I are going to _____ for lunch tomorrow.
7 Thank you for the party. We really _____ .
8 I _____ as hard as I could on the maths lesson, but I still couldn't understand it.

2 Find the mistakes in six of the sentences and correct them.

The manager agreed giving my money back. → to give

1 We encourage all students doing some voluntary work.
2 I've arranged visiting my grandparents on Saturday.
3 I couldn't avoid hitting the dog as it ran out in front of my car.
4 I remember to go to the park every day after school when I was a child.
5 He persuaded me joining the new gym with him.
6 My teacher suggested to learn ten new spellings every week.
7 Please will you stop talking for a minute.
8 He advised to have us an early night before the exam.

3 Complete the sentences with the correct form of the verbs in brackets. There is sometimes more than one correct answer.

If we don't go and see Jane, she 'll be (be) really upset. (or ... she might be ...)

1 If you _____ (not go) to bed late last night, you wouldn't be so tired.
2 You'd feel a lot better if you _____ (do) more exercise.

3 Dogs _____ (behave) very well if you train them properly.
4 If I _____ (bring) enough money, I would have paid for your dinner.
5 He'll miss the beginning of the film if he _____ (not arrive) soon.
6 If you _____ (press) that button, you get cold water.
7 What _____ (you/do) if you lost your passport?
8 I _____ (lie) on a beach now if I'd booked that holiday.

4 Complete the sentences with the correct form of the words in the box. Three of the words cannot be used.

> hype   ~~déjà vu~~   premonition   slogan   make
> interrupt   shriek   convince   blurt   intuition
> mumble   reckon

I was sure I'd seen her before. I had a strong feeling of déjà vu.

1 I'm _____ that recycling is essential for helping the environment.
2 Don't believe all the _____ about that new film. It's not much good.
3 Can you let me finish what I'm saying without _____ me all the time?
4 I _____ he knows something that he's not telling us.
5 The surprise was spoilt because he _____ out the whole plan before I could stop him.
6 Don't worry about other people. Trust your _____ and do what you want.
7 I don't really care what _____ of jeans I wear as long as they're comfortable.
8 I'm not going in a car today. I had a _____ about being in a car accident.

5 Find the misspelt words in six of the sentences and correct them.

1 I'll definately see you tomorrow evening.
2 Finding cheap accomodation in London is very difficult.
3 Having children is an enormous responsability.
4 We went to a great new restaurant yesterday.
5 Could you put the sandwiches in seperate bags please?
6 Have you seen there new house?
7 I can't believe how rude the waiter was!
8 My sister is an extremely sucessful designer.

Communication activities

Lesson 2.3 | Ex. 4b, page 27

B

Mma Makutsi looked at her and then looked down at the typewriter keyboard. She opened a drawer, peered inside, and then closed it. At that moment a hen came into the room from the yard outside and pecked at something on the floor. 'Get out,' shouted Mma Makutsi. 'No chickens in here!' At ten o'clock Mma Makutsi got up from her desk and went into the back room to make the tea. She had been asked to make bush tea, which was Mma Ramotswe's favourite, and she soon brought two cups back. She had a tin of condensed milk in her handbag, and she took this out and poured a small amount into each cup. Then they drank their tea, watching a small boy at the edge of the road throwing stones at a skeletal dog.

At eleven o'clock they had another cup of tea, and at twelve Mma Ramotswe rose to her feet and announced that she was going to walk down the road to the shops to buy herself some perfume. Mma Makutsi was to stay behind in case the telephone rang and in case any clients came in. Mma Ramotswe smiled as she said this. There would be no clients, of course. And she would be closed at the end of the month. Did Mma Makutsi understand what a disastrous job she had obtained for herself? A woman with an average of ninety–seven per cent deserved better than this.

Mma Ramotswe was standing at the counter of the shop looking at a bottle of perfume when Mma Makutsi hurtled through the door. 'Mma Ramotswe,' she panted. 'A client. There is a client in the office. It is a big case. A missing man. Come quickly. There is no time to lose.'

Lesson 4.3 | Ex. 11a, page 56

Student B

Communication 9 | Ex. 2, page 128

6 Explanation

The airplane was on the ground when he leapt.

Lesson 6.2 | Ex. 13b, page 81

Student B

Camel trips at Dakhla Oasis Egypt

Price: $160 per person per night

Where?

Dakhla Oasis is about 850km from Cairo. The hotel is situated at the top of pink cliffs which surround the oasis below. Within the oasis, there are beautiful fields and gardens full of grapes, olive trees, date palms, figs, apricots and citrus fruits. Beyond the oasis, there are the incredible sand dunes of the Sahara Desert.

Accommodation

Dakhla has 32 large rooms all with private bathrooms. The rooms are simply but tastefully furnished in the local style. They all have fans and also heaters for the cold winter nights. Some rooms have a terrace with spectacular views of the nearby mountain range. The restaurant serves delicious local food including the traditional 'falafel'.

Activities

There are camel trips and walking tours available from half a day to 3-plus days. These go across the sand dunes of the desert and also up into the mountains. The guides will help you set up the tents and prepare a delicious barbecue dinner on the campfire with homemade bread, baked in the sand.

Communication 2 | Ex. 4, page 30

London Centre for Business Studies

BSc Business Studies: Full-time, Part-time or Online Learning – a flexible mode of study which allows you to combine online learning with university-based study.

We offer excellent facilities and tuition to the candidate who is committed to taking initiative and studying to his/her full potential.

Many places available for mature students and overseas students.

For more information and to apply, contact:
Ms. A. Owen,
London Centre for Business Studies,
22 Gower Road, London, NW3

Nursing Diploma - Cambridge

Our programme is a full time, 3-year course leading to an academic qualification and professional registration as a nurse. Half the course is classroom or private study and the remaining time is practice-based. Right from the start, students will be working with patients, with appropriate support, and this will involve working some evenings, nights and weekends. The training will be demanding. However, the potential personal rewards can also be great.

You will need to have school-leaving qualifications and to be at least 17 years old at the start of the course.

To apply: request an application pack online from **www.nmas.ac.uk**

Lesson 4.3 | Ex. 2, page 54

MILLION DOLLAR BABY

After a painful separation from his daughter, boxing trainer Frankie Dunn (Clint Eastwood) has been unwilling to risk letting himself get close to anyone for a very long time - then Maggie Fitzgerald (Hilary Swank) walks into his gym. In a life of constant struggle, Maggie has got herself this far on raw talent, clear focus and an incredible strength of will. But more than anything, she wants someone to believe in her.
The last thing Frankie wants is this kind of responsibility - let alone this kind of risk. However, he is won over by Maggie's determination and reluctantly agrees to take her on. Over time, the two come to discover that they share a common spirit that rises above the pain and loss of their pasts, and they find in each other a sense of family they lost long ago.
The pinnacle of their work together comes when Maggie has a chance to fight for the world championship. However, after an illegal punch from her opponent, she falls and hits her head on a wooden stool. She is then paralysed from the neck down. Struggling with the guilt and pain of seeing her in this state, Frankie tries to do everything he can to take care of her. This makes it even more difficult when she asks him to help her end it all.

Lesson 3.1 | Ex. 3, page 34

1 Who is/are described as the hero(es) in the film?
2 Is the reviewer generally positive or negative about the film?

TROY

a review by *Andrew Mansfield*

The film *Troy*, made in 2004, was inspired by Homer's Iliad, an epic work originally written over 28 centuries ago. Homer's Iliad describes the horrors and brutality of war. In this modern-day film, however, director Wolfgang Petersen takes a different look at the story – through the eyes of the real people caught up in a terrifying experience.

In order to achieve such realism, Petersen chose to focus on the people, especially the raging Achilles (played by Brad Pitt) and the honourable Hector (Eric Bana). There is much historical detail, impressive recreations of Troy and the wooden horse and more than 2,000 'extras'. There are also some spectacular battle scenes but the story remains intimate and human.

Both Brad Pitt as Achilles and Peter O'Toole as King Priam have huge presence on the screen but it is Eric Bana as Hector who is brilliant throughout the film. With his nobility and gentle authority, Bana is far more convincing and far more heroic than anyone else. His final confrontation with Achilles is one of the film's most important moments – the most thrilling fight of all.

The film is long and it has had its criticisms. Some people don't approve of the differences between Homer's 'original' and what is shown here. But to my mind, although Homer wrote stories based on truth, we don't know the real truth. The film Troy is another look at those stories. And by focussing on the human angle of this epic story of love and war, in my opinion Petersen has crafted an impressive film.

Star rating: ★ ★ ★ ★
(Maximum ★ ★ ★ ★ ★)

Lesson 3.1 | Ex. 8, page 35

Student A

Place: Verona, Italy
Background: Capulets (Juliet's family) and Montagues (Romeo's family) are two families with long-standing history of fighting each other
Monday:
Romeo and Juliet get married
Wednesday:
Romeo finds out about Juliet and thinks she is dead
Romeo kills Paris
Romeo then drinks some poison and kills himself

Communication 9 | Ex. 2, page 128

3 Explanation
He was riding a horse called "Friday" …

Lesson 3.3 | Ex. 3, page 40

Student A

Communication 6 | Ex. 3a, page 86

You love your creature comforts

You love your holidays but you prefer a touch of home wherever you go. Creature comforts mean a lot to you. Trekking through the desert with a camel for company is probably not your idea of a great holiday. You prefer a complete rest and lots of sun.

You love a touch of adventure

You're a bit of an adventurer compared to some holidaymakers. You hate lying around sunbathing, but prefer something different, such as white-water rafting. However, you also prefer to sleep in a nice bed in a good hotel after a hard day's adventure.

You love to be independent

You're a true independent traveller who probably avoids package holidays and is rarely seen on a Greek island or the Costa del Sol. You love exploring far-flung countries and mixing with the locals. And you've probably got cupboards full of photos and interesting souvenirs.

You're a real explorer

You have the spirit of a Stanley or Livingstone – a real explorer who loves to get lost in places where no tourist has gone before. You love meeting the locals, hate bumping into anyone who speaks your language and don't mind sleeping in the open with the local wildlife for company.

Letters to the Editor

The good old days?

In last week's edition, Oliver Hughes lamented the passing of 'the good old days'. According to him, we now have identical high streets worldwide, local cultures have been eroded and national identities have all but disappeared. I, personally, couldn't believe how negative his article was. I strongly disagree with almost everything he said. Far from the uniformity he was describing, we now live in a world of incredible diversity and that can only be good.

In the old days, we were far more stereotyped and more pigeon-holed by our nationality or where we lived. You were an Italian in Italy, you were expected to be, like and do things like 'an Italian'. The beauty of the new international view is that it can free people from the tyranny of geography. Just because someone lives in France does not mean they can only speak French, eat French food and listen to French music. We can now take it for granted that a Frenchman, or an American, or a Japanese person takes holidays in Spain or Florida, eats sushi or spaghetti for dinner and has friends from around the world.

I see this diversity and availability as an extremely good thing. Look at things on a local level. Oliver Hughes may think that every high street is the same. I disagree. Yes, people from many different countries may recognise some of the shops but I can now go down my high street and I have choice! I can choose to eat many different types of food. I can also buy clothes from shops originally from many different places: we've got shops like Zara from Spain and Muji from Japan, as well as countless brands from all over the world. Far from having limited choice; the choice is almost endless.

There is no doubt that in some ways the world is becoming more uniform but the significance of this uniformity is often exaggerated. Different cultures remain and we can choose to be the same or different. The truth is that we increasingly define ourselves rather than let others define us. Being Italian or American or Polish does not define who you are: it is part of who you are. It seems to me that most people want the best of both worlds – old and new. Admit it, Oliver Hughes! Most of us want to have our cake AND eat it, don't we? And maybe we can!

Paul Hodge, London E5

Lesson 3.3 | Ex. 3, page 40

Student B

I read Oliver Hughes' article 'The good old days' last week with interest. Despite making some sensible points, to my mind his argument is wildly oversimplified in saying that the old days were better. All too often nowadays, we hear these black and white opinions about 'globalisation'. In my opinion, it's a grey area and there are important benefits as well as some inevitable downsides as we move away from the 'good old days'.

I feel that thriving cultures are not fixed and many of the best things come from cultures mixing. For example, Indian food in Britain is not the same as an authentic curry from India, but for some, it's even better. Even branded goods are often changed to suit local tastes, with McDonald's selling beer in France, lamb in India, and chilli in Mexico.

As far as I can see, the same is true of music. According to Oliver Hughes, all we ever listen to now is bland American-influenced music. I know for a fact that the evidence does not back this up. Latin American salsa, Brazilian lambada, and African music are all popular throughout the world, as well as a massive intermixing of musical types. And alongside this incredible diversity now available across the world, in most countries, local artists still top the charts. So, local tastes are alive and well, AND even more variety is being created.

Another point which Mr Hughes failed to convince me about was about English 'taking over the world' as he put it. I don't think so! I agree that huge numbers of people now speak English: around 380 million people speak it as their first language and another 250 million or so as their second. However, in many cases, a new type of English has been created. Many people across the world now speak a 'global English' which facilitates communication in an ever-shrinking, ever-more commercial world. People certainly don't want a single world language, but a new common global language has major advantages for global business, scientific research and tourism.

Some people may be saddened by the passing of the 'old days' but it seems to me that most people are embracing the mixing of cultures and the new things that are being created all the time.

Mr. L. Bishop, Near Manchester

Communication 9 | Ex. 2, page 128

4   **Explanation**
Because Bobby was only 9 months old ...

Lesson 4.2 | Ex. 4, page 51

Student A

To relax and prevent tension build-up in your hands and wrists.

1   With elbows out, push your fingertips together. Keep pressing firmly for 10 seconds. Relax hands together and repeat.

2   Tuck your elbows into your sides. Hold your hands out in front of you, palms down. Beginning with the thumbs and index fingers touching, flick each finger away in turn. Then reverse back from the little fingers.

3   Rest your forearms on your desk, fingers soft and relaxed. Keeping your little fingers in contact with the desk, roll your hands outwards so that both palms face the ceiling. Then roll the hands inwards.

Lesson 3.1 | Ex. 8, page 35

Student B

Sunday:

Juliet's father promises that Juliet will marry Paris (the son of the Prince of Verona)

Romeo and Juliet meet, fall in love and decide to marry

Tuesday:

Juliet is told she will marry Paris the next day

Juliet takes a 'sleeping potion' to pretend to be dead

Thursday:

Juliet wakes up from the effects of the 'sleeping potion'

She discovers Romeo is dead and kills herself

The two families find their two children dead and make peace with each other

Lesson 9.1 | Ex. 11, page 120

Story 1

At 5a.m. one September morning two would-be robbers from Edmonton in Canada, raided a small petrol station in Vancouver. After locking the attendant in the toilets, they made their getaway with a few hundred dollars. Coming from Edmonton, they didn't know their way around Vancouver and twenty minutes later they drove up at the same petrol station to ask directions.

The attendant, Mr. Karnail Dhillon, having just escaped from the toilets, was alarmed to see the two robbers coming into the shop again. "They wanted me to tell them the way to Port Moody," he said. "I guess they didn't recognise me or the petrol station."

He was just calling the police when the pair came back again to say that they couldn't get their car to start. While they were waiting for a mechanic to help them, the police arrived and arrested them.

Lesson 4.3 | Ex. 11a, page 56

Student A

Lesson 4.2 | Ex. 4, page 51

Student B

Do this sitting or standing. It's great for stiff shoulders and necks.

1 Sit on the edge of your chair, feet parallel, flat on the floor and about 30 cm apart.
2 Put your left hand behind your back, palm outwards. Make it go as high up between your shoulder blades as you can (use your other arm to help it up).
3 Breathe in and raise your right hand up to the ceiling. Then relax all of your right side as you breathe out.
4 Breathe in and stretch towards the ceiling.
5 Breathe out and drop your right hand down behind you to take hold of the waiting left fingers. Keep shoulders and elbows back.
6 Hold for two breaths, release hands and repeat on the opposite side.

Tip: If you find that you cannot reach, hold a tie or belt or scarf in the top hand and let it hang down so that the lower hand can catch hold of it. Try moving hands closer together using it and you should improve the looseness of your shoulders.

Communication 9 | Ex. 2, page 128

1 **Explanation**
The teenagers were travelling on the road that crossed the road that the police officer was on. They drove through a green light.

Communication activities

Lesson 4.1 | Ex. 10b, page 50

I blog therefore I am

I'm sure someone's said that before, but hey, I'm new to this. I have been looking through the blogs out there and I knew there were lots but I didn't realise that there were lots and lots and lots and lots and lots. I wasted hours today going through some of them. I hadn't meant to, I just hadn't noticed how the time had gone. The thing is that most of them have links to other blogs and it's easy to get carried away. It's curious though, all these people out there putting their thoughts and lives out for everyone to see. In my case it's just people I don't know who see it as I haven't told anyone I do this. Which of course leads to the question, why do I do this? I have a diary too that I write when I have time, but I find it easier to get to the computer and write it down. But why put it up on the web? It's hard to answer that one. Some people seem to use them as a way of keeping family living elsewhere up-to-date or to stay in touch with friends, but there are many like me who just throw their thoughts out into cyber-space for anyone who feels like reading them. I'm sure that this is a great topic for psychoanalysts everywhere; I wonder what they think?

Posted: Sunday February 13th at 10:37 pm

Communication 9 | Ex. 2, page 128

5 **Explanation**
The man had just been cured of deafness, and the ringing phone is final proof that it has been a success.

Lesson 4.2 | Ex. 2a, page 51

Standing/Basic jump

The Parkour Roll

Wall flip – NOT for beginners

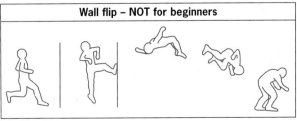

Lesson 6.2 | Ex. 13b, page 81

Student A

Bird watching in Mexico at Yucatan Ecolodge

Price: $100 per person per night

Where? Yucatan Ecolodge is a 5-hour drive from Cancun airport and is surrounded by beautiful coconut trees with wonderful views of the Gulf of Mexico. The whole area is famous for its incredibly varied plant and animal life, especially birds.

Accommodation Stay in a comfortable bungalow with a veranda as well as bedroom, sitting room and bathroom. There are fans but no air conditioning. Meals are served in our main building – half board including tasty Mexican breakfast and 4-course candle-lit dinner. There is a lot of delicious fresh food and seafood available. There is also a bar, a games room and a swimming pool for you to enjoy.

Activities A variety of tours are available including bird watching tours, trips to the famous caves in the area and moonlight safaris. There is also a small Natural History Museum, offering an overall view of the flora and fauna surrounding the hotel.

Communication 10 | Ex. 3, page 142

Types of thinkers/learners

Linguistic: They like to think in words and use complex ideas. They are sensitive to the different sounds and meanings of words and enjoy the process of learning a foreign language.

Logical-mathematical: They like to understand patterns and the relationships between things. They are good at thinking critically and problem-solving. They like to analyse and understand the rules.

Interpersonal: They like to think about other people and are often peacemakers. They are aware that different people have different views on life and probably have lots of friends.

Existential: They like to spend time thinking about philosophical issues and don't like to be bothered with trivial questions. They are always asking questions provoking discussions and debates.

Kinaesthetic: They like to think in movements and find it difficult to sit still for long. They are interested in fitness and health and they learn best when they are physically involved.

150

Communication 4 | Ex. 1, page 58

How to play

1 Play in groups of 3–5.

2 Make a set of fifteen question cards for the game using the topics or grammar from this unit.

   How would you feel about doing something 'extreme' (like sailing alone across an ocean), where your life might be in danger?

   Would you bet a large amount of money on something if a friend said you were certain to win?

3 Each player puts a counter on the Start. When it's your turn, take a question card and answer the question. If you manage to answer well and keep speaking for at least one minute, throw the dice and move forward. If not, leave your counter in the same place and don't move. After you throw the dice and move, if you land on a ladder, go up it and if you land on a rope, go down it.

4 The winner is the player who reaches the Finish first.

Communication 9 | Ex. 2, page 128

2 **Explanation**

   The water in the river only came up to the man's chest

Lesson 2.3 | Ex. 11, page 28

WANTED

INTERNET AND COMPUTER EXPERT

Internet and computer expert wanted.
Can you help this busy Internet café?
Are you good with computers?
Do you know about the latest developments in Internet technology?
Can you communicate well with all kinds of customers?

If you are the right person for us, we will offer you a good salary and free use of all facilities.

Write to: Jenny Keaton, PepeNet Café, 2 Alexandra Gardens, Brighton, BN1 9BG

Assistant organiser
for social activities

Our English language school is looking for an enthusiastic person to help organise our busy social activities programme.

You don't need experience but you do need to be energetic and sociable. You also need to have a good level of English.

The job is part-time with hours to suit you. Good rates of pay to be negotiated. We also offer a discount on our English courses to the successful candidate.

Write to: The Secretary, Oakwood School of English, 16 Bridge Street, Manchester, M60 7TP

Published in 1839, *Nicholas Nickleby* was Charles Dickens' third novel. It was first made into a film in 1947 and there have been various other versions since then. Like many of Dickens' novels, *Nicholas Nickleby* shows his outrage at cruelty and social injustice, but it also reveals his extraordinary talent for comic writing.

Following the death of his father, Nicholas Nickleby and his mother and sister, are taken into the care of his uncle Ralph who is rich but very mean and cruel. The film describes what happens to Nicholas and his family as they struggle to survive.

1   Look at the pictures and read the information above. Then answer the questions.

   1   Have you read any books by Charles Dickens? If so, tell other students about them.
   2   Who do you think the characters are in the pictures? What do you think the connection is between them?

2   Watch the film extract and answer the questions.

   1   What news is in the letter that Uncle Ralph receives?
   2   Who does Uncle Ralph go to see?
   3   What advice does Uncle Ralph give to Mrs Nickleby?
   4   What did Mrs Nickleby hope for?
   5   What does Ralph want Kate to do?
   6   What job does Ralph propose for Nicholas?
   7   What does Ralph say he will do if Nicholas gets the position?

3   Work in pairs. Discuss what you think happens next in the film. Tell another pair of students your ideas.

1   Discuss.

1   Which of the words/phrases in the box below do you associate with the following jobs, and why?
- a model
- a photographer
- a fashion designer

> creative glamorous   hard work   highly-paid
> lonely   pressurised   privileged   self-disciplined
> self-motivated

2   Do you think you might enjoy doing any of these jobs? Why/Why not?

2   a   Lindsay Pressdee (the fashion designer in the bottom photo) has been running her own business since 1996. Watch the film extract and put the things she mentions in the correct order.

do a degree in fashion ☐
set up business on her own ☐
carry a notebook around ☐
have lots of Saturday jobs ☐
show her designs at a trade show ☐
have a glamorous lifestyle ☐
earn less money than her friends ☐
deal directly with large department stores ☐
make clothes for her Cindy dolls ☐

b   Which thing does she NOT mention?

3   Discuss.

1   What is your impression of how Lindsay feels about being a fashion designer?

2   Lindsay says: 'I feel very privileged that I get to do what I want with my life.' What does she mean? Have you ever felt like that about your job or something you've done? Give examples.

3   Do you or does anyone you know have a 'dream career'? What is it and what is so good about it?

4   In which other jobs do you think it might be an advantage to be young?

FILM BANK

The Seventh Voyage of Sinbad was made in 1958, and tells the story of the legendary sailor, Sinbad. To save a princess from an evil wizard, Sinbad must fight several fabulous monsters, created by special effects expert Ray Harryhausen. The film is regarded as Harryhausen's greatest work and despite the age of the film, the special effects are still spectacular.

Ben-Hur was made in 1959 and was the first film ever to win eleven Oscars. It is based on a biblical story and stars Charlton Heston as the Prince of Judea. He is enslaved by a Roman friend, but then returns years later to seek revenge. The climax is a chariot race which is one of the most thrilling scenes in film history.

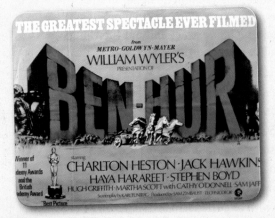

The Lord of the Rings trilogy (2001–2003) is based on the books of J.R.R.Tolkien and directed by Peter Jackson. An ancient ring, which had been lost, is found. It ends up in the possession of the Hobbit, Frodo, who then must go on a dangerous journey to destroy the ring. These are epic films with incredible special effects that hugely deserve their numerous Oscars.

1   Look at the film posters and read the information about them. Then, discuss these questions with other students.

   1   Have you seen any of these films? If so, what did you think of them?

   2   All three films are adventure films. Can you think of any other adventure films? Generally, do you like this kind of film? Why/Why not?

   3   Do you have any favourite types of film? What are they? Give examples.

2   Look at the list of people, scenes and quotes from *The Seventh Voyage of Sinbad* and *Ben-Hur*. Work in pairs. Which film do you think each one comes from?

   1   'Kill! Kill him!'

   2   '… a shout of freedom…'

   3   horses and chariots

   4   a beautiful woman called Esther

   5   the dance of the 'Cobra-woman'

   6   a fire-breathing dragon

   7   thunder and lightning

   8   men sitting on a raft in the sea

   9   men fighting on the deck of a ship

   10   slaves walking across a mountain

3   Watch the film trailers and check your answers.

4   Discuss.

   1   Which of the two films appeals to you most? Why?

   2   Do you generally prefer old or new films? Why?

   3   Do you prefer to watch films at the cinema or on TV/DVD? Why?

   4   What is the best film you've seen recently? Why do you like it?

   5   What is your favourite film of all time? Why do you like it so much?

1   Match each photo to one of the paragraphs 1–4 below.

1   America's most famous flyer grew up in an environment of wealth and privilege, thanks to her grandfather, Alfred Otis. Amelia, known as Milly, was ten years old when she saw her first airplane at the Iowa State Fair, and said of it:
'It was a thing of rusty wire and wood and not at all interesting …'

2   Ellen's passionate relationship with sailing began when she was eight and stepped aboard her aunt's boat to go sailing on the East Coast. For a small child growing up in land-locked Derbyshire, it was an exciting new experience – and it would turn into a lifelong obsession. Over the next few years, Ellen saved as much money as she could to buy her first boat, a 2.5-metre dinghy.

3   He was born in 1919 and grew up in Auckland, New Zealand. It was here that he became interested in mountain climbing. Although he made his living as a beekeeper, he climbed mountains in New Zealand, then in the Alps, and finally in the Himalayas, where he climbed eleven different peaks of over 6000 metres. By this time, he was ready to confront the world's highest mountain.

4   Born on August 5, 1930 on his grandparents' farm in Ohio, he was the eldest of three children. He fell in love with airplanes at the age of six when he took his first flight. He worked at numerous jobs around town and at the nearby airport so he could start taking flying lessons at the age of fifteen and on his sixteenth birthday he was issued a pilot's licence.

2   Look at the photos again and discuss these questions with other students.

1   Who are the people?

2   What made them famous?

3   In approximately which year did each person do the thing that made them most famous?

3   Watch the film extract about Ellen MacArthur. What is the significance of the following:

1   seventy two days

2   Kingfisher

3   the Southern Ocean

4   6000 calories and twenty vitamin pills

5   fifteen minutes

4   Discuss.

1   What do you think drives Ellen to break these sailing records?

2   If you were going on a long solo sailing trip and you could take one special book, one special CD and one special thing to eat – what would they be?

Who Framed Roger Rabbit

Toy Story

Jurassic Park

Home Road Movie

1 **Look at the pictures and discuss the questions.**

1 Have you seen any of the films? If so, what do you know about them?

2 Do you know any other computer-animated films? Do you like this kind of film in general?

2 **Watch the extract from *Home Road Movie* and complete the sentences below.**

1 Dad was an expert on __ .

2 Dad bought a car because __ .

3 Their holiday destinations by car were __ .

4 Dad drove the car at __ mph.

5 When Dad forgot to change gear, the children used to __ .

6 After Dad retired, he would spend a lot of time __ .

7 The children left home to __ or __ .

8 Dad's last journey was on __ .

3 **Summarise what *Home Road Movie* is about in one sentence. Then, compare your sentence to other students' sentences.**

4 **Tell other students about your family summer holidays when you were a child. Were they the same every year or were they different?**

Michael Palin started his career in TV as part of the team behind the comedy series *Monty Python*. Various other comedy programmes and films followed including the film, *A Fish called Wanda*. More recently he has become well-known for his BBC travel programmes. These include *Around the World in 80 days*, *Pole to Pole*, *Sahara* and *Himalaya*. In this latest project, he travels the full length of the Himalaya from the Pakistan-Afghan frontier through India, Nepal, Tibet and Yunnan to China, before re-crossing the mountains to Assam, Bhutan and Bangladesh. The whole journey took six months of hard travelling and he even met the Dalai Lama in Tibet who recognised him from his *Monty Python* days!

Monty Python

A Fish Called Wanda

MICHAEL PALIN
HIMALAYA

As seen on
BBC

Himalaya

1   Look at the photos and read the information above.

   1   Are you interested in watching travel programmes on TV? Why/Why not?

   2   Are you surprised that Michael Palin became a travel show presenter?

   3   What do you think makes a good travel show presenter?

2   How much do you know about Bhutan? In pairs choose the correct alternatives to complete the sentences.

   1   Bhutan is situated between:
       A   China and India   B   China and Russia

   2   Most Bhutanese people wear:
       A   western clothes   B   Bhutan national costume

   3   The population of Bhutan is about:
       A   one million   B   five million

   4   National Park covers about:
       A   25% of the country   B   45% of the country

   5   The King of Bhutan says the most important thing is:
       A   Gross National Product   B   'Gross National Happiness'

   6   Bhutan has many areas and buildings devoted to:
       A   Hinduism   B   Buddhism

   7   Tourists in Bhutan have to pay a minimum of:
       A $75 a day   B $200 a day

   8   The main link between the east and the west is:
       A   a road   B   a river

   9   The main influence on Bhutan's climate and culture is:
       A   the rivers and sea   B   the mountains

3   Watch the film extract and check your answers.

4   Discuss.

   1   Did you enjoy watching this extract? Why/Why not? Does it make you want to watch more of this series?

   2   Do you think Michael Palin is a good travel show presenter? Why/Why not?

   3   Would you like to be involved in making travel programmes like this one?

   4   If you had the chance to travel for six months as part of a travel programme like this, where would you go and why?

FILM
BANK

The Vikings lived over one thousand years ago and came from Denmark, Norway and Sweden. They were mostly farmers, but some worked as craftsmen or traders. The Viking Age – or Dark Ages as they were known – began in Britain about 1200 years ago in the 8th century AD and lasted for 300 years. At the time of the invasions, Britain was mostly inhabited by the Anglo-Saxons who were terrified of these fierce people.

There are people in Britain today (and in Europe and the US) who are fascinated by the Vikings and their whole way of life. Many of these people are members of 'Re-enactment Societies' and they spend their spare time living exactly as the Vikings did. They go to great lengths to be as accurate as they can about every detail including clothes, food and battles. Although some people may regard this type of hobby as excessive, for the 'Re-enactors' it is a fantastic way of spending their free time.

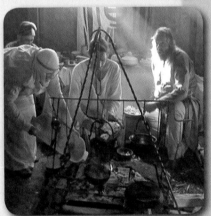

1   Look at the pictures and discuss these questions with other students.

   1   What you know about the Vikings?
   2   What do you think a 'Re-enactment Society' is?

2   Read the information above and answer these questions.

   1   What did you learn about the Vikings that you didn't know before?
   2   What do you think people enjoy about being part of a 'Re-enactment Society'?

3   Watch the film extract and answer the questions .

   1   Which of the reasons below for doing this hobby are mentioned?

> it's fun to dress up   it brings history to life   it's very friendly
> it's a way of making money   it's good exercise

   2   Do the re-enactors try to hurt each other when they are fighting? Why/Why not?
   3   What are the two main reasons for creating the Viking village?
   4   One man says that he knows some people who '... seem to take it a bit far.' What example does he give?
   5   Where do the re-enactors get the costumes from?
   6   What does the blacksmith say about the tools he makes?
   7   What jobs does the film mention that some of these people do in their 'real lives'?

4   Discuss.

   1   Do you think that being a member of one of these societies is 'excessive'? Why/Why not?
   2   Many other 'Re-enactment Societies' exist for different periods in history (e.g. World War I, The American Civil War, The Roman Invasion of Britain). If you were going to join (or start up) a 'Re-enactment Society', which one would it be? Why?

1 Which of the jobs in the box below are represented in the photos?

> a milliner   a web consultant   a quantity surveyor   a card maker   street performers
> an Indian takeaway owner   an Internet entrepreneur

2 Discuss.
1 What are the biggest challenges of starting up your own business?
2 If you had the chance to start up your own business, what would it be? Why?

3 Watch the film and number the following quotes in the order you hear them.

I did some market research on it. ☐

I've an annual turnover of £70,000. ☐

Always believe in yourself. ☐

I'm very passionate about my work. ☐

Last year I decided to set up my own business. ☐

We've been very lucky and very successful. ☐

We've been going for two and a half years now. ☐

4 Having watched the film, can you remember the seven secrets of success? Complete the sentences below using the words in the box.

> boss   give   help   idea   customer   partner   passionate

1 Stay __
2 Get some __
3 Be your own __
4 Have a good __
5 Choose your __
6 Know your __
7 Don't __ up

5 Discuss.
1 Which three tips above do you think are the most important?
2 Can you add one other?
3 What are the advantages and disadvantages of working for yourself rather than working for someone else? Which would you rather do? Why?

FILM
BANK

The Lavender Hill Mob

The Italian Job

The Sting

Ocean's Twelve

1 Look at the pictures. Have you seen any of these films? Which well-known actors are in them? What is the connection between them all?

2 Watch the film extract from *The Lavender Hill Mob* and decide if the following statements are true (T) or false (F).

  1 There are 211 bars of gold in the van.
  2 Mr Holland says he is going to Paris on holiday.
  3 Mr Holland stops the van because he says he is worried about another car.
  4 The man on the bicycle tells the van driver that one of his lights is broken.
  5 The pavement artist jumps in the van and pushes the van driver out.
  6 The robbery takes place near Queen Elizabeth Street.
  7 Mr Holland is part of the criminal gang.

3 Imagine you are Mr Holland. Tell another student the whole story from your point of view.

4 Discuss.

  1 Do you know of any famous robberies?
  2 What happened?
  3 Why are they famous?
  4 Were those responsible ever caught?

Yes, Prime Minister and *Spitting Image* are two of Britain's most well-known political satirical TV series. In different ways they both make fun of key political characters and the political system.

In *Yes, Prime Minister*, Jim Hacker (new elected Prime Minister) attempts to make various bold changes but these generally come to nothing, thanks to the manoeuvring of his manipulative Cabinet Secretary, Sir Humphrey, who opposes action or change of any sort.

In *Spitting Image*, famous characters in British and international life were re-created in the form of latex puppets, which – in the manner of newspaper political cartoons – grossly exaggerated that person's most obvious facial or personality characteristic.

1 Look at the pictures and read the information above. Then, discuss these questions with other students.

1 Do you have any political satirical TV programmes in your country? Do you find them funny? Why/Why not?

2 Do you think programmes like this are a good thing? Why/Why not?

2 Watch the extract from *Yes, Prime Minister*. What does the TV producer, Godfrey, say about the following:

glasses   face   suit   hair   eyes   nose

3 Discuss with other students.

1 What advice would you give to a politician who was making a political broadcast?

2 Have you seen any TV debates between politicians? Who did well? Who didn't? Why?

Writing bank

Informal emails

Lesson 6.1 | Ex. 13, page 78

1 Read the email. Which of the following best summarises Maisie's experience?

   1 She's about to finish an interesting course.
   2 She's nearly at the end of an exciting holiday.
   3 She's coming to the end of her time at university.
   4 She's about to leave a job she's been doing for a long time.

Writing skill | punctuation

2 **a** Look at the email again and find examples of the following:

   1 an exclamation mark
   2 a question mark
   3 an apostrophe
   4 a dash
   5 a full-stop
   6 a comma

   b Match the punctuation (1–6) above with the correct explanations (A–F) below.

   A Used to show the end of a sentence
   B Used at the end of a sentence, to show it is a question
   C Used at the end of a sentence, often to show excitement, surprise or other strong emotions
   D Used in writing to show pauses in speech especially in lists, between adjectives and around clauses
   E Used to show missing letters in contractions and with the possessive 's'
   F Used in informal writing, to add an extra thought or idea to a sentence

---

> Name, date and email address are included at the top, so don't write them in the main part of the email

> Use an informal greeting with or without the person's name

> Use informal language, including contractions (e.g. *I've*), informal words and exclamation marks

From: Maisie Ryland
Date: 07.12.05 19:34
To: leila@hotmail.co.uk
Subject: elephant orphanage
Attach: elephant2.JPG (285 KB)

Hi Leila

Wow! Where do I start? Did I tell you about this amazing project I'm doing before I go to university? I've been on holiday in Sri Lanka for three months working in an elephant orphanage! It's the first time I've been anywhere like this – and although I was a bit daunted at first, now I love it!

We don't work all the time – there's plenty of time to have a real holiday too. It's been great to experience a different culture and to see the places I've only read about in books. The best bit is meeting so many friendly people and it's fascinating being so close to the elephants. I'm attaching a photo of me washing one of the babies!

I've only got ten more days to go. I'm looking forward to seeing you all, but I don't want to leave this place.

See you soon!

Lots of love,

Maisie

Useful phrases

Opening phrases	*Hi Leila/Hello Leila/Hi/Hello/Dear Leila*
Giving news	*Did I tell you about ...?* *It's the first time I've ...* *It's been great to ...*
Attaching photos	*I'm attaching a photo of ...* *I'm sending you a photo of ...*
Closing phrases	*I'm looking forward to seeing you ...* *Lots of love, Maisie/Best wishes, Maisie/* *All the best, Maisie*

Formal letters

Lesson 7.2 | Ex. 12, page 95

1 Read the letter and answer the questions.

1 What are the three problems the customer is complaining about?

2 What does she want?

> Write the name and/or title and address of the person you are writing to.

> Write your address here. Don't write your name.

> Write the date here.

55, Chestnut Avenue
Bristol, BS8 2JH

15th February 2006

Customer services
Film Express
214, Nightingale Lane
London, WC1 2AA

Dear Sir/Madam

> Use *Dear Sir/Madam* if you don't know the name of the person you are writing to. Use *Dear Mr/Mrs Smith* if you know the name. Put a comma (,) after the name, not a colon(:)

I am writing to complain about two DVDs I bought recently from your company on the Internet and about how I was treated by a member of staff when I phoned to complain.

Firstly, I ordered them on 6th January and I was promised they would arrive in three days but they weren't sent to me for over two weeks. Then, when they arrived and I opened the box, I was shocked to see that one of them was broken, as they clearly hadn't been packaged properly.

Secondly, when I phoned to complain, I was very disappointed by the way in which I was treated. The member of staff who I spoke to was extremely rude and did not offer me any form of refund or replacement.

I would be grateful if you could send me a replacement DVD (Kill Bill 2) as soon as possible, or if this is not possible, I would like a full refund of my money. Thank you for your help with this matter.

> Use *Yours faithfully* if you don't know the name of the person you are writing to. Use *Yours sincerely* if you know the name.

Yours faithfully

Diana Jones

> Use formal language. Don't use contractions (I would like... NOT: I'd like)

Diana Jones – customer number: FE3428890/3

email: jonesd@hotmail.co.uk

> Include any relevant reference numbers and email addresses at the end of the letter

Writing skill | formal and informal language

2 Look at the letter again. Is the language used formal or informal? Give two examples from the letter.

3 Mark the sentences formal (F) or informal (I).

1 It would be great to hear from you soon.

2 I would be grateful if a full refund could be sent as soon as possible.

3 I look forward to hearing from you at your earliest convenience.

4 Love, Jenny

5 I'm writing to tell you about something I bought recently.

6 Dear Ms. Harrison,

7 I am writing with reference to the service I received at your restaurant last week.

8 Dear Anna,

9 You know how I feel about all this, don't you?

10 Yours sincerely, Julio Manzanares

11 I am sure that you will understand why I feel so annoyed about this situation.

12 Could you give me the money back please?

Useful phrases

First lines	I am writing with reference to ... I am writing to complain about ... I am writing in order to ...
Ways of complaining	I was promised that ... but ... I was shocked to see/find that ... I was very disappointed by ... The goods clearly hadn't been packaged properly and were damaged. The service I received was not of the standard I would expect from your company.
Last lines	I would be grateful if you could send me a full refund/a replacement as soon as possible. I would like a full refund/a replacement. I look forward to hearing from you at your earliest convenience. Thanks you for your help with this matter. Thank you in advance.

Writing bank

Reports

Lesson 8.3 | Ex. 12, page 112

1 Read the report. Which of the topics in Ex. 10, page 112 is it about?

Writing Skill | paragraphs

2 What is the purpose of each paragraph in the report? Can you give them a short heading?

> **Useful phrases**
>
> | Introduction | This report gives the results of .../is intended to ... |
> |---|---|
> | Reporting results | Approximately 70% of all those who took part in the survey ... |
> | Conclusion | From this survey it is clear that ... |

Divide your report into appropriate paragraphs.

The first few years in school are possibly the most significant for any child. Consequently, the quality and attitudes of their teacher are of extreme importance. This report gives the results of an informal survey into the necessary qualities of teachers of young children.

Approximately 70% of all those who took part in the survey said that they thought the most important thing was that these teachers should care about the children. 60% also referred to the need for classes to be varied and interesting in order to keep the childrens' interest. 20% mentioned the importance of good discipline.

From this small survey it is clear that there is strong feeling that primary school teachers need to be carefully selected for their caring attitudes and creative teaching ability.

Use formal language

State facts. Don't give personal opinions until the conclusion.

Articles

Lesson 9.3 | Ex. 12, page 126

1 Find five different pieces of information between the article and the interview in Ex. 9, page 126.

Writing Skill | referencing words

2 a Find these underlined words in the text and say what they refer to.

1 there (l.3)	4 it (l.11)
2 they (l.7)	5 she (l.13)
3 this (l.9)	6 them (l.18)

b How can using referencing words like those above improve a text?

> **Useful phrases**
>
> | Interest your reader | Oddly enough ... To my surprise ... Unbelievably ... |
> |---|---|
> | Give examples | There was a time when .../On one occasion ... |
> | Give your opinion | As far as I'm concerned ... In my opinion ... |

Think of an interesting title.

The American 'Sherlock Holmes'

Deep in the heart of the United States of America, far from Baker Street in London, lives a man called 'Sherlock Holmes'. In May of this year, I tracked him down <u>there</u> and had the chance to ask him a few questions that I'd been wondering about.

It turns out that Holmes's parents - (he prefers to be called 'Sherlock' by his friends and family) – were great lovers of the work of Conan Doyle. He has memories from his earliest childhood of how <u>they</u> used to read the stories to him. And apparently, they always knew that if they were going to have a boy, they would give him <u>this</u> name. They wanted him to feel special.

Early on Holmes used to get quite angry about people's reactions to his name but he says he's more relaxed about <u>it</u> now. There was a time in San Francisco when a shop assistant looked at his I.D. card and thought he must be the real, original Sherlock Holmes. <u>She</u> looked like she'd seen a ghost.

Oddly enough, Holmes says that people look to him sometimes to solve problems or mysteries. Luckily, he's done some magic himself, so he understands how some of the tricks on TV are done. On one occasion the police called him to help <u>them</u> out with a case they couldn't solve. Fortunately, he was able to find some clues on a computer which helped to work out what had happened to the missing person.

Meeting the American 'Sherlock Holmes' was quite an experience. I'm not sure that I would want to be named after such a famous person but from what I saw he has coped with it extremely well. As far as I'm concerned, parents need to think long and hard about the consequences of the names they give their children for their future lives!

Give some background or context to the title.

Use informal language.

Give examples of the points you make to interest your reader.

Express your opinion.

Tapescripts

Unit 1 Recording 1

K=Keith T=Tina S=Sara

K: Oh hi Alison. Just Keith about tonight. Umm ... you know that Jackie and Steve were coming along too ... well apparently they can't make it now ... something about Steve's Dad not being well or something ... Anyway, just wondering if you still wanted to go to the film or we could do something else. I really don't mind. Perhaps give me a ring? Best to get me on my mobile as I'm out and about for most of the day. All right ... Talk soon ... Bye.

T: This is a message for a Mr. James Stevenson from the Customer Services department of HSBC. We need to confirm a large payment from his credit card before we can go ahead and make the appropriate authorization. Could he please call Tina Jenkins on (01303) 813 843 as soon as possible? Thank you.

S: Oh hello ... umm ... message for Brian Jarvis. ... I'm just ringing in response to the ad. in last week's Hackney Advertiser. I understand that you have a 4-year old VW Golf for sale and ... umm ... I would definitely be interested in coming round to see it .. if that was ok. Perhaps you could give me a call sometime ... The best number for me during the day is 01273 443 750. That's my work number ... and you just have to ask for Sarah Shiali. Hope that's ok. Thank you.

Unit 1 Recording 2

F=Fiona H=Harry

F: So, would you say that you have anyone who is a particularly close friend at the moment?

H: Hmmm ... that's a tricky one. I don't think so ... really. I suppose it's more like I have a few people that I get on really well with and have lots in common with ... But you have a kind of 'best friend', don't you?

F: Well, yes, Angelina ... definitely ... I mean we were best friends at school ... and it's never really changed.

H: So, what makes her so special for you ... you know ... different to anyone else?

F: I suppose it's partly that I can tell her anything ... however awful ... but then also that I tell her pretty much everything that's going on with me. I mean, we text each other all the time!

H: Yeah ... I think that's what's a bit different for me. I mean, you know my closest friends, Jamie, Paula ... probably Alex ... but they're all very different and I usually talk to them about different things.

F: What do you mean?

H: Well ... Jamie's known me for ever ... and he knows my parents and my whole family ... so whenever things are going on there, he's the person I go to ... but then Paula and I have only really got close in the last couple of years ... but we've both been through some quite difficult relationship bits and pieces and talked a lot about that ... so.

F: ... that's who you talk to about all your love life stuff!

H: Exactly ...

F: ... and Alex ...

H: Yes, ... Alex ... well, I suppose she's more like my careers adviser really. Whenever, I have to make sensible decisions about work ... or practical things ... she always has good suggestions.

F: But, hang on, that's not how it's always been for you, is it? I mean you had a best friend at school, didn't you?

H: Yeah, I did have a best friend at school ... Nigel ... but we kind of lost touch when we both left school and went off to college.

F: And you hardly ever see him now, do you?

H: No, that's right. And since then it's basically been like this ... a few close friends ...

F: ... but not the same ones always ...

H: No ... people have come and gone for various reasons ... but that's ok ... you drift apart ... That's just the way life is, isn't it? I mean, you can't keep in touch with everybody, can you?

F: So, do you reckon your friends are as important to you as your family?

H: Hmm, that's a hard one ...

Unit 1 Recording 4

1 She's getting very tall, isn't she?
2 They don't seem to like their present, do they?
3 You haven't been waiting long, have you?
4 We can't leave the party early, can we?
5 Let's go and see a film, shall we?
6 Do sit down, won't you?
7 Nothing seems to be going right, does it?
8 I'm being a bit silly, aren't I?

Unit 1 Recording 5

P=Presenter

P: Being in a large family usually means learning to juggle several tasks at once – making dinner while helping children with homework, bandaging a knee, keeping an eye on the games outside, and lending a caring ear.

However, in addition to normal family life, the Boehmers juggle clubs, rings, torches, balls, and anything else they can get their hands on. It all started 22 years ago when Larry Boehmer's job as a pipeline worker took him away from his wife, Judy, and his 4 children, and he had a lot of spare time on his hands. Adam was in the first grade, Judy says. He came home and said there was a circus at school. Adam wanted to know what his dad could do.

This was all the motivation Larry needed and he decided to occupy his evenings in his motel room constructively, by learning to juggle. And here is a man who, once he puts his mind to something ... he usually finishes it. Then, at home, when his children saw him practising, they wanted to join in. Larry is a big family man so he was only too happy about that.

Larry and three of the children gave their first family performance at an amusement park in 1989. From there it all went from strength to strength. And today they are the largest family of jugglers in the world. At the moment they have 4 boys and 7 girls but they're hoping for more.

As Judy puts it: we didn't plan on this all happening. When the kids saw each other, they picked up on different things. One would do rings, another would do clubs, acrobatics or the unicycle. Before we knew it, we had everybody doing something.

Larry insists the children's talents aren't inherited; it's simply a matter of practice and persistence. It's not in the genes. This is a skill that basically anybody can do. Most people who try to learn juggling give up too soon, but almost anybody can learn, Larry says. Everyone has a speciality but they all have to practise ... a lot! In the end though, doing the shows is the fun part. They all love it. We're all very excited because we've just been asked to perform at the Vatican in Rome ... all 13 of us! We plan to go in April.

Unit 1 Recording 6

M=Man W=Woman

M: So, do you think it makes any difference ... where you're born in the family?

W: Definitely, I think the first born children always have a harder time than the others. Parents have lots more rules then ... and expect so much more ...

M: I totally disagree. In my family, and in others I know, the parents were really careful to treat all the kids the same. You can't be a very good parent if you treat all the children differently.

W: No, that's not true at all. You can be an excellent parent but once you've been through the experience of having one ... well, things change ... you will be different ... approach things differently.

M: That's probably true ... so, maybe parents get better and better ... the more children they have?

W: I think there's some truth in that ... well that's certainly what my oldest sister says!

Unit 1 Recording 9

Dialogue 1

M=Man W=Woman

M: Hi, it's me. Look, I'm really sorry but I had this meeting and we ran over. My boss went on and on ... anyway, I'm out of it now and I won't be long I promise.

W: How much longer do you think?

M: Half an hour max ... I promise. I know we said 3 o'clock but really there was nothing I could do ...

Dialogue 2

W: So ... how's it all going?

M: Fine, fine ... we're all having a really good time.

W: But I suppose you haven't been able to get out much.

M: Well, no, true ... but it's a lovely old house and there are lots of games and things to do inside ... and the kids love exploring up in the attic and so on so that's been ok

W: They say it should clear up a bit in the next few days.

M: Yes, I hope so ... we really want to do some walks ... the countryside around here is supposed to be amazing.

Dialogue 3

W: So, what do you fancy doing?

M: Well, I need to finish off this essay before I come out.

W: Ok, but then?

M: I don't know ... Do you fancy getting something to eat or ...?

W: Well, there are a couple of films I wouldn't mind seeing ...

M: On around here?

W: Yeah ... Would you be up for that?

M: Perhaps, it depends which ones because ...

Dialogue 4

M: So, we've now rearranged to meet up on Friday.

W: Ok ... and what exactly went wrong today.

M: Well, I thought we had it all arranged but apparently he was expecting an email confirmation ...

W: So, you didn't send him one.

M: Well, no, I mean you see, as far as I was concerned ...

Dialogue 5

M: Hi ... Jenny?

W: Yep ... oh hi, Mick. Where are you? You're very late!

M: Ah yes, well ... I did set off quite late and I've had one or two ... shall we say ... interesting diversions along the way.

W: Are you alright?

M: Yeah, yeah ... fine ... now ... you did say you were in Stanhope Road, didn't you?

W: No ... not Stanhope Road ... Stanhope Street. Where exactly are you?

M: I'm not entirely sure but I'm in very busy shopping street ... I think I'm near Willesden.

W: Willesden? But that's miles away ... what are you doing there?

Unit 1 Recording 11

M=Morgan F=Friend

M: So, have you come across, Genes Reunited on the web?

F: Genes what?

M: You know, like Friends Reunited ... only this is a website where you can try and find old relatives and build a family tree.

F: Oh really ... I've always thought I'd like to know a bit more about my family in the past.

M: Well, this is just the thing. It's great. I've started putting together my own family tree.

F: So, how far back do you know?

M: Well, I'm pretty confident about as far back as my great-grandparents, Cicely and John.

F: You didn't actually know them, did you?

M: No, unfortunately, they died in the 1970s. By all accounts they were an amazing couple, devoted to each other ... and of course they'd been through two World Wars.

F: Yes ... that generation went through such a lot ... Do you know when they were actually born?

F: Funnily enough I do ... because my great-grandfather, John, was born right on the turn of the century in 1900 ... and my great-grandmother, Cicely just a year before that in 1899.

F: Wow ... So did they have children.

M: Yep, they had two children Laura and Ben, both around 1930 I think.

F: So, Laura's your grandmother, isn't she? I've heard you talk about her, haven't I?

M: Yes, that's right. I go and visit her about once a month ... up in Leeds.

F: Is her husband still alive?

M: Julian? No, he died a couple of years ago. So, she's on her own now.

F: So, obviously Laura is your ...

M: ... my mum's mother. Laura and Julian had 3 kids: my mum Alison and my aunts Sue and Deborah.

F: Gosh, 3 girls!

M: Yep ... but all very different in character!

F: Really?

M: Oh yes ... have I never told you about Aunt Sue?

F: I don't think so.

M: Well she was ... is ... an anthropologist, a kind of adventurer really. She's spent most of her life in and around Borneo, studying the culture, religion and so on. She's quite an expert apparently.

F: And wasn't there some story about your grandmother's brother ... you know, Ben?

M: Oh yes. Well, that's all a bit mysterious. No-one will talk about him. Apparently, he just went off in his early 20s and no-one ever heard from him again. I'm sure something big happened but I've never been able to find out exactly what.

F: Weird!

M: So, then my mum and dad had just me ...

F: Great being an only child isn't it!

M: Sometimes ...

F: And you've got some cousins, haven't you.

M: Yes, my aunt Deborah had a son and a daughter, Leon and Esther. Esther's a year or so older than me ... and I'm a few years older than Leon. We actually all got on really well. I used to see them quite a lot as a kid because Deborah and her husband split up when the kids were quite small ... and they used to come round to us in the holidays a lot.

F: And now?

M: Well Esther met a doctor in New Zealand while she was travelling around in her year off ... and Leon divides his time between being a diving instructor in the summers mainly around Egypt and Turkey ... and a skiing instructor in the winters.

F: Hard life!

M: Yeah, I know ...

Unit 2 Recording 1

1 Recently, I've realised that investigating and writing about important issues is what I really want to do, so I'm now considering a change of career. I'd like to get a job with a newspaper or perhaps a specialist magazine.

2 You could call my job a labour of love I suppose. I don't get paid much and it's very hard work but I really love working with children and I really wouldn't want to do anything else.

3 There's a pretty strict career path for my field of work. After the basic five-year training, you have to work in various different hospital departments to build up experience. That's what I'm doing now but eventually I'd like to specialise in heart operations.

4 I've finished my training now and I'm going to take a year out before I apply for a job. What I want to do is work in the field of road building and town planning but I'd like to travel before I get stuck into the whole work thing.

5 What I really like about my job is being able to help people. I mean I get a great deal of job satisfaction from knowing that I've helped individuals and families with some pretty serious problems – like having nowhere to live.

Unit 2 Recording 2

M=Mark J=Julia

M: Hi Julia. What's the matter? You look a bit upset.

J: Oh I don't know. I'm so fed up with work at the moment. It's so stressful here and I'm working longer and longer hours. I'm not being paid to do all this extra admin. Basically, it's got to the stage where I'm totally overworked and underpaid!

M: I know. It's been awful for ages, hasn't it?

J: I'm thinking about resigning actually. I'd like to have a complete break ... you know.

M: That's a good idea. That would be great. Have you got any plans?

J: I'm not sure yet but I think I'll leave soon – maybe in the next two months. I can use the time to think about what to do next ... perhaps I'll do some voluntary work or something. One idea is to do some voluntary work abroad. I've seen an ad recently and I'm going to get some more information about it ...

M: You could research some stuff on the Internet ...

J: Yes. That's a good idea! I think I'll go to the library now and do it there. It's my lunch break and I've got at least half an hour.

M: Good idea! Let me know how you get on ...

J=Jane S=Simon

J: How are you, Simon? What have you been doing?

S: Oh I'm fine. I've been making plans! I'm really excited.

J: Oh? Really? What's going on?

S: I've decided I'm going to leave work and go back to college. I'm planning to retrain and do something completely different.

J: Retrain? Really? What are you going to do?

S: Well, I've always wanted to be a vet ... And life's too short ... you know, I want to get on and do it now! I know it's going to be hard work but I've decided I'm just going to do it.

J: Wow, that's great. When are you going to start?

S: Well, it depends on being accepted on the course this year. I have to take an exam first, but if all goes to plan, I'm probably going to start in September.

H=Helen F=Fran

H: Hi, Fran. Do you fancy coming out for a meal tonight?

F: Well, I'd love to but I can't I'm afraid. I'm having an interview tomorrow so I'm going to have an early night.

H: An interview? What for? I thought you liked working for yourself from home.

F: Well, it's been OK, and I suppose I like the flexible hours and not having to commute and stuff, but to be honest, I'm feeling a bit isolated.

H: Yes, I know what you mean.

F: I really miss having colleagues, you know. So I've applied for this job – it's to work for a small firm of architects. It's a small open plan office and they seem really friendly on the phone. I'm meeting them at 10 o'clock tomorrow morning and then having the interview in the afternoon.

H: Oh, well. Good luck. I hope you get it.

P=Patrick J=John

P: I think I'm going to try and look for another job.

J: Why? Don't you like where you are?

P: Yes, it's OK. But I want to be promoted and take on more responsibility. I really want a more senior position now and there are lots of other people who I work with who will get those jobs before me.

J: Oh, you don't know that.

P: Well, I do. I think they'll offer Sally the job of departmental manager. She's really good and she's been there ages.

J: OK ... but what about assistant manager?

P: No, David's going to be assistant manager. He's a bit of a rising star, isn't he? He's bound to get the job. It's obvious. He's being fast-tracked for It ... you can tell ... I heard him talking to James about it.

J: That's just because he wants the job ... you don't know if he'll get it.

Unit 2 Recording 3

1 That's a good idea! I think I'll go to the library now and do it there.

2 I've decided I'm going to leave work and go back to college.

3 I'm meeting them at 10 o'clock tomorrow morning.

4 I think they'll offer Sally the job of departmental manager. She's really good and she's been here ages.

5 David is going to be assistant manager. I heard him talking to James about it.

6 He's bound to get the job. It's obvious. He's being fast-tracked for it.

Unit 2 Recording 4

P=Presenter

P: I'm standing in the extraordinary Rock Gardens of Chandigarh in India. And I've spent the morning talking to Nek Chand, India's most visionary artist and creator of these gardens. He is a small, elderly man with a wrinkled face and silvery hair, and is extremely modest about his work. I've been trying to find out what has driven him to create these gardens, but he told me, simply, One day I started, and then I continued. His modest manner, however, hides an incredible story.

Nek Chand was the son of a poor farmer and in 1958 he started work as a Government road inspector. At that time, his city, Chandigarh, was being designed and built by a famous Swiss Architect. Chand was fascinated by the process of design and construction using concrete, and decided to build his own 'kingdom'. He started to collect rocks and other bits of 'rubbish' from the building sites. Secretly, he took these things to a forest area outside the city and began to build his garden. It had to be done in secret because he was building on land which belonged to the Government.

At first, he spent the time making walls and paths and buildings. And then he moved on to the second phase, creating over 5,000 sculptures. These sculptures provide an incredible array of different figures: people, animals, birds and many other strange and wonderful creatures. Each one is different and they are all made of material that had been thrown away. Chand recycles anything he can find; old bicycles, bricks, lumps of concrete, broken plates, old sinks, electric plugs, pebbles ... the list goes on.

For 18 years, Chand worked on his secret garden, every day after work and every weekend. Every minute of his free time was filled with working on this huge project that nobody else knew about. Then after 18 years, the garden was discovered by accident. At first, Chand was afraid that it would be destroyed as he had built it illegally on Government-owned land. But quickly, people became interested in it and the Government realised that the garden could become a tourist attraction. They paid Chand a small salary to work on the project full-time and one year later the Rock Garden was officially opened.

Now it is India's second most popular tourist attraction, after the Taj Mahal, with 5,000 visitors every day. His huge achievement doesn't seem to have changed Chand at all, however. He told me, I am just doing my work. Everyone has work they do. This is mine. He says his life is utterly regular – I eat. I sleep. I work. Tomorrow morning, he will be doing the same as he's doing today. And the day after, he will be doing the same. He says it makes him happy, just doing it. Which is a good thing, because soon, he will have spent half a century just doing it.

Unit 2 Recording 6

P=Presenter

P: As part of our efforts to improve the work/life balance of the people who work here, we've done a small survey of twenty of our employees. One of the things we wanted to find out was how people spend their time when they're not working. Everyone in the survey was aged between 21 and 30 and these are the results.

Firstly, nearly half the group regularly works late at the office. In fact, 9 out of 20 people stay at work late at least three times every week. However, hardly any of them thought this was a bad thing. Only 3 of them in fact. 25% of the group had done voluntary work at some time in their lives, but only 10% were doing it now.

Next, about evening classes: the group as a whole was keen on doing extra classes or activities. The vast majority say they do at least one evening class, mostly either some kind of sport or art class. Only a small minority of the people questioned would like to do more evening classes, however. It's not surprising too perhaps, that many people are doing, or have done, some kind of online course, mostly to improve their career prospects by getting further qualifications.

Everyone said that a good way of relaxing was watching TV or a DVD, but nobody liked doing this every evening. Only a few people said they switched their computer on every evening, with visiting chat rooms being the most popular reason.

The majority of the group preferred being with friends or family rather than being on their own as a way of relaxing. 60% said they found it easy to switch off after work but the vast majority of people said they would like to change their work/life balance. Most said they want to work less and make more time for themselves.

Unit 2 Recording 9

Dialogue 1

I=Interviewer K=Karen

I: It's Karen Goodman, isn't it?

K: Err ... yes ...

I: Hello Karen. Pleased to meet you. My name's Michael Harrison. Come and sit down.

K: Thank you.

I: So, thank you for applying for the job and coming to the interview today. First, I'd like to ask you about your experience. In your letter, you say you've worked in an office before. Tell me about that ...

K: Oh well, it was ages ago actually.

I: OK ... well, what did you do there?

K: Nothing much really ... I was just an assistant ... You know, answering the phone and stuff ...

Dialogue 2

I=Interviewer J=Jenny

I: Ah ... there you are...

J: Oh dear. I'm so sorry ...

I: Let's see ... You are Jenny, aren't you? Jenny Scott?

J: Yes, that's right.

I: Well, come in Jenny. I'm Peter Manning, Head of the Economics department and I'll be interviewing you today. Very nice to see you. Thank you for coming.

J: I'm really very sorry. I thought it would be a much quicker journey. The traffic was terrible and then I couldn't find the building.

I: OK ... can I start then by asking you about your reasons for applying for the course? What do you think you'd get from studying Economics in this particular university, Jenny?

Dialogue 3

I=Interviewer L=Liz

I: OK ... let's move on, Liz. You've talked about your experience to date. Now, I'd like to know about your plans for the future. What are your plans for the future, let's say, for the five years following the course?

L: Oh, umm ... well, I'd really like to do this and then, maybe stay in the same business for a while when I've finished my degree ... umm ... I'm not really sure what I want to do after that really. I mean, I'd love to study here. I think I'd get a lot out of it as well as having a lot to offer, but ... er ... after that, well, I don't know at the moment. I haven't really thought about that.

I: Do you see catering as a long-term thing in your life or just for the short-term?

L: I'm just thinking short-term at the moment ... I really haven't thought about the future ... I don't know how I'm going to feel. I suppose I should think a bit further ahead but ...

Dialogue 4

I=Interviewer L=Linda

I: Well, thank you very much for talking to me today, Linda. We're coming to the end of the interview now. Is there anything that you'd like to ask me?

L: Yes, I do have a question, if that's OK.

I: Of course. Fire away.

L: Well, I was wondering about promotion prospects. Obviously I'm keen on staying in the journalism business and I'd like to know what kind of opportunities there might be.

I: That's a good question. We are very interested in the professional development of our staff and offer many opportunities for further training and promotion within the company. The right person can be promoted to a position such as senior editor and we are always looking for people to manage completely new magazines. Anything else?

L: Could you tell me when you're going to make your decision?

I: I've got some other candidates who I'll be interviewing this afternoon, but we'll let you know by tomorrow afternoon.

L: Thank you very much.

Unit 2 Recording 10

I=Interviewer

I: Thank you for applying for the job and coming to the interview today.
I'd like to ask you about your experience.
You say you've worked in an office before. Tell me about that.
I'm Peter Manning and I'll be interviewing you today.
Can I start by asking you about your reasons for applying for the course?
What are your plans for the future?

Unit 3 Recording 1

P=Presenter

P: Until the 3rd century BC, Carthage had been a powerful city which controlled most of the Mediterranean Sea. For the previous few hundred years, the Carthaginians had been trading with people in India and the Mediterranean area. There had been many battles between the Romans and the Carthaginians to try to control the area. Although, Carthage had taken control of many important places, they hadn't managed to take Sicily, the island on their doorstep. So, when the Romans won total control of Sicily, Carthage decided to attack Rome.

The leader of the attack was a brilliant young general called Hannibal. He had 40 war elephants, trained to charge at the enemy. As Hannibal's army was marching northwards towards the Alps, soldiers from Spain and other areas joined them. The icy mountains were difficult to cross, however, and by the time they reached Italy in 218 BC, many of his soldiers and elephants had died. They famously won three battles but in the end the Romans were stronger and they took the city of Carthage.

Unit 3 Recording 3

Dialogue 1

W=Woman M=Man

W: Brrr ... it's really cold today, isn't it?

M: Yeah ... do you want to borrow my jumper?

W: Well, I don't think I will, thanks. Trouble is ... I can't wear wool because it makes my skin itchy ...

M: Oh dear ... does it? Well, I've got a cotton jacket in the back of my car ...

Dialogue 2

W1: Hey, I like your jeans ...

W2: Thanks they're nice, aren't they? I bought them yesterday ...

W1: They really suit you.

W2: Mmm ... I think the denim's got Lycra in it, so they feel quite stretchy and very comfortable.

Dialogue 3

M: What's the matter?

W: Oh ... it's a real pain. I got these lovely earrings for my birthday, but I think I'm allergic to them. Look, my ears have gone red and sore ...

M: Oh yes, they look really painful. You mustn't wear them ...

W: No, I think I can only wear real gold or silver jewellery ... they seem to be OK.

Dialogue 4

W: I bought my nephew a really nice toy train made of wood for his birthday ... but I don't think he ever plays with it ...

M: Oh? Really? Why not?

W: Oh I don't know ... I love wooden toys ... but I think most kids prefer plastic ones ... you know, the adults like wood, but the children want plastic! Or better still, computer games ...

Dialogue 5

W: You know my friend Sylvia? She's a vegetarian ...

M: Oh, yes ... I met her at your party, I think.

W: Yes, that's right. Well, she was telling me ... obviously she doesn't agree with eating animals, but she also won't wear animal products ...

M: Oh ... right. No fur coats then!

W: No, certainly not fur ... but she won't use anything made of leather either ... shoes, bags, coats ... nothing.

Unit 3 Recording 4

P=Presenter E=Expert

P: Hello, welcome to today's edition of *Then and Now*. Today we're talking about an incredible country, with a fascinating culture and a long history going back over 3000 years ... China is hugely rich in art and culture, and its food and traditions are well-known around the world. But two aspects of China are perhaps lesser known. Firstly, this vast country has a long history of inventing things and secondly, in recent years has started to flourish as an important global economy with ultra-modern cities and many booming industries. Today we've got China expert Sandra Benning here to tell us all about this flourishing 'Land of invention'. Hello Sandra.

E: Hello.

P: Well, this programme is called Then and Now ...., so let's start with 'Then' ... China's history, and this idea of a 'land of invention' ... I knew that the Chinese invented paper, but I must admit, I didn't know that they invented so many other important things. Before we talk about those, can you remind us about the story of paper?

E: Yes. It was in 105 AD that papermaking was perfected in China. The first paper was made of silk. Well, it was really the waste from silk making, which they pulped up to make paper.

P: Of course, paper had an enormous impact on China, didn't it?

E: Yes, with paper, and then printing, it meant people could get information much more easily.

P: So, what else did the Chinese invent?

E: Well, quite a few simple but important things ... I think one of the simplest inventions was the wheelbarrow, invented around 220 AD, which meant that enormous loads could be carried by just one person ... As well as other things that we take for granted today, like silk, porcelain, the kite and even the umbrella!

P: And we have the Chinese to thank for fireworks, don't we?

E: Yes, that's right! In the 8th century, the Chinese discovered gunpowder. And by the 10th century, it was being used to make fireworks, the gun, the rocket and the bomb ... so it eventually had a huge influence on the whole world of course. Another major invention was a machine for making cast iron, which they first developed in the 6th century BC.

P: Wow! That really is a long time ago! That must have made a big difference to people's lives too.

E: That's right. A lot of iron was used for agricultural tools, so production was increased hugely ... which brings me quite nicely to the present really ... to the 'Now' ... to present-day China ...

P: Is agricultural production big in China now?

E: Well, yes, there's a lot of agriculture ... about 15% of the economy is based on agriculture. You know, things like rice, tea, cotton and fish ... But it's certainly not just countryside and agriculture. There are some huge, modern cities like Shanghai and industry is huge in China now, and expanding all the time. Production of iron is growing at a rate of about 22% a year in China at the moment.

P: That's certainly a booming industry ... So what other industries are important in China now?

E: Well, so many of the things we buy are made in China, aren't they? Industrial production accounts for over half of China's economic wealth, including such consumer items as toys, clothes, shoes, cars and electronic goods, as well as the heavier industrial products like iron.

Unit 3 Recording 5

W=Woman M=Man

W: So, what do you think?

M: Well, I think the first one is easy. I mean, we have to decide on the three most important inventions ever ... So, for the first one, do you agree that the computer is definitely the most important?

W: Well, maybe ... but isn't it true that we wouldn't have computers without electricity? So, really I think that the invention of the light bulb and discovering electricity is incredibly important. What about you?

M: Mmm ... I suppose you're right ... How do you feel about the television then?

W: It's similar to the computer really. I mean, again, we wouldn't have the television without electricity, would we?

M: OK, so shall we decide on the light bulb for the first one?

W: Yes, fine. And what else do you think is important?

Unit 3 Recording 8

D=Debbie M=Martin

D: Hi Martin. How's it going?

M: Oh hi. Yeah, I'm fine but a bit tired, you know ...

D: Oh? Are you very busy at the moment?

M: Well, yes ... didn't I tell you I'm doing a

course? Mostly online, and also one day a week in college. It's really hard work.

D: No. I didn't know. What is it?

M: It's a long story, but what I'm doing is trying to get a basic qualification in maths ...

D: Maths? But I thought you hated maths!

M: Well, yes. It was definitely my worst subject at school. I really hated it then, I had an awful teacher and I didn't understand a thing!

D: So why do you want to do it now?

M: I don't want to ... but I need to. Looking back, I wish I'd studied harder at school and just done it, because I really need it now. I want to retrain to be a teacher.

D: A maths teacher?!

M: No! I want to be a history teacher, but in the UK, you have to have a basic maths qualification to train to be any kind of teacher.

D: Really? That doesn't seem fair.

M: Well, that's the rules! Now I'm older – and wiser! – I realise that studying hard and passing exams gives you more choice in life ... That's one of the biggest lessons I've learned.

D: I suppose you're right. But it's only with the benefit of hindsight that you realise these things ... When you're young, you often can't see the point of some things ... I mean, it IS difficult to see the point of it really ... How were you to know that doing well in maths then, would help you become a history teacher now!

M: I know.

Unit 4 Recording 1

W=Woman

W: I'm very different to my brother I think ... I'm not very good at taking risks whereas he loves it. The maddest thing I think he's done was just after he finished university. He and a friend decided to go by motorbike from the top of Africa to the bottom. For years it had been a kind of obsession with him, something he just had to do ... and he did it. I mean, it wasn't all plain sailing but they made it one piece and had some amazing adventures along the way. I do think he's incredibly brave. Actually, I've just been offered a chance to be part of a sailing expedition to the Galapagos Islands. I've always had a dream of doing something like this but never thought it might really happen. It will mean giving up my job and I'm not sure what I'll do when I get back but I'm sure it would be an amazing experience.

Unit 4 Recording 2

W=Woman

W: ... and now here's one for all of you in offices working at desks or computers ... Basically it relieves tension in the neck, back and shoulders and it also increases lung capacity.

First place your fingertips on your shoulders with elbows bent in front of you. Then, breathe in deeply.

Now, while breathing out, drop your chin onto your chest and bring your elbows together in front of your body.

Finally, while breathing out, lift your head up and back, drawing your elbows back as though they want to touch behind your back.

Repeat this ten times.

Unit 4 Recording 3

M=Man

M: One of the best things we did on holiday was to go whitewater rafting. However, I was a bit nervous at first when they told us we had to sign something which basically said we wouldn't hold the company responsible if we got injured or died! Anyway, the guy in charge of our boat gave us some instruction before we started off. We had to wear lifejackets of course but I was quite surprised that we didn't have to wear any kind of crash helmet. We were also supposed to wear trainers but I'd forgotten mine so I had to wear my sandals. Finally, we got going and the whole thing was fantastic. There were 8 of us in a boat and there really was a lot of 'white water'. It was a bit like being on a rollercoaster and I nearly fell in at one point. The one thing I'm sorry about is that I didn't get any photos. I should have taken my camera but I was afraid I would drop it in the water.

Unit 4 Recording 4

M=Man W=Woman

M: So ... did you go and see it in the end?

W: Yeah, yeah ... I said I would, didn't I?

M: You often say you'll do things but ...

W: Ok, ok ... well this time I did ...

M: And?

W: You were right ... it was pretty good.

M: Pretty good!? Come on ... it was much, much better than that. I think it's the film which I've enjoyed most this year.

W: Really? I do like Clint Eastwood but I suppose I've never really been that into films about boxing.

M: Ok ... but it's not really about boxing is it?

W: Isn't it? ... I mean one of the main characters runs a boxing gym ... and the other wants to be a boxing champion.

M: That's all true but there's a lot more to it than that. There are so many different themes running through the film.

W: Such as?

M: Well, risk, for one.

W: What do you mean?

M: Well you know at the beginning of the film, one of Clint Eastwood's most promising boxers leaves him just as he has a chance to make the big time ...

W: Oh yes, that's right ... doesn't he go off with another promoter or something..

M: Yep ... after years of training in the gym with the Clint Eastwood character. And actually, it's because Clint won't take a risk with him.

W: He won't put him up for a big championship fight ... and the other promoter will ...

M: Exactly. The Clint character plays safe. He's just too cautious. And then this young woman hopeful turns up ...

W: She'd been working in a café before she went to the gym ... but dreaming of being a champion boxer.

M: But I thought he didn't want to take her on because she was a woman or a 'girlie' as he puts it ... not because it was a 'risk' ...

M: Well, at first yes ... but when she actually turns out to be really good ... then he faces another risk.

W: You mean, he'll train her up and then she'll leave him.

M: Exactly ... and that nearly does happen, doesn't it?

W: Oh yes, that's right ... but she sticks with Clint in the end ... thank goodness!

M: Then there's a kind of emotional risk he takes too ...

W: You mean about getting too involved with her?

M: Well, yes ... you remember how he keeps writing to his daughter and never getting any replies ...

W: Yes, I never worked out what that was all about ... I mean, there's obviously some story ... something has happened which we never really find out about.

M: Yes ... well ... in the film ... I think there's a growing emotional connection between them ... and given what happened with his daughter ... that's a big risk that's he's taking too ...

W: I see what you mean. I hadn't really looked at it like that before ... but now you say it ...

M: I mean obviously there's lots of other stuff too ... weren't you shocked by what happened in her big championship fight?

W: Oh wow yes ... I couldn't believe it ...

Unit 4 Recording 7

W=Woman

W: Well ... obviously both photos are of someone doing the same thing but in very different situations!. I guess the first guy is one of those people whose really into risk-taking ... you know, extreme sports and stuff! Not like the second guy!

So ... they're both ironing. In the first picture, I can see a young man ironing some kind of brown t-shirt or sweatshirt or something. But the ironing board is somehow fixed between the sides of a ravine. I can't imagine how he got there with the ironing board ... and how he manages to stay there himself. It's amazing. On the other hand, the second picture is of a much more ordinary situation. A middle-aged man is doing the ironing in his kitchen – his wife might be out at work. He is also looking after his children ... but not very well! Strangely, the guy in the first picture looks more relaxed than the man in the second picture, even though it must be very dangerous. Maybe it's because he doesn't have so much ironing to do ... and he doesn't have to look after any children! I know I hate ironing but I am also scared of heights and climbing ... so I wouldn't like to be in either situation!

Unit 4 Recording 8

P=Presenter

P: long, length, lengthen; short, shorten; wide, width, widen; broad, breadth, broaden; high, height, heighten; deep, depth, deepen; low, lower.

Unit 5 Recording 2

S=Simon C=Camilla

1 **S:** Oh ... I'd forgotten about this photo. Gosh ... this brings back a few memories.

C: Really ... so who is this? It's not your mum is it? And where is it? Is that when you lived in

5 south London?

S: Yes ... that's right. That's where my parents lived for years and where I was brought up.

It was this huge rambling old house. Actually
we just rented one floor of it ... but a lot of the
10 rest of it was just empty ... and we had this
enormous garden, pretty much to ourselves.
C: So is that you in the garden.
S: Yep ... haven't changed a bit have I? That's
actually Muriel I'm with. I've told you about
15 her, haven't I.?
C: Umm ... maybe ... remind me ...
S: Well, basically, my mum wasn't very well
after I was born and so she employed Muriel to
come in and look after me a lot of the day. She
20 was a trained children's nanny. The idea was
that she'd just be around for a few months ...
but in the end she stayed until I was nearly 7.
She was really important to me ... and I'm still
in touch with her and her family.
25 C: Wow ... that's brilliant.
S: Yeah ... In fact I think this is one of my
favourite photos of all. She was an amazing
person and partly because of her I have really
great memories of my childhood. I mean ... she
30 was really good fun.. We were always doing
interesting things but at the same time you
couldn't mess around with her. When she told
you to do something, you did it. No arguing ...
that was for sure!
35 C: She sounds great ... So, what kind of child
were you. I bet you were naughty!
S: Me?? No! I was a model child. Actually, I did
a lot of things very quickly for my age ...
C: Like what?
40 S: Well, my mum tells me I said my first few
words by the time I was nine months and I was
able to walk, more or less, by 10 months.
C: Gosh ...
S: Then later I was quite musical ... I could play
45 simple tunes on the piano reasonably well by
the age of 4 which apparently is quite early ...
C: So where did it all go wrong?
S: Yeah, I know ... Shame really ...

Unit 5 Recording 3

C=Camilla

C: My brother, Clive, and I were always pretty
competitive even as quite young children. I
remember we both got bikes one Christmas
and he could ride his on his own before me.
I was really cross! He was only 5 I think.
Swimming was good though. He's always been
quite nervous about being in the water but I've
always loved it. I was able to swim well by the
age of 8 but even now he's quite tentative. I
mean he can swim but he doesn't really like it.
What else? Oh yes, our granddad was a great
chess player, so we got into that at one point
– I think we were about 13 or 14. Anyway, I
was really good at it ... so good in fact that he
never managed to beat me ... not even once.
He hated that ... and said he'd never play
me again. And he never did! More recently,
we've taken up skiing. Clive loves it and he's
great at it – a real natural. I'm ok ... I mean
I'm improving. In fact, last time I succeeded
in coming down my first black slope without
falling over ... which I was really proud of!

Unit 5 Recording 4

S=Simon C=Camilla

S: ... and I think this photo must have been
taken a few years later.
C: So, who are all these people? You're in both
the photos though, aren't you? In this one it's

you on the ground, with the dogs ... right?
S: Yep, as usual ... And, on the left is my father
... then my mum ... At the far right is Aunt Joan,
she was my father's older sister ... and next
to her, her husband, Uncle Jack. This photo's
actually taken outside the hotel that my aunt
and uncle had ... down in the south-west of
England. We used to go and stay with them in
the summer quite often.
C: So, did you like being down there?
S: Oh, the hotel was great. As a kid I found
it really exciting. Usually, in the summer at
home I'd get quite bored. There wasn't much
to do whereas at the hotel there was no end
of possibilities. I used to go round everywhere
exploring ... They had tennis courts and a
wood at the back. And sometimes I remember
I'd go in the kitchens and the chef would let
me try some of the desserts! That was until I
ate so much of the chocolate mousse one time
that I threw up! But no, overall, It was brilliant
... much more fun than just hanging around at
home.
C: And how did you get on with the dogs?
S: Oh they were a lot of fun. Sammy, my cat ...
you know, in this picture ... he was just so ...
how can I put it? ... superior and independent.
Like all Siamese cats probably. And he wasn't
very interested in kids I don't think. On the
other hand, these two dogs were just so
friendly. I think they just liked the attention
... but they became like my best friends. They
used to come exploring with me. I was always
really sad to leave them when we had to go
home.

Unit 5 Recording 5

1 This year hasn't been great but I'm sure
things will be better next year.
2 I saw this great film last night
Oh yeah ...
3 but I don't really understand what you're
saying. Do you mean that ...
4 Kate ... Kate ... thank goodness you're home
... I've been so worried ...
5 Listen ... I think we're lost ... and we
shouldn't be walking round here late at
night ... I'm not sure that it's safe you know
...
6 So, go on, why exactly did you agree to go
out on a date with him?
7 Well, of course, he said that was why he
was late home but you don't believe him, do
you?
8 I can't believe it. We're flying off to Australia
for a month on Monday to see my twin
sister. I can't wait ...
9 You're always late ... why can't you be on
time for once in your life?
10 Can you see that young guy ... standing ...
looking into that car? What on earth do you
think he's doing?
11 She said ... what??!! I can't believe it. That's
terrible ...

Unit 5 Recording 6

W=Woman

W: Well ... where shall I start? Well ... the
basic story is that a girl, Catherine, is left a
box by her mother, who died when she was a
baby. Catherine discovers the box when she's
31, the same age as when her mother died.
Inside the box are 11 objects, like a red hat,

a map of part of England and so on ... all of
them meaningless at first, but when Catherine
begins to examine each object, she finds new
truths not only about her mother but also
about herself. Through these objects Catherine
finds that her mother was not the sweet
and innocent woman that everyone likes to
remember her as.
So, what did I think of it? Well ... overall ...
I really enjoyed it – it's a really interesting
idea for a story – and I thought it was very
well-written. Not only that but there are lots
of aspects of Catherine's life that I can totally
relate to – different events, feelings and
thoughts which so accurately mirror my own
life that I found myself constantly underlining
parts of the text.
However, sometimes I found it a bit slow.
I wanted to know about the objects and it
seemed to take ages to work out what they
were all about. Still ... apart from that one
small thing ... it was very easy to read and I'd
certainly recommend it.

Unit 5 Recording 7

W=Woman

W: Well first of all it's very important to make
sure that your time capsule container is going
to last for a very long time ... obviously! So,
it mustn't rust, it mustn't leak and it must be
very hard-wearing. We were told to avoid any
kinds of plastics and go for a material like
aluminium or stainless steel.
We put in various books, newspapers and
photographs ... all of which I still think were
a good idea. With books and papers, it's
important to make sure they're printed on
the highest quality paper – so they don't
deteriorate any faster than absolutely
necessary.
One mistake we made was to put in colour
photographs. I mean, photographs are very
good information carriers across time and
cultures ... but apparently, black and white
photographs are much more stable and
long-lasting than colour prints ... so that's
something worth bearing in mind.
The other thing which we should have thought
about was that some kinds of technology
become redundant. We put in an old video
tape and they probably won't be able to view
that when the capsule finally gets opened. So,
it's probably best not to include any items that
require any technology or equipment to use ...
other than eye and hand.
Finally, and again, pretty obviously I guess,
do make sure that the outside of the capsule
is clearly labelled using a permanent marker
pen ... saying what it is and any necessary
instructions.

Unit 6 Recording 1

W=Woman

W: I was about 25 and I'd been working at the
same company for five years. A friend showed
me his photos of an amazing holiday he'd had
in Central America. One photo in particular
really struck me. It was when he went diving
and saw the most beautiful fish you've ever
seen! I began to have itchy feet and wanted
to leave work and do something exciting. I'd
never been out of Europe before then and I
was a bit worried about going straight into

uncharted territory! I mean, I didn't know anything about countries so different and far away from mine. So, I decided to go to Spain first, to learn a bit of Spanish and get used to being away from home. I went as an independent traveller on my own, because I really wanted to do it all by myself. I spent a month wandering around the town where I was living and learning Spanish and loving every minute! I was bitten by the travel bug then and wanted to explore lots of other places. About six months later, after saving up some money, I went off to Guatemala, feeling very confident and pleased with myself. The first two months were difficult and I experienced real culture shock, I think. It seemed that everything was different. Lots of things went wrong too, like I was robbed twice, I couldn't find anywhere to live and I was really homesick and missed my family like mad! So I had a bit of a bumpy ride to start with, but after a while, I found a job teaching English, made some friends and started to really enjoy myself. In fact, I grew to love it so much I stayed there for three years!

Unit 6 Recording 5

1 The summer is generally hot and very <u>humid</u> and quite uncomfortable. It's often <u>overcast</u> too and there is no <u>breeze</u> to cool things down. It's very different in the winter, when it's <u>cool</u> and the sky is <u>clear</u>.

2 I'm not so keen on <u>mild</u> weather – when it's not really hot or cold. I much prefer it when the weather is quite dramatic. Like when you get <u>scorching</u> days and then it suddenly <u>pours</u> for hours. Or when it's hot in the day and then you get <u>subzero temperatures</u> at night.

3 The weather is very <u>changeable</u>. In the summer, the days are often <u>bright</u> but can be <u>showery</u> and the nights are sometimes <u>chilly</u> but not very cold. In the winter, it seems to <u>drizzle</u> a lot and the sky is often grey.

Unit 6 Recording 6

P=Presenter J=Jamie W=Woman M=Man

P: Hello everyone. I think we'll make a start as it's 7.30 already. Let me introduce Jamie. He's our 'Bhutan expert' … He's spent a substantial amount of time in this amazing country and I'm sure he'll be able to help you with whatever queries you may have.
J: Hello. Thank you. Well, I'll do my best … Please feel free to ask whatever you want and if I can't answer anything . Well, I'll say so!! … So, fire away …
W: Err… yes … when is the best time to go?
J: Well, in the winter it can be up to about 15c in the daytime but you often get subzero temperatures at night. There is a lot of snow in winter, which can make travelling difficult. It's hot in the summer, sometimes really scorching, but it's often very wet too. In my experience, the best seasons to visit are spring and autumn. Spring is beautiful with wonderful flowers and lovely sunny days. And autumn is fantastic too with mild weather and clear views of the Himalayas … Yes?
M: What activities do you recommend?
J: One of the most popular activities for visitors to Bhutan is to go trekking in the Himalayas. The high mountains and deep valleys are truly spectacular and you can sometimes walk for several days before coming to the next village. You'll see a huge variety of plant life ranging from dense forest to tiny mountain flowers. I've been many times … You won't be disappointed, I can assure you!
M: Thank you.
W: Excuse me … I'd like to know whether we need to take anything special.
J: Ah yes, good question. The changeable climate means that you will need an assortment of clothes, including rain gear and good walking boots. The sun can be very strong especially up in the mountains, so you'll need a hat and sunglasses. I'd also recommend warm clothes for the evenings … it can get pretty chilly, even in summer.
M: Would we need to carry all our equipment on a trek?
J: No. Trekking is done in organised trips and they provide yaks to carry your luggage. They also carry the food and camping equipment, which is all provided. I've always found them very well-equipped and helpful.
M: and who goes with the trekking group? I mean do they provide a guide?
J: Oh yes … There's always a guide who speaks English and a cook and other assistants to help make the trek run smoothly. They're all very friendly … you really don't need to worry about getting lost or anything …
W: Could I ask you what the food is like?
J: Mmm … interesting, yes. The Bhutanese eat a lot of meat, dairy foods, vegetables and rice. The national dish is a fabulous chilli pepper and cheese stew called Emadatse. In fact, chillis are very common in Bhutan and you'll find that a lot of their dishes are flavoured with spicy chilli peppers. I love the food, I must say.
M: I'm thinking of going in the autumn. Do you know if there are any interesting festivals at that time?
J: Well, yes, this year there are, although the dates of festivals vary according to the moon. The most popular one for tourists is held in Thimphu, the capital and this year it's in October. People dress in their colourful, traditional clothes and there is a lot of music and dancing, including the masked sword dances. All the festivals are important religious events for the people to offer thanks to their gods.
M: I've seen pictures of strings of flags in the mountains. Can you tell me what they are?
J: Yes, they are prayer flags. As I said, the Bhutanese people are very religious and they use the flags as a way of communicating with the heavens …

Unit 6 Recording 7

1 When I'm abroad I always have a go at speaking the language.
2 We're going away for the weekend. Could you look after our cat?
3 Don't worry. It goes without saying that I'll meet you at the airport.
4 There's something going on in the city centre. It's full of people.
5 Although they argue a lot, they want to make a go of their marriage.
6 I promise I won't go back on what I've said.
7 Can you help with dinner please? I've been on the go all day.
8 Your teacher can't be here today. She's gone down with a bad cold.
9 I couldn't decide which kitten to go for. They were all gorgeous.
10 He went to great lengths to make sure he was totally prepared for the interview.

Unit 7 Recording 1

1 Sharon Osborne has reportedly spent over €180,000 on cosmetic surgery and she says it was worth every penny. Her weight fell from 102 to 54 kilos, after surgeons dramatically reduced the size of her stomach, forcing her to eat much less than before. She then had multiple operations to remove excess flesh from her face, neck, stomach and other areas of her body.

2 Craig Flatman is a teenager known to his friends as 'Jam Boy'. Since early childhood, he has refused to eat any form of meat, fish, fresh fruit or vegetables. Instead, for the last 11 years, he has had five rounds of jam sandwiches a day, plus 1 litre of milk. Doctors are confused, however, as he is over 1.8 metres tall, weighs a healthy 70 kilos and has no fillings in his teeth.

3 Sir Christopher Gent was the boss of the mobile phone empire Vodafone for 17 years. While in the job, his salary increased hugely, rising to a massive £2.9million in his last year. Now, he lives off his Vodafone pension which totals £10.4million – meaning that he can expect an annual pension of around £662,000 for the duration of his retirement.

Unit 7 Recording 3

W=Woman

W: Well, we have a really big meal on Christmas Day in our family. It's lovely but we always end up eating too much and feeling too full! Our traditional Christmas dinner is roast turkey, roast potatoes, carrots, parsnips, gravy and cranberry sauce, followed by Christmas pudding of course. I suppose some people in Britain probably have slightly different things, but that's what we have. I love it! My favourite bit is the roast potatoes … and there is a particular way of cooking them to make them taste really delicious. First, you peel them and boil them for a short time – about 5 minutes, or 10 minutes maximum. Then you cover them in flour. Then, you put them on a tray in the oven but the important thing is that the oil on the tray is very hot and that you roast them in a very hot oven …

Unit 7 Recording 4

P=Presenter

P: And now, news of more celebrity items and film memorabilia going under the hammer … In the last few years, some items have hit the headlines as they have been sold at auctions for absurdly high prices.
You'll probably remember that back in 2001, the white bikini worn by Ursula Andress in the James Bond film Dr No was put up for auction. The actress reportedly decided to sell the two-piece after she discovered it in the attic at her home. Andress is now in her sixties, but she shot to fame when she played the first 'Bond girl' in the first James Bond film in 1962. The bikini was bought for a huge $61,000 by the

Tapescripts

American, Robert Earl, co-founder of Planet Hollywood.

More recently, one of the six stormtrooper helmets used in the original Star Wars films was sold at an auction in London. It was put up for auction after it was found by chance at a second-hand sale and bought for just $75. The lucky owner ended up getting around $25,000 for it!

Of course, traditional auctions are not the only way to bid for things. Thousands of people now buy and sell things on eBay, the popular Internet auction site. And sometimes the most incredible things go for extraordinary prices! One seller put a piece of chewing gum which had been spat out by pop star Britney Spears up for sale on eBay. The seller said he found the gum on the pavement outside a London hotel when he saw Britney spit it out. The description that went with the gum on the Internet read: It is completely preserved as you can see, with Britney's teeth marks highly visible! This is the chance to own a piece of pop history – right from the mouth of the princess of pop herself!

There is no guarantee that the gum is authentic, but potential buyers can contact the seller direct and then use their own judgement to decide. It may not just be the gum which is fake; the bids may be fake too. During the bidding for Britney's gum, fake bids went up as high as $14,000 although the winning bid for the gum was reportedly closer to $100.

It is not only celebrity items that have been making news on eBay. Three boys in Texas, USA got a shock last Christmas after their father had given them constant warnings about their bad behaviour. He had bought them $700-worth of video console and games for Christmas but when there was no improvement in their behaviour, he decided to auction off their Christmas presents on eBay. The father sold the items for $1,700 and gave the profit to the local church.

So, it seems that almost anything can be bought and sold and that ridiculously high prices will be paid for sometimes completely useless items ...

Unit 7 Recording 5

1 One man bid £5,000 for a small antique chair.
2 Ten CDs for only £50 – that's a bargain!
3 I asked for a discount, but the shop assistant said no.
4 I'd like to buy a motorbike but I can't afford it.
5 This DVD player broke after only a week. I'd like a refund please.
6 I always try and haggle with market traders.
7 The rent on that tiny flat isn't worth it.
8 Don't forget to keep the receipt.

Unit 7 Recording 6

W=Woman R=Recorded message M=Mark
W: Hello. I'd like to speak ...
R: Hello. Welcome to FDS. In order to deal with your call efficiently, please listen to the following options. If you're phoning to arrange a delivery date, press 1. If you're phoning to change or cancel an existing appointment, press 2. If you're phoning about a fau!ty machine, press 3. If you're ...

W: Hello ...
R: Hello. For all hi-fi, television, DVD and video player faults, press 1. For all kitchen appliances faults, press 2. For all ...
M: Hello, Customer Services. Kitchen appliances. Repairs and replacements. Mark speaking. How may I help you?
W: Oh, hello. I'd like to speak to the manager please.
M: Well, this is Customer Services. Can I be of any assistance? What seems to be the problem?
W: Well, I bought a washing machine from you about three weeks ago and there have been problems with it ever since I first used it.
M: Oh, I'm very sorry about that, madam. Can I take your customer number please?
W: Oh, yes. It's 45002315.
M: ... Thank you ... OK. Alison Bentley, is it?
W: Yes. That's right.
M: So, you've had problems with your washing machine. What sort of problems?
W: Well, it often stops for no reason in the middle of a cycle and then starts again, but it keeps making strange noises. Now it's stopped completely and there's a load of washing stuck inside ... I phoned to make an appointment for one of your engineers to come and look at it yesterday, but your computers were down and I couldn't get through. Now it's really urgent ...
M: We did indeed have technical problems yesterday. I can only apologise for the difficulties you experienced in getting through. Would you like to make an appointment now?
W: Yes, please. I need an engineer urgently – today.
M: Just bear with me and I'll see if we've got any appointments available ... It looks like the earliest appointment we've got is Friday morning between 8 and 1. Shall I book that in for you?
W: Friday morning? That's three days time! What am I supposed to do about the clothes stuck inside the machine? They'll be ruined. Haven't you got anything sooner?
M: ... I'm afraid not. If you had the 3-star Service Plan, you could've got a priority appointment on the same day. But you've got the basic guarantee which says that we'll repair your appliance within a week if we can. And if not, we'll provide a replacement free of any extra charge. Shall I book an appointment for Friday for you?
W: Well ... I suppose I'll have to.
M: ... OK. That's fine. That's all booked for you. An engineer will be with you Friday between 8 and 1. Is there anything else I can help you with?

Unit 7 Recording 7

A feathers
B wings
C beak
D claws
E fur
F tail
G paws
H whiskers
I horns
J hooves
K fins

Unit 7 Recording 9

1 I'd forgotten to set the alarm clock that day so I overslept and woke up three hours later than I was supposed to ... Then, I'd seriously underestimated the time it would take me to get there. On the way, it started pouring with rain and I got completely soaked to the skin. In the end, it took me nearly two hours which meant that I was really, really late. When I did finally arrive – wet through – I walked into the interview room and who was sitting there, waiting to interview me, but my ex-boss from my previous job! I felt so awful because I know for a fact that he hates me and I'd made such a fool of myself.

2 A couple of years ago I decided to have a change of career. Having been a Spanish teacher for nearly 20 years, I decided to retrain as a translator and interpreter. It's a really difficult job and I found the training very hard work, but I'm really pleased with myself for having done it. I was brought up bilingual so the language itself wasn't difficult for me, but you have to learn completely different skills. I now work for a huge multinational holiday company specialising in organised trips around South America and I really love it! It's the best job I've ever had.

3 I can't believe the trouble I've had over this jacket I ordered off the Internet. It was unusual because I've ordered stuff from the same company before and never had one single problem. But this time, I ordered a waterproof rain jacket and when it came it was an extra-large even though I'd ordered medium. When I sent it back, the same thing happened. I sent it back about three or four times. So, eventually I phoned the customer services department but the man I spoke to was so rude I couldn't believe it. Throughout the whole conversation, he spoke to me in a sort of bored, monotonous voice and clearly wasn't interested in my problem at all. He didn't even apologise!

Unit 7 Recording 11

Dialogue 1

W=Waitress M=Man C=Woman customer
W: Good evening. Have you got a reservation?
M: Yes, we booked a table for two in the name of Morrison.
W: Madison ... I don't think we've got a booking from ...
M: Er ... no, it's Morrison ...
W: Sorry, Morrison ... ah, yes. If you'd like to follow me ...
M: Thank you ...
W: Can I get you some drinks?
M: Yes, please. A bottle of the house red and some mineral water please.
W: Sorry ... Did you say a bottle or a glass of red?
M: A bottle ... of the house red.
W: Certainly, Sir.
W: Are you ready to order?
M: Yes ... I think so.
W: Madam?
C: I'll have the steak please.
W: How would you like it?
C: Rare please.
W: Rare. Thank you. And for you, Sir?
M: I'll have the grilled tuna, please.
W: Sorry, the tuna's finished ...

M: Oh! Well, I'll have the swordfish then.
W: Mmm ... I'm very sorry but there's no swordfish either.
M: Oh!! Is there any fish on the menu today?
W: Yes, we have the grilled seabass.
M: I'll have that then please. And I'll have new potatoes with it, please.
W: I'm terribly sorry but we've run out of new potatoes but you can have it with rice.
M: Well, OK ... but I'm not very happy about all this ...

Dialogue 2
A=Assistant C=Customer
A: Can I help you?
C: Oh, yes ... I'd like to try these on, please.
A: Yes of course. What size are you?
C: Umm ... well, usually a 38 but sometimes a 39. Perhaps I could try both ...
A: Yes, that's fine. I'll bring both for you. I won't be a minute. Was it black you wanted?
C: Yes.
A: OK fine. Would you like to take a seat over there?
OK. I've got black in size 38, but not in 39. I've brought brown in size 39 for you to try.
C: Thanks. I'll try the 38 first.
A: Oh, they look really nice on you. How do they feel?
C: I really like them but they feel a bit tight actually. I think I'll try the 39s, though I don't like brown.
C: Ah, yes ... these are better ... mmm. The 39s fit much better, but I really don't like the colour. Are you sure you haven't got black in 39?
A: I'll just make sure if you like.
C: Yes, please. I really prefer black.
A: No, I'm sorry ... only brown in 39.
C: Oh! Can you phone your other branch and see if they've got them. I don't like brown ... they don't go with any of my clothes ...
A: Yes, of course ...

Dialogue 3
C=Customer R=Receptionist
C: Good morning. I'd like to book an appointment to have my hair done please.
R: Yes, of course. When would you like to come?
C: Have you got anything for tomorrow morning before 12.00?
R: Umm ... yes, there's 10.30, 11.15 or 11.45?
C: Oh, 10.30 please.
R: Fine, 10.30. That's with Tina. And what would you like to have done? Just a cut and blow-dry?
C: Well, a cut and blow-dry yes ... but I'd also like some highlights done. In fact, I was thinking of having multicoloured highlights this time. Would that be possible?
R: Oooh yes. That sounds fun. There's also a special offer on tomorrow. We're offering all customers an Indian head massage. I'm sure you'll like it. It's very relaxing.
C: Oh, yes please. That would be great.
R: Lovely. We'll see you tomorrow at 10.30.
C: Thank you. Bye.

Unit 8 Recording 2

B=Boss E=Employee
B: So, generally things are going fine. We've talked about your attitude to work, which is very good. Over the three years that you've worked here, you've shown a consistently professional approach to your work.

E: Thank you ... I must say that I've enjoyed it very much. Testing computer games is great fun ... and my colleagues are very helpful and supportive.
B: So, the next part of this appraisal is to think about the future. What do you see yourself doing next?
E: Well, as I say, I've really enjoyed the games testing work that I've been doing, but I feel that it's time I moved on now ... I mean I think I'd like to have a bit more responsibility.
B: Yes, I think we need to think about that. You've shown some good leadership skills and I wonder how you would feel about becoming a team leader. You know, then you'd be supervising a team of games testers and making sure everything gets done properly.
E: Oh, yes ... I'd like to very much ... though I'm not sure that I've got all the necessary skills to be honest. I mean, I'd like the responsibility, but err ... would there be any management training?
B: Yes, of course. We run some excellent in-house courses which I think would give you confidence. There's one coming up next week and then another in 2 months' time. And I think I'd rather you did the first one, so that we don't waste any more time. What do you think?
E: Well, yes. I'd be very interested. It would be great to get some training underway as soon as possible. I mean, I'd rather not wait for two months, if that's OK with you. I'd like to be as prepared as I can.
B: OK. Great. In that case, I'd better get your name on the list for the one next week immediately. I hope it's not full up already. I don't think it will be. Perhaps I'll just check with Jeannie now. Excuse me just one minute ... Oh, hello Jeannie. I just wanted to check if you've still got places on the Management Skills course for next week ... ah, you have ... great ... Could I put Will Scott's name down please? ... Yes, S-C-O-double T ...

Unit 8 Recording 3

1 I feel that it's time I moved on now.
2 I think I'd rather you did the first course.
3 I'd rather not wait for two months.
4 I'd better get your name on the list immediately.

Unit 8 Recording 5

1 She isn't very strict and she hardly ever gets upset or worried.
2 He's the kind of person who has one aim and works hard to achieve it, doesn't he?
3 She's determined to do what she wants and won't listen to advice from anyone.
4 He uses words in a funny, intelligent and interesting way.
5 She really enjoys meeting and talking to people, doesn't she?
6 He's one of those people who is always honest and doesn't keep secrets from anyone.
7 He has very strong views about a lot of things in a way that annoys a lot of people.
8 She's the kind of person who cares only about herself rather than other people.
9 He's good at making things happen and change. He doesn't just react to events, does he?
10 She's one of those people who is good at

secretly controlling or tricking people to get what she wants.

Unit 8 Recording 6

P=Presenter T=Tony Greenwood
P: Today on *Sports Alive* we are looking at success and achievement in sport. Who are the most successful sportspeople in the world and just how do they achieve their success? There is a huge sports psychology industry working with almost all athletes these days. But does it work? Is it all really necessary? We've got sports psychologist, Tony Greenwood here to help us answer these questions. Hello, Tony. Welcome to the programme.
T: Hello ...
P: So, first of all, Tony, let's think about that question. Is sports psychology really necessary? Some people would say that you've either got the determination to succeed or you haven't. What do you think?
T: Well, I suppose that's sometimes true. There are examples of sports people who are extremely successful and have never needed any help with their mental determination. Mohamed Ali was probably the most famous of all. He had complete self-belief that he was the best and absolutely unbeatable.
P: That's right. Nobody needed to remind him to focus on the goal!
T: No ... and there are other examples of sportspeople who seem to be totally committed to their own success: tennis player Bjorn Borg, racing driver Michael Schumacher and basketball player Michael Jordan to name a few. But these people are actually quite rare ... most sportspeople do a lot of work on mental preparation and get a lot of help with staying focussed on winning.
P: OK ... so what do the sports psychologists do? How do you help people to succeed?
T: Well, our basic job is to prepare the mind and we can do this in different ways depending on who we're working with. One of the most important things we do is to help people change negative thoughts into positive ones. I did some work with a footballer recently. He missed a really important goal and started thinking that he couldn't do it anymore. I told him he could do it by thinking about something different, not on missing the goal. After practising thinking about the way the ball was turning instead, his whole game improved dramatically.
P: Kelly Holmes is a good example of that too, isn't she?
T: Yes, that's right. For much of her career, she was constantly getting injured and then worrying that it would happen again. I remember that she admitted feeling totally out of control when she got injured all the time. But the fact is, athletes have to get over that and start to take control mentally. That's exactly what she did – and then of course won two gold medals at the Athens Olympics, which was a fantastic achievement!
P: Yes, she was really brilliant!
T: There are other things we can do to help with mental preparation too. Things like routines to get the players focussed and working as a team can really help.
P: Routines? What do you mean?
T: Well, the New Zealand All Blacks rugby team

do their Haka war dance to focus themselves and to try and worry the other team. Then there are people who have their own personal lucky routines. Footballer Andy Cole said he always wanted to be the last player onto the pitch. It might seem a bit silly, but if it works ...

Unit 8 Recording 7

1 Kelly Holmes must be really ecstatic about her success.
Kelly Holmes must be absolutely ecstatic about her success.
2 The sports psychologist who worked with Kelly Holmes must be really ecstatic about her success.
The sports psychologist who worked with Kelly Holmes must be absolutely ecstatic about her success.
3 An extremely big sports centre near here has just opened.
A very big sports centre near where here has just opened.
4 If you want to get to the top in athletics, it's really vital to get yourself a professional trainer.
5 Whenever he plays football, he comes back with really filthy.
Whenever he plays football, he comes back absolutely filthy.
6 She was absolutely exhausted at the end of the race.
7 I love running. I'd be really devastated if I had to give it up.

Unit 8 Recording 8

1 I want to be the last player onto the pitch.
2 I won the race easily.
3 I'm not going to train today.
4 You can do it by thinking about something different.
5 Why are you feeling so negative?
6 Will you help me tomorrow?

Unit 8 Recording 10

Dialogue 1
H=Host J=Julie
H: ... and our next caller is Julie. So, what's on your mind, Julie?
J: ... Well ... guys basically, Chris ...
H: Ahh ... now where have I heard that before?
J: I know, I know ... but it feels like I've tried everything and I'm just not getting anywhere.
H: So ... what exactly do you mean when you say you've 'tried everything'?
J: Well ... I mean ... there was this guy I fancied a couple of months ago ... at work ... We used to have a bit of a laugh and a joke around the office ... and had lunch together a few times. It all seemed to be going pretty well. I'd text him now and then ... but then he seemed to just start avoiding me .
H: What ... like overnight?
J: Well ... I don't know about that ... but it was pretty strange.
H: And nothing had really changed?
J: No ... well ... like I said I had been texting him quite a bit..
H: What kind of things?
J: ... oh nothing much ... silly things ... telling him I thought he was really cute ... you know ...
H: Anything else?
J: Well ... I did send him the odd card ... and a

big cake on his birthday ... to the office ...
H: To the office?
J: Yeah ... well ... maybe that was a bit over the top ...

Dialogue 2
H=Host M=Martina
H: So Martina ... apparently you're some kind of sportsperson ... is that right?
M: Yeah, well, I do a lot of long-distance running ... you know marathons and stuff.
H: Oh yeah ... so what exactly were you phoning about?
M: Well, just recently, I had this race ... you know, a really big one, televised and everything and ... well, how can I put it, I, you know, I just couldn't do it.
H: What do you mean ... 'couldn't do it'?
M: Well, it was really hot ... but about half-way, I was losing touch with the leaders and I just had to stop – which is really unusual for me ... and then I just couldn't get going again ... and I just gave up.
H: Wow ... I see ...
M: And since then, I've lost all my confidence ... I'm thinking I may have to give up running altogether ... But really, it's been my life until now.
H: That sounds really difficult. Have you talked to anyone about how you're feeling.
M: Yes, well, I work with a sports psychologist but she's just telling me to ...

Dialogue 3
H=Host T=Tim
H: So what's your issue today Tim?
T: ... my job I suppose ...
H: And what do you suppose about it?
T: Well ... I've been in my company for quite some time now ... and it's just ... well ... I seem to have got a bit stuck I think ...
H: Stuck?
T: Yeah well ... Other people who started around the same time have got promoted and moved up ... and I'm still doing exactly the same job as when I started ...
H: And you feel like you've been doing your current job ok?
T: Umm ... well ... I suppose there have been one or two problems. I mean I didn't really get on with one of my biggest clients ... but that wasn't all my fault as they were really annoying ... but, anyway, they didn't renew their contract with us so I got into a bit of trouble about that ... and then I have been told off a few times about being late ..
H: So, are you late for work often?
T: Yeah, well, I guess so ...
H: Just how often, Tim?
T: Well, maybe a couple of times a week ...
H: What ... every week?
T: Pretty much I suppose ... it's just that I sleep really well ... and I never hear my alarm clock ... I've tried different types but it doesn't seem to make any difference ...

Unit 9 Recording 2

M=Man W=Woman
M: Did I tell you about this really funny lawyer story that a friend of mine sent me on email the other day?
W: No, go on.
M: Well ... the way it goes is that ... there's this lawyer in the USA ... North Carolina or

somewhere ... and he buys this box of really rare and very, very expensive cigars ...
W: Ok ...
M: And because they're so expensive he decides to insure them ... against fire amongst other things.
W: Fair enough.
M: Yes ... except that, within a month, having smoked his complete collection of these fantastic cigars and without having made even his first payment for the insurance policy, the lawyer made a claim against the insurance company.
W: What on earth for?
M: Well, in his claim, the lawyer stated that the cigars were lost in a series of small fires.
W: How ridiculous!
M: And unsurprisingly, the insurance company refused to pay for the obvious reason that the man had smoked the cigars in the normal way. But then, the lawyer sued the insurance company ... and won! When he gave his decision, the judge agreed with the insurance company that the claim appeared ridiculous BUT concluded that the lawyer had a policy from the company in which it guaranteed they could be insured against fire, without defining exactly what did or did not count as 'fire'. And so the company would have to pay the claim.
W: No! You're kidding.
M: But that's not all! You see, rather than going through a long and expensive appeal, the insurance company accepted the decision and paid $15,000 to the lawyer for his loss of the valuable cigars in the 'fires'. But now comes the best part!
W: Go on ... I can't wait ...
M: Then ... after cashing the cheque, the lawyer was arrested! The insurance company had him charged with 24 counts of arson! With his own insurance claim and evidence from the previous case being used against him, the lawyer was convicted of deliberately burning his insured property and so – can you believe it? – he was sentenced to 24 months in jail and a $24,000 fine.
W: No! Is that really true?
M: Cross my heart! My friend said he got it from a real newspaper.
W: How amazing.

Unit 9 Recording 3

W=Woman M=Man
W: Did you see these photos in the paper? It says they're of someone who was in the middle of stealing computer equipment from someone's house ...
M: Really? So, how did they manage to do that?
W: I'm not sure, I suppose they must have fixed up some kind of security camera.
M: What ... inside their own house?
W: Yeah. That would be pretty unusual. Do you think the thief realised he was being caught on camera?
M: He can't have done, can he? Otherwise, he'd have taken the camera too!

Unit 9 Recording 5

P=Presenter
P: ... and finally today, a house burglar was given an 11-month prison sentence today

after admitting breaking into a local house and stealing thousands of pounds worth of computer equipment.

The householder, Duncan Grisby, who had been burgled on a previous occasion, set up a webcam which would start recording as soon as it detected movement in the room. But the particularly clever thing was that even though the burglar stole the computer and webcam, the images had already been sent via the Internet to a private email address.

The police officer in charge of the case, commented after the trial: After the break-in was discovered, Mr Grisby simply gave us the email address and we were able to watch several minutes of footage and identify the thief who is quite well known to us. When he initially denied breaking in to the property we were simply able to show him the footage. The webcam made our job really easy. It was a pleasure to show him the pictures and see his expression when we interviewed him.

Unit 9 Recording 6

I=Interviewer S.H.=Sherlock Holmes

I: Mr. Sherlock Holmes, I must ask you first ... How is it that you have the same name as Sherlock Holmes, the great detective from London?

S.H: Please, call me Holmes – that's what my friends and family call me – well, you see, my parents were great fans of the original Conan Doyle stories. Both parents, my father, especially, would spend hours reading the adventures to me – even as a child.

I: Really!?

S.H: Yes ... and when I was born, they discussed a number of first names. They wanted to give their son a name that was uncommon – but also that represented something special. They didn't take long to decide on Sherlock Holmes as he was their favourite literary figure – and they knew no one would forget me once they'd heard my name. And boy, were they right!

I: So, how do people in general react when you introduce yourself to them?

S.H: Well, I get all kinds of reactions really – everything from the usual 'Where's Dr Watson' type comments to people just thinking I'm being funny.

I: I can imagine ... And do you mind?

S.H: No, not at all. I never have done. I think, the best reaction was when I was in San Francisco one time. I went into an electronic store to buy a TV. The clerk behind the counter was a young lady about 18 or so. When she saw the name on my credit card she stared at it for about 10 full seconds. She slowly lifted her face to look at me and she said, in all sincerity, I didn't know you were real! Wait 'til I tell my friends I saw the real Sherlock Holmes!

I: No!

S.H: Yes! You could have knocked her over with a feather. The expression on her face was as if she'd seen a ghost. It was very amusing.

I: Given your name, do you feel that you have any special talent or ability to solve mysteries in everyday life?

S.H: Well, I will say that having such a name does mean that people often turn to me if anything unusual happens. For example, if I'm watching TV with a friend or family member

and a magician comes on and does some kind of trick – all eyes turn to me to explain how it's done.

I: Really? How funny!

S.H: It's not as if I've even ever been interested in magic! Anyway, about two years ago, an old family friend suddenly disappeared from work with about $7,000. His mother hadn't heard from him for days. Even though we hadn't been in touch for years, she called me after the local police said they couldn't help. To keep her calm, I met her at her son's house, pulled out my torch and magnifying glass, and slowly went through the house looking for clues.

I: And did you actually find any?

S.H: Well, fortunately, he had left some of his email messages un-deleted in his computer system. It seemed to suggest that he'd deliberately taken the money to leave town and live in a warmer climate which was what I told his mother. In the end, it turned out that he realized he couldn't really start a new life on only $7,000 and he returned to face the justice system. It was hard for him, but I was pleased to have worked out what happened!

I: Just like your namesake ...

Unit 9 Recording 7

P=Presenter

P: Nick Leeson's life started as a classic rags-to-riches story. He was born into a working class family and left school with almost no qualifications. Nonetheless, in the early 1980s, he got a series of clerical jobs with different banks, ending up with Barings, a well-known investment bank, where he did well and received rapid promotion.

Before long, he was making millions for Barings by betting on the future direction of the Japanese stock exchange. His bosses back in London were delighted with his large profits and put more and more trust in him. By the end of 1993, he had made more than £10m – about 10% of the total profit of the bank for that year. However, what the bank didn't know was that Leeson had a special account where he was hiding his losses.

By December '94 the losses hidden in that account totalled $512 million. As the losses grew, Leeson requested extra funds to continue trading, hoping to get himself out of the mess by more deals. In the end, Leeson managed to lose the bank $1.3 billion and effectively destroyed Barings

As the direct result of his actions, he had wiped out the 233 year old Barings investment Bank, who proudly counted the Queen as a client. Investors saw their savings wiped out, and some 1,200 of Leeson's fellow employees lost their jobs.

What became of Leeson? After going on the run, the world's most wanted man, on the cover of every newspaper, checked in on a flight to Europe using his own name and hiding beneath a baseball cap. The German authorities were alerted and the police were there to arrest Leeson as he touched down. In December 1995 a court in Singapore sentenced him to six and a half years. In jail, he is said to have spent a lot of time doing exercise and he also, apparently, found God.

He was released early, in the summer of 1999 and, after his return to the UK, found that

he was effectively homeless and without a job. Leeson though, has managed to bounce back and make the most of his experiences. He has made an estimated £50,000 from his book, and the fee for selling his story to the newspapers is reported to be about three times that amount. The story has also been turned into a film called 'Rogue Trader', starring Ewan McGregor.

Unit 10 Recording 1

1 Once I had a premonition that something awful was going to happen to an old school friend of mine, Carola, who'd moved to Australia and I hadn't seen for ages. I somehow knew something was going to happen and then later that day, another friend of mine phoned to say that Carola had had an accident and was in hospital. A few other things like that have happened recently, so nowadays I take my premonitions a bit more seriously than I used to!

2 It was really weird the other day because I was at my brother's 30th birthday party and was talking to some people there ... And then in the middle of the conversation, I suddenly had a really strong feeling of déjà vu. I just felt that the whole thing ... you know, the place, the people, the exact conversation, had all happened before in exactly the same way. It made me feel quite strange for a couple of minutes.

3 More and more in my life, I think I've learned to trust my intuition ... It could be anything really, like deciding which job to apply for, or knowing which road to take if I get lost, or having a feeling that someone's lying to me. I find if I start analysing things and trying to work it out, I get confused. But if I go with my gut feeling, without thinking about things too much, it's funny but I find I'm usually right.

4 My cousins are twins and they have always been incredibly close. Now they are older, they still have an amazing sixth sense about each other. They always seem to know when something happens to the other one, even if they're miles apart. One of them knows if something important has happened to the other one, especially if they're in trouble or hurt in some way.

5 I've only been unconscious once in my life and that was when I was playing football with some friends. We used to play every Sunday and I really enjoyed it, but I often got injured! One day, I was knocked unconscious by someone ... I still don't really know how it happened ... I just remember waking up, lying on the grass looking up at a group of about twenty people all staring down at me, and I hadn't got a clue what was going on!

6 I think that I'm a very single-minded person – I mean, I really drive myself hard to succeed at everything I do ... The other day, I was wondering why I let myself work so hard and get so stressed about things, and I think it's maybe because I have a subconscious fear of failure. I think that deep down, without really being aware of it most of the time, I'm really scared of not succeeding in everything I do. Maybe it's to do with my parents. They always expected me to be the best at school.

Tapescripts

Unit 10 Recording 2

Dialogue 1
I=Interviewer W=Woman M=Man
I: How do you feel about Paul McKenna?
W: Well, I reckon he's probably genuine myself. It sounds as if his clients go away satisfied. So even if we don't really understand how he does it, if you ask me, it doesn't really matter. He must be doing something right! Some people want to know how everything works, but I'm in favour of just accepting it if it works for you, and not analysing things too much!

Dialogue 2
I: What are your views on hypnosis? Do you have any strong feelings about it?
M: Yes, I do. I've always believed that people like Paul McKenna are just good showmen. To my mind, it's all rubbish – he's just good at being nice to people, so they're a bit happier at the time. But, I have my doubts about how much he can actually do for people in the long-term. I'm sceptical that hypnosis has any effect at all and I'm against people paying for a service and getting nothing real in return. I mean, I doubt hypnosis actually works for anyone.

Dialogue 3
I: What do you think of hypnosis?
M: From my point of view, I have to say that when I went for a session to a hypnotist, it was fantastic. It saved me my job. I mean, I was able to deal with the stress of my job much better after that and I'm convinced that it was the hypnosis that helped me. In fact, if I hadn't gone to the session, I suspect I would've left my job by now.

Unit 10 Recording 3

I=Interviewer E=Expert
I: Welcome to *Modern World*. On the programme today, we're talking to Jo Carlson about the power of persuasion. All around us, there are images on television, jingles on the radio, adverts in magazines, sound bites on the news, offers in the shops. They're all hard at work – trying to make us believe something or persuading us to buy something. Fear not, however, Jo Carlson is here to reveal their secrets and show us how to resist all this persuasion! Hello, Jo.
E: Hello.
I: First, persuading people is big business, isn't it? I mean, supermarkets and politicians, advertisers and salespeople, they all take it very seriously, don't they?
E: Yes. They spend a lot of money on working out the best psychological tricks to guarantee that even the most cautious among us are open to manipulation.
I: Let's take supermarkets then. How do they make us buy things we don't necessarily want? What are some of their tricks?
E: Well, firstly, they try to relax us by playing music and by pumping the smell of freshly-baked bread into the store. Studies have shown that the smell makes people buy more.
I: I know I've done that without even thinking about it …
E: Exactly … most of the time, we are completely unaware of what's happening. It's subconscious persuasion …
I: And what about 'reward' cards?

E: Ah yes! Well, from the supermarket's point of view, reward cards are a huge success story. As customers, we think we're being rewarded for shopping at that particular supermarket. What's really happening, however, is that the store is basically not only tempting us to shop there again, but also getting vital information about what we're buying.
I: More information to help them work out how to persuade us to buy even more things …
E: That's right!
E: So, what about the advertising industry? What secrets can you reveal about that? In what ways does it persuade us to buy particular products?
E: Well … there's so much. And no matter how much we think we know about what the advertisers are doing … they still tend to win! We still fall for the advert and end up buying the product.
I: Yes …
E: Basically, there are two types of ads … those that appeal to the thinking part of our brain and those that appeal to the emotional part.
I: So, for what type of products would they advertise by appealing to the thinking part of our brain?
E: Well, they are mostly used for things which have little emotional appeal, for example, cleaning products. They give us information about the product and try to influence us that way. However, adverts which go for our emotions are usually much more successful. In using emotion, adverts exploit psychoanalytical theories about the subconscious. I mean, they know that images can reach our emotions at a level that we are not aware of and so are much more powerful in persuading us to do things.
I: So, what kinds of emotions are used?
E: Well, adverts for different brands of clothes often want to make us feel that we belong, for example by showing us how to buy the right clothes to fit in with our friends. And adverts for insurance play on our need to feel safe. For example they might show a family happily spending their insurance money buying new things when their house has been burgled. Self-esteem is an important one too. Many ads for luxury products like expensive cars, work on making us feel good about ourselves and the lifestyles that we could have.
I: Celebrities are used a lot too, aren't they?
E: Yes, that's very popular. Celebrities are often used as a quick way of getting the message across. Their success and familiarity makes them feel safe, interesting, cool, … whatever … We see our favourite pop star drinking a particular fizzy drink and we're immediately persuaded to buy it!

Unit 10 Recording 5

1 They persuade us to buy things we may not want.
2 We carry on using reward cards at the same supermarket.
3 Adverts for clothes often want to make us feel that we belong.
4 I try to resist buying expensive designer clothes but it's difficult!
5 You could try leaving your credit card at home if you don't want to spend so much.

Unit 10 Recording 7

S=Student
S: I can't believe that spelling is so difficult in English. In Spanish, it's so easy! There are so many exceptions in English that every time I think I've learned a rule, I find a word that breaks it!
But I do think there are some quite nice words in English. I mean, they are hard to spell, but I like the fact that some of them are so strange … like the g-h-t words, for example … brought, caught, fight, … you know … why do they have g-h-t?
I think the best way to remember how to spell words, is just to repeat them … I write them down lots of times and I also chant the spelling to myself … You know, like, for example, brought … I say … B – R – O – U – – G – H – T. B – R – – O – U – – G – H – T.
B – R – – O – U – – G – H – T. It's a bit like brainwashing … or mind control … in the end, it works!